Inside
the Registry
for Microsoft
Windows 95

Günter Born

Microsoft Press

PUBLISHED BY
Microsoft Press
A Division of Microsoft Corporation
One Microsoft Way
Redmond, Washington 98052-6399

Library of Congress Cataloging-in-Publication Data
Born, Günter, 1955-
    Inside the registry for Microsoft Windows 95 / Günter Born.
        p.   cm.
    Includes index.
    ISBN 1-57231-424-9
    1. Microsoft Windows (Computer file)   2. Operating systems
(Computers) I. Title
QA76.76.063B643   1997
005.4'469–dc21   96-37067
                                                                 CIP

Printed and bound in the United States of America.

1 2 3 4 5 6 7 8 9   MLML   2 1 0 9 8 7

Distributed to the book trade in Canada by Macmillan of Canada, a division of Canada Publishing Corporation.

A CIP catalogue record for this book is available from the British Library.

Microsoft Press books are available through booksellers and distributors worldwide. For further information about international editions, contact your local Microsoft Corporation office. Or contact Microsoft Press International directly at fax (206) 936-7329.

TrueType is a registered trademark of Apple Computer, Inc. IBM is a registered trademark of International Business Machines Corporation. MS-DOS, Microsoft, Microsoft Press, Win32, Windows, Windows NT, Visual C++ are registered trademarks, and ActiveX is a trademark of Microsoft Corporation. Novell is a registered trademark of Novell, Inc. Other product and company names mentioned herein may be the trademarks of their respective owners.

Acquisitions Editor: Stephen G. Guty
Project Editor: Victoria P. Thulman
Technical Editor: Jean Ross

TABLE OF CONTENTS

Acknowledgments

This book could not have been finished without the help of many people, to whom I want to say thank you. First of all I have to mention Thomas Pohlmann and Stephen Guty (my acquisition editors at Microsoft Press Germany and USA, respectively). Both editors encouraged me to develop my initial ideas into a book, and Stephen gave me a chance to actually publish the book—even though I am living in Germany, my native language isn't English, and the schedule for writing the manuscript was pretty short (excellent conditions for a project). I want to give my special thanks to Victoria Thulman and Jean Ross, my editors at Microsoft Press. Both editors spent many hours editing and polishing my text. I also want to thank my wife and my children Kati and Benjamin, who supported me during the time the book was written.

Günter Born

Introduction

Why I Wrote This Book

This book is the end of a long story. Nearly two years ago I received an early copy of Chicago (the press called it Windows 4.0 at that time). I wasn't exactly ecstatic about the software, but after playing with it for two days, I was convinced. Time went by, and I installed new builds of this software (named Chicago, Microsoft Windows 95 Preview and Microsoft Windows 95 Retail). I also installed and uninstalled many other preliminary software packages for test purposes and realized that my Registry was cluttered with a lot of unused entries. I wrote two books about Windows 95 and learned how to customize Windows—hacking in the Registry a little bit to troubleshoot and get my old settings back.

Some months later I translated Nancy Cluts's book *Programming the Windows 95 User Interface* and wondered why some examples that shipped with the book didn't work on my system. After a few hours of debugging, I found the culprit—an incorrect Registry setting. I surfed the World Wide Web to glean tricks and learn how to hack in the Registry, but most of the tricks didn't work properly on my computer. During the hours I spent exploring why, I became more familiar with Registry issues. One important lesson I learned was that I didn't need to hack directly in the Registry; often it was smarter to set an option on a property page to get the same results. (I *always* came to this conclusion after spending unproductive hours in the Registry Editor.)

So I decided that a book about the Windows 95 Registry and related topics was really needed. I started writing down the knowledge I had gained while troubleshooting, customizing, and programming with Windows 95.

The Goals of This Book

This book is not a complete reference to all entries in the Registry, although we'd all like such a reference. Such a book simply can't be written. Because the Registry is used by so many hardware and software components, everybody's Registry is different. My goals in this book were to examine the most important parts of the Registry, to show how to backup and recover the Registry, and to provide some background knowledge about related topics. This book will be helpful for system administrators, troubleshooters, programmers, and users who want to customize Windows 95.

> **NOTE:** Keep in mind that you can seriously damage your system when you alter Registry settings. Always back up your system before you attempt to modify the Registry. (See pages 35–42 to learn how to back up your system files.) Any change you make is at your own risk—neither Microsoft nor I (the author) can support you with Registry issues. So proceed with modifications cautiously.

Book Sample Files and Useful Tools

Throughout this book, you will find listings for sample files that you can either type in or download from the World Wide Web. The archive file is called REGFILES.EXE, and it can be downloaded from the following Web site:

http://www.microsoft.com/mspress/products/1039

Place this file in its own folder—\RegBook, for example. (Do not use long filenames when naming this directory, because some of the INF files will not run properly from a folder with a name of more than eight characters.) Select Run from the Start menu and type *C:\RegBook\RegFiles -d* to expand the sample files into a directory structure designating the chapters. For example, the sample files for Chapter 3 are in \RegBook\chapter3. Be sure to include the -d switch when you run REGFILES or you will end up with all the sample files in a single directory.

On the Web site, you will also find direct links to other Web sites that contain some useful tools for working with the Registry, such as the following:

- *Microsoft Power Toys.* Power Toys is a collection of helpful tools, provided for free by the Windows 95 developers, that extend the Windows 95 User Interface. In this book, I've used the Tweak UI module of Power Toys extensively.

- *EzDesk.* EzDesk is a shareware tool developed by Melissa Nguyen that saves and restores the position of all icons shown on the desktop. You'll find this helpful if the icon positions you prefer are reset to the default after a Safe Start.

- *Microsoft Kernel Toys.* These are tools developed by Microsoft for advanced Windows 95 users. The tools are useful for optimizing performance and for other aspects of the Windows 95 kernel.

- *RegClean.* This tool is shipped with Microsoft Visual Basic 4.0 and later, and is also available free from Microsoft over the Internet. You can run REGCLEAN.EXE to identify and clean out many unused keys in the Registry.

Getting in Touch with the Author

If you'd like to get in touch with me regarding the book, feel free to visit my home page at this address:

http://ourworld.compuserve.com/homepages/Guenter_Born

6810×8850

1080-1170

This book brings together all the scattered details about the Registry and provides a comprehensive look at how it works and how you can use it. Fortunately, the concept of the

The Registry is the central database in Microsoft Windows 95 that stores and maintains configuration information and is thus one of the most interesting and important components of Windows 95. Until now, details about the Registry haven't been readily available, and developers, administrators, and end users have all faced the challenge of trying to find information about it.

The MCA Bus

C H A P T E R   O N E

The Basics

The Registry is the central database in Microsoft Windows 95 that stores and maintains configuration information and is thus one of the most interesting and important components of Windows 95. Until now, details about the Registry haven't been readily available—developers, administrators, and end users have all faced the challenge of trying to find information about it. This book brings together all the scattered details about the Registry and provides a comprehensive look at how it works and how you can use it. Fortunately, the concept of the Registry is pretty straightforward, and with a little help you can decipher the database entries.

This chapter discusses the basic Registry architecture and explains why the Registry has replaced the old INI (initialization) files. We'll also examine when—and how—you should modify the Registry.

Why Abandon INI Files for the Registry?

If you're accustomed to using the old INI files in Microsoft Windows versions prior to Windows 95, you're probably asking this question: Why did the Windows developers drop the INI files and create the Registry? After all, the INI files were printable, and only a simple text editor was needed to change initialization settings. To understand why the Registry was developed, let's take a look at the old INI structure by examining a small section of the WIN.INI file:

```
[windows]
load=...
NullPort=None
run=...
device=HP Deskjet
⋮
```

Each section in an INI file begins with a keyword enclosed in brackets (such as [windows] in the WIN.INI file) followed by several lines of settings.

Although this approach worked well enough in earlier, less complicated versions of Windows, it caused problems in Windows 3.1 and Windows 3.11. The disadvantages are apparent if you take a closer look at the INI file concept:

- INI files are text-based, so their size is limited to 64 KB. As you install programs on your PC the WIN.INI file gets longer, restricting the number of programs you can install. (You can't exceed 64 KB.) In addition, programs often have problems reading entries properly beyond the first 32 KB. So, although there is a system limitation of 64 KB, to be sure all your programs run properly, your INI file shouldn't be larger than 32 KB.

- All information stored in INI files is nonhierarchical—files contain only section headers and some additional text lines—so accessing lengthy INI files is a slow process. To keep their programs from being slowed by lengthy INI files, software developers started creating a separate INI file for each program they wrote. As a result, each tested program leaves an unused INI file in the Windows directory. Such a disorganized file structure can't be managed easily by the user.

- Each INI file initializes settings that affect the computer as a whole, so user-specific information can't be stored easily in a single INI file. Also, remote access from other network devices to the INI files of a local machine is not possible (nor available from the APIs).

These issues became more and more critical in Windows 3.1. So due to these restrictions and the complexity of OLE, Microsoft developers created a different structure to store the information necessary for OLE in Windows 3.1: REG files. Information was stored in REG files by using a Registration Editor or during the installation of new software. (The REG file feature seemed to be overlooked by many people; I, for one, have never played with the REG files in Windows 3.1.) So as you can see, the Registry isn't a new concept for Windows 95. The Windows 3.1 REG file structure was the parent of the Windows 95 Registry.

Requirements for the Registry

The design goals of Windows 95 included support for Plug & Play, remote access to system settings, multiple user configurations, and so on. It was clear that a new hierarchical database was necessary to meet all these requirements.

The Windows developers based their hierarchical centralized configuration database on an advanced version of the Windows 3.1 REG structure, which met the following objectives:

- All configuration information (user and system data) should be stored in a single (logical) source.

- Multiple configurations of user and system data can be stored in one database.

- Hardware and operating system parameters can be stored in one database.

- The database should be recoverable after a system crash.

- The size of this database should not be limited to 64 KB.

- Administrators can configure this database with Control Panel tools or other utilities.

- A set of network-independent functions will allow examination of the Registry locally or via remote (over a network).

- Developers can access Registry entries by using a set of API calls.

The Registry Architecture

The information stored in the Registry's hierarchical database is organized in keys, where each key contains a value or a subkey:

```
key
    subkey 1 | value
    subkey 2
    subkey 3 | value
```

A key can contain several subkeys, in order to group settings, and one or more values. This results in a hierarchical tree, which you can see in the Registry Editor, as shown in Figure 1-1.

NOTE: The Microsoft Windows Explorer uses a similar structure to show the directory hierarchy. The Registry can be compared with a directory tree: The keys are similar to the directories in the file system. Key values are comparable to files in a directory.

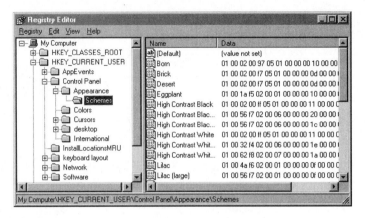

Figure 1-1.
Example of a Registry branch.

The Six Root Keys

The Windows 95 Registry consists of six root keys, each of which reflects a different aspect of the configuration data (that is, user data and machine-dependent settings). Each root key is named *HKEY_XXX* and can be followed by several subkeys. These root keys are shown in Figure 1-2. A branch represents a type of information about the user, the hardware, the application, and so on.

> N O T E :   This structure is also used in Microsoft Windows NT 3.51 and Windows NT 4.0. The difference is that in Windows NT 3.51 only four *HKEY* entries are used in the Registry. Also, the tools for editing and displaying the Registry are different in Windows 95 and Windows NT.

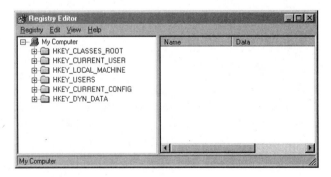

Figure 1-2.
The six root keys of the Windows 95 Registry.

What Does Each Root Key Contain?

Each branch of the Registry contains information that logically belongs together. Following is a description of the contents of these six branches within the Registry.

HKEY_CLASSES_ROOT This branch contains all data used in Windows for OLE and drag-and-drop operations, including the names of all registered file types and their properties. Registered file types enable the user to open a file by double-clicking. Properties of registered file types include the icons shown in Windows 95 and the commands (Open, Print, etc.) that users can apply to files of those types. This branch also contains information about Quick Viewers, property sheet handlers, copy hook handlers, and other OLE components (OLE servers).

Many subkeys (*.bat*, *.bmp*, and so on) pertain to file extensions. For each of these subkeys, a second file type subkey exists (*batfile, exefile,* and so on) in *HKEY_CLASSES_ROOT*. This second subkey contains properties such as the icon, Class ID, and commands.

Most of the entries in *HKEY_CLASSES_ROOT* can also be found in *HKEY_LOCAL_MACHINE\SOFTWARE\Classes*. We look more closely at the structure of *HKEY_CLASSES_ROOT* in Chapter 3.

This branch of the Registry was derived from the Windows 3.1 Registry structure (although the formats differ) and is also available in Windows NT 3.51.

HKEY_USERS Any user-specific information (customized desktop settings, for example) is located in *HKEY_USERS*. This branch always contains the default settings (*HKEY_USERS\.Default*) for the desktop, Start menu, applications, and so on. When a new user logs on to the system, these settings are copied to a separate subkey that is identified with the user's name (*HKEY_USERS\Born*, for example). All changes that the user makes are stored in this subkey. Windows NT 3.51 also supports this entry.

HKEY_CURRENT_USER User settings are built from *HKEY_USERS* during the login process, so all information found in *HKEY_CURRENT_USER* is a copy of the subkey *HKEY_USERS\name*, w here *name* is the name of the active user (or *Default*). *HKEY_CURRENT_USER* contains several subkeys:

- *AppEvents*. Contains paths to sound files that are loaded for particular system events (for example, when an error message occurs).

- *Control Panel*. Contains data that can be altered in the Control Panel window (for example, display settings).

5

- *Network.* Defines the network state (if available).

- *Software.* Describes the properties of user-installed software. (This information was previously stored in WIN.INI.) This branch also references *HKEY_LOCAL_MACHINE.* Applications settings are stored in here.

- *InstallLocationsMRU.* Contains values defining the paths used during the last install processes. The values named *a, b, c,* and so on define the paths, and *MRUList* contains the order of these entries. The paths defined in *a, b, c,* and so on will be used in the list box of the Install From Disk dialog box.

- *keyboard layout.* Contains information about the keyboard layout (layout scheme and optional DLLs to load).

- *RemoteAccess.* Optional subkey available only if the Remote Access service is installed. It defines the Remote Access settings.

These subkeys are discussed further in other chapters of this book. Windows NT 3.51 also supports this entry.

HKEY_LOCAL_MACHINE   This branch defines all specific information for the local machine, such as drivers, installed hardware, port mappings, and software configuration. This information is valid for all users logged on to the system. This branch is also available in Windows NT 3.51.

The key *HKEY_LOCAL_MACHINE* has several subkeys containing the following data:

- *hardware.* This subkey contains the settings for the serial ports available on the local machine. The subkey *devicemap* contains entries for devices installed in the system.

- *Config.* The machine configuration is maintained in this subkey. This information is necessary for docking stations with varying hardware and is updated during Windows 95 Setup and during a Windows 95 startup. The subkey contains two entries: one for display settings and one for available system printers.

■ *Enum.* Windows uses a new feature called *Bus Enumeration* for the bookkeeping of all installed hardware components. The data for these components is stored in this subkey and can be used to build the "hardware tree" shown in the Device Manager. (Select System from the Control Panel.)

■ *Network.* When Windows 95 runs in a network, this subkey contains user-login information (user name, network provider, logon validation, policy information, and so on).

■ *SOFTWARE.* All information about the software installed on the machine is stored here. Parts of this subkey (*\Classes*) are used to construct *HKEY_CLASSES_ROOT*.

■ *System.* This subkey contains all data that is required for Windows 95 to start. The subkey contains the key *CurrentControlSet*, which contains the subkeys *control* and *Services*. The *control* subkey contains information such as the computer name, the settings for the file system, and so on. *Services* lists the services used in Windows 95.

■ *Security.* This subkey is available for networked computers and contains information about the security provider.

HKEY_CURRENT_CONFIG   This branch handles Plug & Play and contains information about the current configuration of a multiple hardware configuration computer. Dockable stations are a typical example. The settings in this branch match one set of *Display* and *System* settings stored in the *HKEY_LOCAL_MACHINE\Config* key.

HKEY_DYN_DATA   This branch defines the keys that store the dynamic status information of several devices. This data can be used by monitor programs to detect hardware problems, device status, or changing configurations. The Device Manager uses this data to show the current hardware configuration.

All data is read and modified by the system. Some data can also be altered by the user, whereas other data is updated only by the system itself. Details about the altering of data are reviewed in later chapters.

Why Do Identical Keys Appear in Different Branches?

You've probably noticed that in the Registry, key names can appear in more than one branch. This is because certain keys are built from keys in other branches. Windows automatically stores any modification made by the user in all of the related keys. So, for example, a change in *HKEY_LOCAL_MACHINE\SOFTWARE\Classes* would also appear in the *HKEY_CURRENT_ROOT* key because *HKEY_CURRENT_ROOT* is built from *HKEY_LOCAL_MACHINE\SOFTWARE\Classes*. Likewise, because the contents of *HKEY_CURRENT_USER* are built from *HKEY_USERS\name* (*name* refers to the user's name) when a user logs on, the keys would share the same user information.

An exception to this is the *\Software\Microsoft\Windows\CurrentVersion* subkey, which is available in *HKEY_CURRENT_USER* and in *HKEY_LOCAL_MACHINE*. (The subkeys *\SOFTWARE* and *\Software* are identical. Registry entries are not case-sensitive. You need to worry about correctly identifying upper and lowercase letters only when you are referring to entries that are part of the user interface.) Although the names are identical, their content is distinct; entries in the *HKEY_CURRENT_USER* branch contain user-specific settings (recent file lists, for example). Entries in *HKEY_LOCAL_MACHINE* contain settings that are global for the local machine, the software, or all users (for example, application paths, the Windows tip list, and so on). These issues are discussed in more detail in later chapters.

How Can I Access the Registry Database?

You can access the Registry database from a program by using the Windows API calls or a tool called the Registry Editor with which you can display, print, and modify the Registry database. (The Registry Editor is discussed in more detail in Chapter 2.) Each software installation changes the system settings (or in Windows 95 notation, the contents of the Registry). Following is an explanation of the files that are affected.

SYSTEM.DAT and USER.DAT

For an independent computer user, a single file is adequate to store the Registry. In a network, however, a single file would enable an individual user to modify not only typical user-specific data but also the system configuration—which might be quite different from the settings that the network administrator prefers. To keep all system configuration data in a separate file, which prevents the end users from configuring the system and maintains some global settings for all users, Windows 95 separates and stores the two categories of Registry data in two files: SYSTEM.DAT and USER.DAT.

- SYSTEM.DAT contains the system configuration and settings of data (hardware configuration, Plug & Play settings, and application settings). These settings are required during system startup to load the device drivers and to determine which hardware is available. SYSTEM.DAT is always located on the local machine in the Windows 95 directory.

- USER.DAT contains user-specific data (login names, desktop settings, start menu settings, and so on). During the Windows setup, USER.DAT is automatically stored in the \Windows directory, but the file doesn't have to remain there. If user profiles are enabled, individual users can have their own settings (for the desktop, Start menu, and so on) stored in their own directory structure under the \Windows\Profiles subdirectory (see Figure 1-3), which contains a copy of the USER.DAT file for this user. In a network environment, this file can be located on a central server for roving users and can be downloaded if necessary.

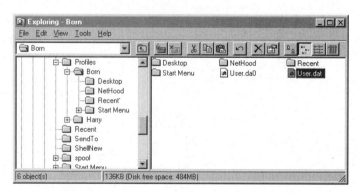

Figure 1-3.
Location of the USER.DAT file.

What's a DA0 File?

Figure 1-3 shows a second file, USER.DA0, in the user subdirectory. The DA0 files are the second set, or backup set, of Registry files. The current Registry database is built during system startup from USER.DAT and SYSTEM.DAT. If this startup fails, Windows 95 can recover the previous version of the Registry (during safe startup) from the USER.DA0 and SYSTEM.DA0 files. If the startup process is successful, the current values from USER.DAT and SYSTEM.DAT are copied into USER.DA0 and SYSTEM.DA0.

DA0 files are helpful only if the Registry is corrupted or deleted and you can't access the backup you've made independent of the DA0 files. This DA0 "backup" isn't a preferable backup source because it can sometimes contain the wrong data. Backing up and recovering the Registry are discussed in detail on pages 17-22 in Chapter 2. DA0 files in particular are discussed on pages 18-19.

The INI Files in Windows 95

If we examine the \Windows directory, we still find WIN.INI and SYSTEM.INI together with other INI files. For compatibility reasons, Windows 95 maintains the WIN.INI and SYSTEM.INI files. These settings are used for Win16 applications. When a Win16-based application is installed, its setup program creates INI settings but doesn't update the Registry because Win16 applications were designed to be compatible with earlier versions of Windows.

During an upgrade, the Windows 95 Setup program deletes several entries from the old WIN.INI and SYSTEM.INI files and adds these entries to the Registry. Table 1-1 describes these entries.

Entries Moved from the INI Files into the Registry

Key	Entry	Subkey Location
[*Desktop*]	*GridGranularity*	*HKEY_CURRENT_USER \ Control Panel \Desktop*
[*Desktop*]	*Pattern*	*HKEY_CURRENT_USER \ Control Panel \Desktop*
[*Desktop*]	*TileWallpaper*	*HKEY_CURRENT_USER \ Control Panel \Desktop*
[*Windows*]	*ScreenSaveActive*	*HKEY_CURRENT_USER\ Control Panel\Desktop*

Table 1-1. *(continued)*

Table 1-1. *continued*

Key	Entry	Subkey Location
[Windows]	*ScreenSaveTimeout*	*HKEY_CURRENT_USER\ Control Panel\Desktop*
[Sound]	*event*	*HKEY_CURRENT_USER\AppEvents\ Schemes\Apps\event\current*
[Network]	*MaintainServerList*	*HKEY_LOCAL_MACHINE\System\ CurrentControlSet\Services\VxD\VNETSETUP*
[Network]	*LogonDomain*	*HKEY_LOCAL_MACHINE\Network\Logon*
[Network]	*LogonValidated*	*HKEY_LOCAL_MACHINE\Network\Logon*
[Network]	*Comment*	*HKEY_LOCAL_MACHINE\System\ CurrentControlSet\Services\VxD\VNETSETUP*
[Network]	*LMAnnounce*	*HKEY_LOCAL_MACHINE\System\ CurrentControlSet\Services\VxD\ VNETSETUP*
[Network]	*LMLogon*	*HKEY_LOCAL_MACHINE\Network\Logon*
[Network]	*Username*	*HKEY_LOCAL_MACHINE\Network\Logon*
[Network]	*WorkGroup*	*HKEY_LOCAL_MACHINE\System\ CurrentControlSet\Services\VxD\VNETSETUP*
[Network]	*EnableSharing*	*HKEY_LOCAL_MACHINE\Services\VxD\ VNETSETUP*
[Network]	*ComputerName*	*HKEY_LOCAL_MACHINE\System\ CurrentControlSet\control\ComputerName\ ComputerName*
[386Enh]	*Transport*	*HKEY_LOCAL_MACHINE\Services\VxD\ transport_entry*
[386Enh]	*Network*	*HKEY_LOCAL_MACHINE\Services\ VxD\VNETSETUP*

NOTE: After the Windows 95 setup, you will find the SETUP.INF file in the \Windows\Inf folder. This file contains entries for moving INI settings into the Registry.

Conflicting Parameters

After the Windows 95 installation, you (or some install programs) can add entries to the INI files. However, changing the INI files can sometimes lead to a curious situation. Suppose you (or an install program) change some settings in the INI file. You then alter Registry settings with the Registry Editor, test the result, and find that everything seems to be okay. But when you restart the system, the new configuration is lost. Your inspection of the Registry reveals that the old settings are back.

What has happened? Well, there is a big trap in the system: Windows keeps data in the INI files and in the Registry consistent. During each system reboot, Windows examines the INI settings and checks each entry against the Registry entries. If an entry is available in the INI file and in the Registry, the value from the INI file is copied over the Registry value. This will overwrite entries previously altered in the Registry. The only way to fix this problem is to manually change the entries in both the INI file and the Registry.

> NOTE: The best solution to conflicting parameters in INI files and the Registry is to remove all entries from the INI files that are also available in the Registry. The Win32 applications don't use INI files, and Microsoft discourages developers from using INI files for future developments.

When Should the Registry Be Modified?

The safest answer to the question above is "Never!" Modifying the Registry can be dangerous—you have the critical responsibility of storing all values in a consistent manner or your system could crash permanently. But the safest answer is not always the most realistic, so if you've got to modify the Registry, let installation routines, setup programs, and utilities do it for you whenever possible.

How Should the Registry Be Modified?

The way you modify the Registry depends on what you need to modify. Most of the time, your safest and simplest bet will be to use the Display Properties property sheet, the Control Panel, the System Policy Editor, or other third-party utilities that enable you to modify Registry settings—for example, customizing the appearance of screen elements, establishing screen saver parameters, and fine-tuning certain parts of the Windows operating system. These methods (described in Table 1-2) are all pretty risk-free and are discussed later in the book.

You can also modify the Registry using the Registry Editor, which is a powerful (and thus potentially dangerous) tool that allows you to modify *any* entry in the Registry. Using the Registry Editor should really be your last resort—use it only when you can't get results via property sheets or other tools.

(Whenever I've forgotten that rule in the past, I've spent hours digging inside the Registry. I finally figured out that I could get the same effect simply by checking a box on a property sheet.)

Whichever method you use, always back up the Registry before you change anything. Modifying the Registry is discussed at length on Chapter 2.

Safe Methods for Modifying the Registry

Modification Method	Settings to Be Modified
Control Panel	Most of the system settings
Display Properties property sheet	Background, appearance of screen elements, graphic adapter, screen saver parameters
System Policy Editor	User access to settings, several system settings
Third-party utilities	Application-specific settings, mouse, menus, and many others

Table 1-2.
REG and INF files used by setup programs may help novice users change Registry settings.

Why Do My Registry Entries Differ from Those in the Book?

Throughout this book, the subkeys and values listed (in tables, mostly) might not exactly match what you see on your computer. Every Registry is different depending on the computer setup and the software that has been installed. The keys, subkeys, and values shown in this book constitute the basic structure of the Windows 95 Registry.

6810×8850

1060-1170

This book brings together all the scattered details about the Registry and provides a comprehensive look at how it works and how you can use it. Fortunately, the concept of the

The Registry is the central repository in Microsoft Windows 95 that stores and maintains configuration information and is thus one of the most interesting and important components of Windows 95. Until now, details about the Registry haven't been readily available. Developers, administrators, and end users have all faced the challenge of trying to find information about it.

The MCA Bus

The Registry Editor and Other Registry Tools

This chapter describes how to use the Registry Editor to display, modify, and recover the Registry. You'll also learn about the tools and techniques for backing up your Registry and setting the system and user policies.

The Registry Editor

The Registry Editor is the tool provided by Microsoft for displaying and editing the Registry database. You can't display the contents of the USER.DAT and SYSTEM.DAT files with a simple text editor because Microsoft uses a special format to store these files. The following sections describe how to use the Registry Editor.

Locating the Registry Editor

After installing Microsoft Windows 95, you won't find the Registry Editor in the Start menu or on the desktop—setup doesn't automatically create a shortcut to the Registry Editor, in order to prevent novice users from using it. But during installation, the REGEDIT.EXE file is copied into the \Windows folder.

Starting the Registry Editor

To start the Registry Editor, do the following:

1. Open the Microsoft Windows Explorer window and search for the REGEDIT.EXE file in the \Windows folder.

2. Double-click REGEDIT.EXE. The Registry Editor starts.

If you use the Registry Editor frequently, you might want to create a short-cut on the desktop. This can be accomplished by following these steps:

1. Open the Explorer window, and search for the REGEDIT.EXE file in the \Windows folder.

2. While pressing the right mouse button, drag the REGEDIT.EXE icon to a free place on the desktop.

3. Release the right mouse button, and select the Create Shortcut(s) Here option from the context menu. The Registry Editor is established on the desktop.

You can change the icon title if you want to (to Regedit, for example). To start the Registry Editor, double-click this icon on the desktop.

TIP: Some people prefer to start programs from the Start menu. To add the Registry Editor to the Start menu, follow the preceding steps, but instead of dragging the REGEDIT.EXE icon onto the desktop, drag the icon to the Start button.

Editing with the Registry Editor

The Registry Editor displays the Registry contents in a window containing a menu bar, a status bar, and two panes. (See Figure 2-1.)

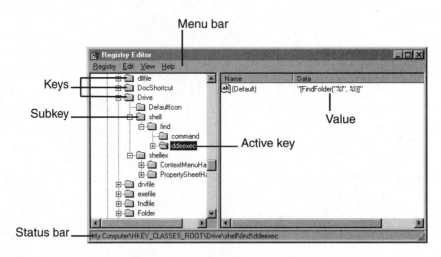

Figure 2-1.
The Registry Editor window.

The menu bar consists of the following commands:

- Registry, which allows you to print, import, and export the Registry data.

- Edit, which allows you to create, delete, rename, and find keys or values.

- View, which allows you to switch the status bar on and off, to change the pane sizes, and to refresh the display.

- Help, which provides help topics about the functions.

In the left pane, the Registry structure, which consists of keys and subkeys, is visible. When you open the Registry Editor for the first time, the six root keys discussed in Chapter 1 are visible. (See Figure 2-2.) Each key is represented by a folder symbol in the left pane. The active key is shown as an open folder icon.

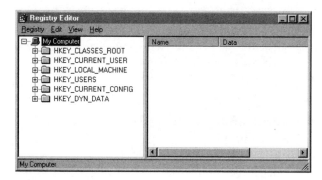

Figure 2-2.
The root keys shown in the Registry Editor.

Displaying Key Values

The values of the active key appear in the right pane of the Registry Editor window. Each key contains at least one value with the name *Default.* Each additional value for a key must have both a name and a data value. The names appear in the right pane in the first column, titled Name. Valid characters to include in a name are *a* through *z*, *0* through *9*, blank, and underscore (_). The actual values appear in the second column, titled Data. (See Figure 2-1 on the facing page.) A value cannot exceed 64 KB, so large strings and binary data streams cannot be stored in the Registry. The total size of each subkey is also restricted to 64 KB, so if a single value is 64 KB, the subkey can't contain any other values. For a subkey whose total value exceeds 64 KB, use a file to store the data and maintain a pointer to this file in the subkey.

The Registry Editor can handle text, binary, and DWORD data types:

- Text data types are stored as characters (such as *"C:\WINDOWS\ Notepad.exe %1"*). Text values are enclosed in quotation marks. An empty text value is indicated as *""*.

- Binary data types are represented as a sequence of hex bytes (for example, *00 03 10 33*). An empty entry is shown as *(zero-length binary value)* in the Registry Editor. A defined value must have at least 4 bytes (32 bits).

- DWORD data types are a special case of a binary value. They are restricted to 4 bytes, and the value is shown in hexadecimals and decimals in the format *0x00000000 (0)*. The first number, *0x00000000*, is the hex representation of the value, whereas the number in brackets, *(0)*, contains the decimal representation.

NOTE: The data types for key values mentioned above are shown by the Registry Editor. A programmer can define additional types as special variants of these values (for example, REG_EXPAND_SZ for a zero-terminated string with Unicode or ANSI characters). Some information about these data types can be found in Nancy Cluts's book, *Programming the Windows 95 User Interface,* published by Microsoft Press.

If the *Default* entry contains no value, the string *(value not set)* is shown. The representation and meaning of the value's data depends on the key. A binary sequence can be interpreted as a single byte, a double byte, or a byte sequence. Some numerical values are stored as strings (for example, the screen resolution).

The whole hierarchy of the active key is shown in the status bar of the Registry Editor. This display can help you keep track of where you are in deeply nested structures when the hierarchy isn't completely visible in the left pane.

Changing an Existing Value

Before you start to modify the Registry values, you should read "Backing Up and Recovering Your Registry" on page 35. If settings get changed and Windows or an application no longer runs correctly, you will have a chance to recover the old Registry settings.

To change any value, you must first activate the key and display its values in the right pane by clicking it in the left pane of the Registry Editor. Then you can do one of the following:

■ Double-click the value name (in the Name column of the right pane).

■ Click the value name and use the Modify command in the Edit menu.

■ Right-click the value name and select the Modify command from the context menu.

The Registry Editor opens a dialog box showing the name and value of this entry. The contents of the dialog box depend on the value type. Figure 2-3 shows the Edit String dialog box for a text value.

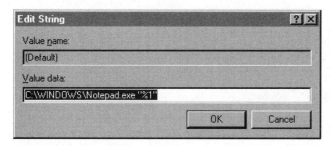

Figure 2-3.
The Edit String dialog box for a text value.

Editing a text value   If you open the Edit String dialog box and the key already contains a value, that value will be highlighted in the Value Data text box. You can type a new value into the Value Data text box and close the dialog box by clicking OK. The new value is immediately stored in the Registry.

> N O T E :   Text values are automatically enclosed in quotation marks (*""*)by the Registry Editor. You should never enter these quotes in the Value Data text box; otherwise, the value will be included in double sets of quotation marks (*""..."")*, which causes an error.

Editing a binary value   If the key contains a binary value, the Registry Editor opens the Edit Binary Value dialog box (see Figure 2-4 on the next page). The value's name appears in the Value Name text box and cannot be modified.

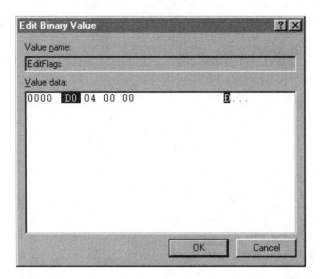

Figure 2-4.
The Edit Binary Value dialog box.

The Value Data text box displays the value in hexadecimal format. The four digits on the left indicate the offset into the data stream. The data itself is shown as a series of byte values (hex digits) followed by their character representations.

To change an existing value, select it first (which highlights it). Any highlighted value (as shown in Figure 2-4) can be overwritten by a new value. Click OK to close the dialog box and store the new value in the Registry. The modified value is displayed in the right pane of the Registry Editor window.

> NOTE: Be careful to edit only highlighted portions of a binary value in the Edit Binary Value dialog box. If no number is highlighted, your insert will be considered a new value. For example, suppose you moved the cursor to a new position but didn't highlight the next value. If you entered a new value, that value would be inserted as a new byte and wrong data would be stored in the Registry.

Editing a DWORD value   A DWORD value is altered in the Edit DWORD Value dialog box (shown in Figure 2-5). You can enter this value as a hexadecimal or as a decimal number. Select one of the Base options, and enter the value in the Value Data text box. A DWORD can never exceed 32 bits (or 8 hex digits).

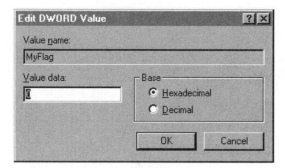

Figure 2-5.
The Edit DWORD Value dialog box.

Adding a New Value

A key can have one or more entries. Their values can be other subkeys (shown in the left pane of the Registry Editor) or data values associated with a name (shown in the right pane). If you want to add a new key, you have to define only the key name. If you want to add a new value, you must specify the name and the value. Follow these steps:

1. Right-click the desired key, or right-click anywhere in the right pane of the Registry Editor window to display the context menu.

2. Select New and one of the following commands: Key, String Value, Binary Value, or DWORD Value.

A new entry is inserted in the Registry. The entry type is defined by the selected command. Choosing Key adds a new subkey called *NewKey* in the left pane. Choosing String Value, Binary Value, or DWORD Value creates a value name (*New Value*) and a null value for the active key. (See Figure 2-6 on the following page.) You should change the default name by typing over the highlighted entry. The new name can be the name of a key or the name of a value (for example, *shell, open,* or *edit*).

After defining a value name in the right pane, you can enter the value for this new entry. (Follow the procedures on pages 19–21.) A string value initially has no value (*""*), whereas a binary value is empty. The initial value of a DWORD entry is zero. Examples of these initial values are shown in Figure 2-6 on the following page.

21

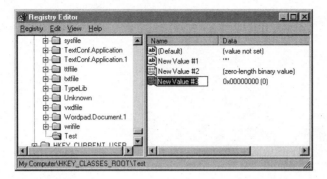

Figure 2-6.
New entries are displayed as "New Value" *in the Registry Editor.*

NOTE: You cannot change the type of a value. To change the value type, you must delete the value and create a new entry.

Deleting an Entry

The Registry Editor allows you to delete keys, subkeys, and values. To delete a key or a subkey:

1. Right-click the key in the left pane, and select Delete from the context menu.

2. Click Yes in the Confirm Key Delete dialog box.

The Registry Editor removes the key and all its associated values and subkeys from the Registry. But be careful—you cannot recall a key once it is deleted.

To delete a value:

1. Right-click the entry in the Name column in the right pane, and select Delete from the context menu.

2. Confirm that you want to delete this value by clicking Yes in the Confirm Value Delete dialog box.

NOTE: The Registry Editor does not have an Undo function. All changes are written directly to the disk. If you want to remove a special item in the Registry, consider renaming the key rather than deleting it. If something goes wrong and you can no longer run certain programs or Windows doesn't run correctly, you can simply rename the key to the old name and all the original data becomes available again.

If you accidentally delete the wrong key, you can restart the computer in Save mode. (Press the F8 key if the message "Windows 95 is loading" appears, and choose the Save Mode option.) This will restore the previous settings from the DA0 files.

The root items *HKEY_XXXX* can't be deleted.

Renaming a Key or a Value

Rename keys cautiously—a new name can dramatically affect system functionality, particularly if the key is necessary for starting Windows or for some other equally important task.

To rename a key or a value, right-click the item and select Rename from the context menu. The name you want to modify will be highlighted, and you can type over the string. To write the new name to the Registry, press Return or click outside the highlighted area.

Finding Information in the Registry

The Registry contains thousands of entries, so it can be difficult to find a desired key or value. You could search for it manually by scrolling through the hierarchy, but you'd have to know where this information is located and how to navigate there to avoid spending a lot of time clicking subkeys to find the one you want.

The more efficient approach is to delegate this searching job to the Registry Editor, which has a Find command on the Edit menu. When you select this command (by clicking it or by pressing Ctrl-F), the Find dialog box shown in Figure 2-7 opens. In it you can define what you want to look for. Enter a key, a subkey, a value name, or an actual value (text or binary) in the Find What text box.

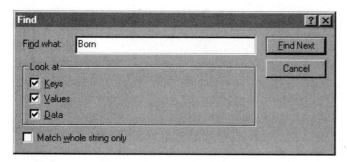

Figure 2-7.
The Find dialog box.

The Find function uses a pattern-matching algorithm to find substrings within a string. If you don't know the proper spelling of the value you are searching for, enter only a partial word and leave the Match Whole String Only checkbox blank. If you know the proper spelling, you can prevent the function from recognizing thousands of potential matches by selecting the Match Whole String Only checkbox. The Find function shows only those entries that match the entire pattern. To restrict the search, you must check the appropriate Look At options. All three of these options are activated by default, which means that the Registry Editor searches for matches in the whole Registry.

- The Keys option finds all key and subkey matches for the pattern.

- The Values option finds all value name matches. Values does not refer to the value of an item; it is the item displayed in the Name column in the right pane of the Registry Editor.

- The Data option extends or restricts the search to the data values of all keys. Data refers to the values shown in the Data column of the Registry Editor.

Click Find Next to start the search. The next match found is highlighted by the Registry Editor (see Figure 2-8). (If you search for data, the value name for a match—not the value data—is highlighted.) To find the next match, press F3 or select Find Next from the Edit menu.

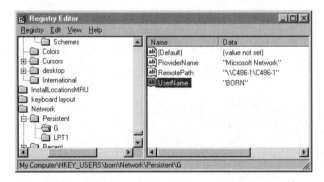

Figure 2-8.
A highlighted match in the Registry Editor.

Printing Parts of the Registry

The Registry Editor provides a function that allows you to print parts of or all of the Registry. Open the Registry menu and select the Print command, or press Ctrl-P.

The Registry Editor displays the Print dialog box shown in Figure 2-9. This dialog box is similar to Print dialog boxes in other Windows 95 applications.

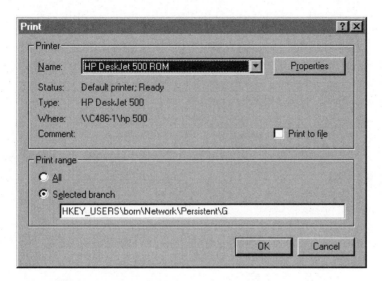

Figure 2-9.
The Print dialog box in the Registry Editor.

Select the range of the Registry Editor that you want to print by clicking one of two options in the Print Range section. By default, the Selected Branch option is marked. The name of the currently selected branch is displayed in the Print dialog box, so it is handy to select a key in the left pane of the Registry Editor before you invoke the Print command. If you want to print the whole Registry, check the All option box (but be careful—you'll be printing several hundred pages).

Importing and Exporting Registry Data

Depending on the computer, the file size of the Registry database can reach several hundred KB, which is a lot to manage. Depending on what you want to do or how the Registry is configured, you should consider storing and reading parts of the Registry in files. For example, you might want to share specific Registry entries (such as the settings for file extensions) between two computers. You could export the entries from one computer into a file and then import that file into the second computer. You could even edit the file and import it to both computers. You can access import and export functions from the Registry menu.

Importing a REG File into the Registry

There are two ways to import data into the Registry: via the Registry Editor and via ActiveX functions. Both methods need files with the REG extension, which are created by the Windows 95 Registry Editor. Both methods produce the same results and are simple to use, so the choice is up to you.

Using the Registry Editor

The first method is implemented by selecting Import Registry File from the Registry menu. After invoking this function, the Import Registry File dialog box is shown. (See Figure 2-10.) Select a folder, click on the requested filename (or enter the filename), and click Open.

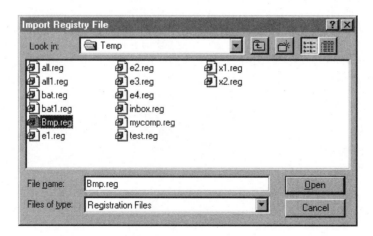

Figure 2-10.
Importing a Registry file.

Using ActiveX Features

The other method of importing REG files takes advantage of ActiveX features included in Windows 95. You must have a valid REG file stored on your hard disk or on a diskette. Either double-click the file or right-click the file and select the Merge command from the context menu.

Whichever method you use, all information required to import the data must be in the imported file. The Registry Editor opens this file, reads the information contained in it, and adds this data into the Registry. You cannot select a destination where the data will be stored, so if there are entries in the file that are already defined in the Registry, the Registry keys and values will be overwritten by the matching imported keys and their values. No query message warns you before the data is overwritten, so proceed cautiously.

The imported files must have a REG extension, and a special format is required. Valid Windows 95 REG files contain only ASCII characters in a predefined format. Each Windows 95 REG file contains the word REGEDIT4 in the first line; the second line must be blank. The following format is valid for a REG file:

```
REGEDIT4

[HKEY_CLASSES_ROOT\.bmp]
@="Paint.Picture"

[HKEY_CLASSES_ROOT\.bmp\ShellNew]
"NullFile"=""
```

All the lines that follow the first blank line can contain entries for Registry settings. Each entry starts with the name of the destination key enclosed in square brackets []. The next line is used for the value of an entry (which is the value shown later in the right pane of the Registry Editor). This value is included in quotation marks (for example, "NullFile"). Some lines start with @= followed by a value in quotes. The @ character indicates a default value for an entry. These entries are marked as *Default* in the right pane of the Registry Editor.

After a REG file is successfully imported, a message box informs you that the REG file was valid, indicating that it was formatted properly, that it was a valid Windows 95 REG file, and that all information was included in the Registry. However, it does not indicate that the information contained in the file and entered into the Registry is valid. (The Registry Editor can't check the contents of a REG file for logical consistency within a system. Chapter 3 addresses this in more detail.)

Importing REG Files Created in Windows 95

All REG files can be used to change the Registry settings of your own computer or to share the information with other machines. Some software packages come with REG files that modify the Registry after installing the files to the hard disk.

Here are a couple things to be careful of with REG files created in Windows 95:

■ Don't import a Windows 95 REG file into older versions of Windows or Windows NT.

■ Import only valid Windows 95 REG files to the Registry, which always contain the REGEDIT4 signature in the first line.

Exporting a REG File

As we have seen, you can easily import new values from REG files into the Registry. REG files are pure ASCII files that can be edited in text editors such as Notepad or WordPad.

REG files can also be created by using the export function of the Registry Editor, which allows you to share settings with other computers or to re-use old settings after you've changed them. To export parts of the Registry, follow these steps:

1. In the Registry Editor, select the branch or subkey that you want to export.

2. Open the Registry menu and select Export Registry File. The Export Registry File dialog box opens (see Figure 2-11).

3. Select the folder that you want to save the REG file to in the Export Registry File dialog box.

4. Enter the new filename.

5. Click Save.

After clicking Save, the Registry Editor creates a REG file containing the information of the selected branch. This REG file can now be imported as described in the previous section.

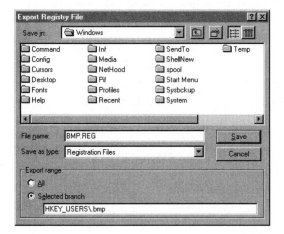

Figure 2-11.
Exporting a Registry branch.

By default, the Registry Editor exports only the active branch. (This is the branch you selected before you invoked the export function.) You can export the whole Registry by selecting All in the Export Range section, but keep the file size in mind. Such a REG file would be too big to edit with Notepad, and in WordPad you would have to be careful to store the altered text in the text file format.

Using Export as a Backup Tool

Perhaps I haven't warned you enough to create backup copies of your Registry before you modify any entries. Okay—before you modify, back up the Registry! You can store the DAT files on a separate disk, which allows you to recover the previous Registry settings from the backup files. In the section titled "Backing Up and Recovering Your Registry," beginning on page 35, I discuss this technique and other topics.

You may be asking, "Why should I back up the whole Registry if I just want to change one entry?" We have seen that the Registry Editor offers functions to export and import parts of the Registry, so why not save time and disk capacity and create a partial backup? The steps for creating a backup are straightforward. From the Registry Editor, select the subkey to be changed, and export this part of the Registry to a REG file. All information contained in the subkeys is stored in the REG file. This file can then be imported later to recover the Registry.

Unfortunately, this approach has a trap (and I was caught several times in my first days working with Windows 95). To illustrate the risks, let's run a small experiment. Let's assume we must change something in the Registry. The *HKEY_CLASSES_ROOT* branch contains the registration for the file extensions. Let's modify the settings of the BMP file type. In Figure 2-12, this branch of the Registry is shown. (In Chapter 3, we'll learn how to register new file types or add commands to a file type.)

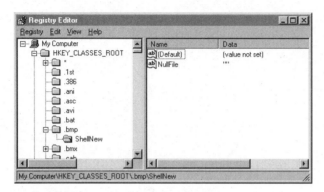

Figure 2-12.
The branch for BMP files with the original data.

Before we modify anything, we have to save the information contained in this branch by using the export function. After exporting this branch, you have a REG file with the following contents:

```
REGEDIT4

[HKEY_CLASSES_ROOT\.bmp]
@="Paint.Picture"

[HKEY_CLASSES_ROOT\.bmp\ShellNew]
"NullFile"=""
```

This is the information we find in the two panes of the Registry Editor. Now we are prepared to modify some entries in the *.bmp* branch. I change the value of the *NullFile* entry, and I add one subkey and one new value. Both the new subkey and the new value are named *Born*, and both data entries (*Born* and *NullFile*) contain values such as *"Hello"*. You can see the new Registry structure in Figure 2-13.

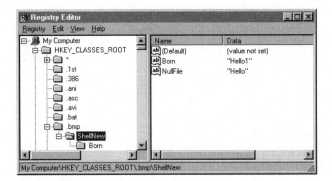

Figure 2-13.
The modified structure of the branch.

Of course, the keys I've added are nonsense, but I use them to illustrate my point. To avoid trouble running Windows or any applications, we want to remove these nonsensical keys from the Registry, so we should import the REG file with the previous data (expecting the modifications to be deleted during the import). No problem—the old settings are only a mouse click away. (We exported the original settings in a REG file, so we will use the Import Registry File command to import it.)

The result is shown in Figure 2-14 on the following page: Only the value for *NullFile* is set back to the previous value. Neither the new subkey *Born* nor the new name *Born* are deleted. What's wrong with our REG file? Well, there's nothing wrong. Importing a REG file does not replace the data in the Registry—it adds to it. If a value name (or a key name) that is not in the Registry exists in the REG file, that value is added to the Registry. If a value name is in the Registry and also in the REG file, the value in the REG file overwrites the data of the matching value in the Registry. So values that are in the Registry but not in the REG file, such as our *Born* value, are left untouched in the Registry. (The word "Merge" on the REG file's context menu expresses this.)

> **WARNING:** The import function does not delete or reset new entries in the Registry. You can change only an existing value (to *""*, for example), so it is not safe to back up the Registry with the export function of the Registry Editor and recover the old settings with the import function!

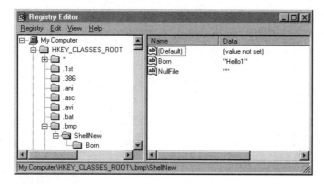

Figure 2-14.
The branch after importing the old values.

Accessing the Registry via Remote

Windows 95 provides a feature to allow remote Registry access from other computers. This feature, called the Microsoft Remote Registry service, is helpful in networking environments where the network administrator might need to change Registry entries on several PCs.

Installing the Remote Registry Service

The Remote Registry feature isn't installed during the standard Windows setup. This feature can be enabled only in networks that support user-level access control with a server such as Windows NT or Novell NetWare. (Windows 95 clients don't have a user-level access control.) To access the Connect Network Registry command from the Registry menu, you must install the Remote Registry service on both computers.

To install this service, do the following:

1. Select the Network icon in the Control Panel.

2. Click Add on the Configuration property page.

3. Select the Service icon in the Select Network Component Type dialog box and click Add.

4. In the Select Network Service dialog box, click Have Disk.

5. Enter the CD-ROM drive letter and the path \Admin\Nettools\Remotreg.

6. Click OK in the Install From Disk dialog box.

Windows installs the necessary components. After a successful installation, select the Access Control property page on the Network property sheet and set the option box to User-Level Access Control. To access the Registry of a remote computer, open the Registry Editor's Registry menu and select Connect Network Registry (see Figure 2-15).

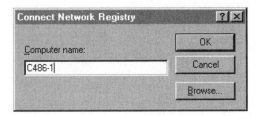

Figure 2-15.
The Connect Network Registry dialog box.

Enter the name of the remote computer, or click the Browse button to scan the whole network. After successfully connecting to the remote computer, you can alter the Registry.

Accessing the Registry in Real Mode

Suppose the Registry is completely corrupted and Windows 95 won't start. You can't start the Windows version of the Registry Editor. How can you inspect the Registry under such circumstances?

The answer is pretty simple: The Registry Editor also runs in MS-DOS real mode, so if you can boot your computer and enter DOS mode, you can access the Registry Editor. You can find a copy of the Registry Editor (REGEDIT.EXE) in two places:

■ On the Windows Start disk (see "Using the Windows 95 Startup Disk" on page 37)

■ In the \Windows folder

Only one version of the Registry Editor is available for Windows and DOS. If you invoke REGEDIT.EXE under Windows 95, the Registry Editor window is displayed. Under DOS, the Registry Editor will have only a command line interface.

When you run REGEDIT.EXE from the DOS prompt without any command line options, a help screen advising you how to use this tool appears.

To import a REG file into the Registry, use the following command:

```
REGEDIT /L:system /R:user filename
```

The first switch, /L:system, is optional and specifies the location of the SYSTEM.DAT file. (This file is located in the Windows folder.) The second switch, /R:user, is also optional and specifies the location of the USER.DAT file. This file could be in the Windows folder or in other folders. (The location depends on the configuration of your computer, as we have seen in Chapter 1.) *Filename* is the name of the REG file that will be imported. For example, the following command will import the contents of GLOBAL.REG into USER.DAT and SYSTEM.DAT:

```
REGEDIT /L:C:\Windows\ /R:C:\Windows\Profiles\ A:Global.REG
```

This command can be used to add keys to the Registry and overwrite data in existing keys.

If you want to create a new Registry database, you must use the /C switch. The following command will create two new files, USER.DAT and SYSTEM.DAT, in the Windows folder from the GLOBAL.REG file located on the A drive:

```
REGEDIT /C A:Global.REG
```

This command is completely different from the previous version because the whole Registry is re-created from GLOBAL.REG, rather than being only modified.

NOTE: Using the /C option to rebuild the Registry database is dangerous. When you import the REG file, if the REG file contains only one branch of the Registry, the complete SYSTEM.DAT and USER.DAT files will contain only this branch. Always be sure that you have a REG file containing the entire Registry database before using this option.

You can also export some parts of the Registry in DOS mode:

```
REGEDIT /L:System /R:User /E filename
```

The /L and /R switches specify the location of the SYSTEM.DAT and USER.DAT files. The /E switch advises REGEDIT.EXE to export the Registry into a new file, which is named in the last parameter as *filename*. This creates a copy of the whole Registry.

Optionally, you can specify a Registry key to export:

```
REGEDIT /E filename regkey
```

The parameter *regkey* defines the Registry key that will be exported into the REG file.

NOTE: I don't recommend that you use REGEDIT.EXE within the DOS command prompt. There are too many parameters, and the risk is high that you would destroy part or all of the Registry. The real-mode version of REGEDIT.EXE also has problems importing large keys. (You get an error message.) Using the real-mode version should be the last choice to recover the Registry. (See the section "Backing Up and Recovering Your Registry" to learn about more convenient methods for backing up and recovering the Registry.)

I use real mode only when I need to update the Registry during a system startup, in which case I include a REGEDIT command in AUTOEXEC.BAT.

Backing Up and Recovering Your Registry

A corrupted Registry prevents the system from starting properly, so backing up and recovering the Registry are two important tasks you need to know how to perform. You can perform these tasks in several ways, but some methods are riskier than others.

Manually Backing Up

The simplest way to create a backup of your Registry is manually—by starting the Windows Explorer and copying the SYSTEM.DAT and USER.DAT files onto a bootable disk—but this could present a file size problem. I've seen several versions of the Registry that need more than 700 KB of disk space. If you want to store multiple versions on one disk, you must use a compression program such as Nico Mak Computing's WinZip or PKWARE's PKZIP.

To recover a corrupted Registry from a disk, you must use the DOS copy command (remember—Windows won't restart properly). The SYSTEM.DAT and USER.DAT files are stored with the attributes Read-Only, Hidden, and System. Reset these before you copy the backup version to your hard disk. After you copy the files, you have to set the correct attributes again. You can do all this with a simple batch program:

```
cd c:\Windows
attrib -h -r -s system.dat
attrib -h -r -s user.dat
copy a:\user.dat
copy a:\system.dat
attrib +h +r +s system.dat
attrib +h +r +s user.dat
```

Once USER.DAT and SYSTEM.DAT are on your hard disk, you can restart the computer or, if the computer is in MS-DOS mode, start Windows 95 with the WIN command.

> NOTE: You can keep a copy of this batch program and a copy of the DOS program ATTRIB.EXE (found in \Windows\Command) on your backup disk. The batch commands shown in the preceding program rely on the fact that the batch program starts from the hard disk of your computer and that your hard disk is your C: drive. If you prefer to start the batch program from the backup disk, you must change the drive letters in the commands.

I have seen this backup method published in magazines and WWW pages. This procedure will work, of course. The risk is that you will backup and recover the wrong data. I mentioned in Chapter 1 that SYSTEM.DAT is always stored in the Windows folder along with a copy of USER.DAT. Unfortunately, Windows can keep several versions of USER.DAT in different locations. If you enable user profiles, each user gets his or her own copy of USER.DAT. During the user logon Windows determines which copy to use. This copy is located in the Windows subfolder \Profiles*name*, where *name* is the name of the active user. Be careful to copy the correct USER.DAT file back to the correct folder.

Using the DA0 Files

The USER.DA0 and SYSTEM.DA0 files are helpful as backup files only if the Registry is corrupted or deleted and you can't recover the Registry using other methods. This DA0 backup isn't a preferable backup source because the DA0 files can sometimes contain incorrect data. For example, let's assume a file extension is registered by an application. Then a new application is installed that overwrites this setting and establishes an association between the file extension and the new application. If the new application is deleted, double-clicking on a file with this extension that was created with the original application results in an error message. The Registry now contains incorrect data, and if it is not corrected before the first restart, the old DA0 files will be overwritten. So it is always wise to create a separate backup of the Registry before something is changed in the system.

> NOTE: During the installation of Windows 95, the setup program analyzes the system hardware and uses that information to create the SYSTEM.DAT file. Setup leaves a copy of the initial settings after the installation in the root directory of the hard disk in the file SYSTEM.1ST. This file can be helpful if SYSTEM.DAT is destroyed.

Using the Windows 95 Startup Disk

If you're having trouble with your computer, boot your computer in the MS-DOS mode. The setup process creates a startup disk during the Windows 95 installation. This disk contains a mini–DOS operating system (including ATTRIB.EXE) as well as copies of the system files (AUTOEXEC.BAT, CONFIG.SYS, SYSTEM.DAT, and USER.DAT). You will also find a copy of REGEDIT.EXE on this startup disk. If your computer can't boot with Windows 95, you should try to restart the system with this startup disk. After this procedure, you can recover the Registry using the batch commands in MS-DOS.

There is only one problem with this approach: The Registry has likely changed in the time between the day you installed Windows and the day you run into serious trouble. Each software installation will change parts of the Registry, so it's highly probable that the startup disk contains an outdated version of your Registry. Reinstalling all the software after recovering the Registry from the startup disk is tedious and time-consuming.

Creating a New Startup Disk

Fortunately, you can easily create an updated startup disk. All you need is a spare disk and a few minutes. After you have successfully installed new software or changed something in your system, you can create the disk as follows:

1. Open the Control Panel, and double-click the Add/Remove Programs icon. Windows 95 opens the Add/Remove Programs Properties dialog box shown in Figure 2-16 on the following page.

2. Select the Startup Disk property page, insert a disk in the disk drive, and click Create Disk.

Follow the Windows 95 prompts to create a new startup disk that contains a copy of the current Registry. Label this copy with the current date, and use this backup later on to restore the Registry.

NOTE: The startup disk contains only a minimal system with the standard files. If you need special device drivers to access some hardware (for example, MSCDEX.EXE for a CD-ROM drive), you must add these drivers and modify the CONFIG.SYS and AUTOEXEC.BAT files on the startup disk. Otherwise, you can't access these devices under MS-DOS.

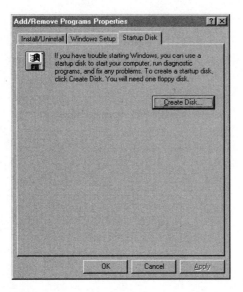

Figure 2-16.
The property page for creating a startup disk.

Using the Error Recovery Utility

Backing up and recovering the Registry manually can be a little bit tricky, but it's your only choice if you have the diskette version of Windows 95. If you change the Registry settings frequently (to test software packages, for example), more handy methods are required. Fortunately, the developers anticipated this situation and created a neat program called Emergency Recovery Utility, which is designed to back up your system configuration on a disk each time you successfully change the Registry. Use this utility to create a backup before you make any significant system changes such as adding new hardware or software. This utility makes it easy to recover a previous version of the Registry.

This Emergency Recovery Utility is located on the Windows 95 CD-ROM in the \Other\Misc\Eru folder. To use this utility, perform the following steps:

1. Create a new folder with the name \ERU, or a similar name, on your hard disk.

2. Copy the files ERU.EXE, ERD.E_E, and ERU.INF from the CD-ROM into this new folder.

Creating a Backup of Your Configuration

To create a backup of all or some system configuration files, you must run the ERU.EXE utility. Start the utility by double-clicking the ERU.EXE icon. (This can be done in the Explorer window, or you can create a shortcut on the desktop.) The ERU program invokes a wizard that guides you through the following backup steps:

1. Click Next to move to the first step, and select the destination (floppy or hard drive) for the saved files (see Figure 2-17). I recommend you use a formatted floppy, which can be labeled with the backup date and other details, as a backup medium. Click Next to progress to the next dialog box.

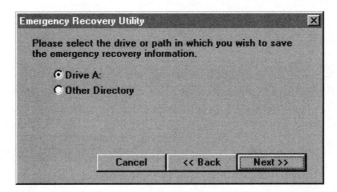

Figure 2-17.
Select the backup drive or directory.

2. If you selected Other Directory, enter a directory name for a network or local drive. Click Next.

3. Select a full backup by clicking the Next button, which saves all system files, or select a Custom backup (see Figure 2-18 on the following page). If you install a new software package, I recommend a full backup. If you change just a few Registry settings (edit a branch, for example), you should create a custom backup.

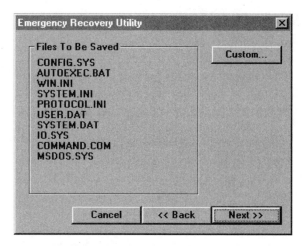

Figure 2-18.
Select the type of backup you want to perform.

4. Click Custom, which invokes the dialog box shown in Figure 2-19.
   This dialog box contains a list of all system files used in the backup
   set. Selected files are checked and will be included in the backup.

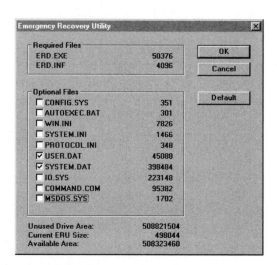

Figure 2-19.
Select the backup files for a custom backup.

5. Deselect all files that you do not want to include in the backup.

6. Close the dialog box by clicking OK. ERU backs up all selected files into the destination folder or onto the floppy disk.

NOTE: ERU stores the selected files with a modified extension (SYSTEM.D_T and USER.D_T, for example). The destination also contains the files ERD.EXE and ERD.INF, which are necessary to recover the system files.

Recovering the System Files

To recover your configuration, reboot the computer and start with the DOS prompt (real mode). (To invoke the DOS prompt, you can press F8 during the boot process when you see the Starting Windows 95 message. Then choose the Safe Mode Command Prompt Only option.) Insert the backup disk or change to the backup directory, and start the ERD.EXE program. ERD is a DOS utility that lists the files to recover (see Figure 2-20). This list shows the files that were backed up with ERU.

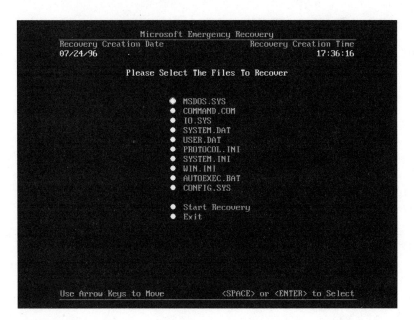

Figure 2-20.
The ERD screen, which lists the files that will be recovered.

ERD recovers all files by default—all system files will be overwritten. I don't recommend you overwrite all files every time. If you want to restore only the Registry, you need only SYSTEM.DAT and USER.DAT. You can select or deselect backup files that you want to recover by pressing the Spacebar next to the selected item. Entries marked with a yellow bullet are included in the recovery. Entries marked with a gray bullet are excluded from the recovery.

Pressing Return toggles the bullet to the previous state. After you have selected the files that you want to recover, move the cursor to the Start Recovery item and press Return. ERD restores all selected files from the backup set. After recovering the system files, you need to reboot the system again; the computer should start with the old configuration.

NOTE: The ERU/ERD utility combination is smart. ERU saves the date of the backup and the location of all files in ERD.INF. During recovery, ERD.EXE examines this file and restores the backup files to the exact location they were copied from. Invoking ERD.EXE from the correct backup set prevents you from overwriting the wrong DAT files.

The System Policy Editor

During startup, Windows reads the data stored in SYSTEM.DAT and in USER.DAT, which can be different for each user. System administrators customize user settings in USER.DAT. For example, they might restrict access to certain desktop components or Start menu commands, or change the location of the USER.DAT file.

The tool for changing these settings is the System Policy Editor, which is shipped on the Windows 95 CD-ROM. Changing a setting with the System Policy Editor influences the Registry settings. We'll review how to install the System Policy Editor in this chapter; the different system settings available through the System Policy Editor will be discussed in later chapters.

Installing the System Policy Editor

The System Policy Editor is available on the Windows CD-ROM in \Admin\Apptools\Poledit. To install the System Policy Editor on your hard disk, follow these steps:

1. Open the Control Panel.

2. Double-click the Add/Remove Programs icon.

3. Click the Windows Setup tab.

4. Click Have Disk on the Windows Setup property page. The Install From Disk dialog box is displayed.

5. Enter the path \Admin\Apptools\Poledit. Click OK.

6. Select the System Policy Editor option shown in the Have Disk dialog box. (See Figure 2-21.) Click Install. The files contained in the \Poledit subfolder are installed in the \Windows folder on your hard disk.

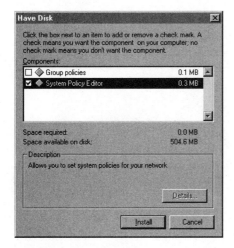

Figure 2-21.
The Have Disk dialog box.

After the files are successfully installed, you can start the program by double-clicking the POLEDIT.EXE file icon.

Enabling User Profiles

Before you can use individual user profiles, you must enable them in Windows 95. To enable user profiles, follow these steps:

1. Open the Control Panel and double-click Passwords.

2. Select the User Profiles tab (see Figure 2-22 on the following page) and check the second option, which allows users to customize their preferences and desktop settings.

3. Select the applicable options under User Profile Settings, and click OK.

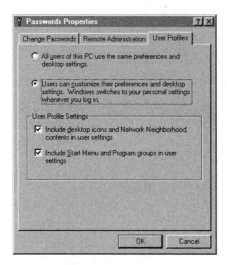

Figure 2-22.
The User Profiles property page.

After restarting the system, each user can log on with a user name and a password. Now you are prepared to change user profile settings with the System Policy Editor.

Using the System Policy Editor

When you start the System Policy Editor for the first time, a blank window is displayed. You can read the current Registry by selecting Open Registry from the File menu. The System Policy Editor will show two icons: Local User and Local Computer (see Figure 2-23).

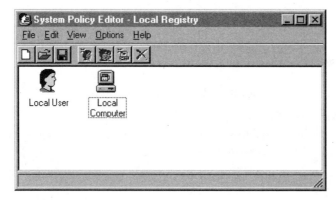

Figure 2-23.
The System Policy Editor.

Double-clicking these icons opens dialog boxes that display the Registry options. Double-clicking the Local Computer icon displays the Local Computer Properties property sheet, which has system settings. (See Figure 2-24.)

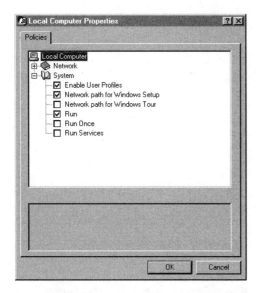

Figure 2-24.
The Local Computer Properties property sheet displays system settings.

Double-clicking the Local User icon displays the Local User Properties property sheet (see Figure 2-25 on the following page), which allows you to set restrictions for the active user, customize the shell, and so on. Any values you change are stored in the Registry. (I discuss several topics concerning the System Policy Editor in later chapters.)

> N O T E : You can also use the System Policy Editor to set up profiles for other users. More information can be found in the *Windows 95 Resource Kit,* which is available from Microsoft Press.

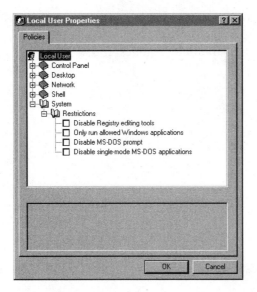

Figure 2-25.
The Local User Properties property sheet displays user-specific settings.

Other Tools for Changing Registry Settings

The Registry Editor and System Policy Editor are only two tools for changing Registry settings. Following is a description of additional tools:

- *The Open With dialog box.* Use this with the Windows shell to change registered file types. This technique is discussed further in Chapter 3.

- *The File Types property page.* Select Options from the Explorer's View menu to access the property page File Types, which allows you to inspect and alter the Registry settings for registered file types. This technique is discussed further in Chapter 3.

- *The Control Panel.* The Control Panel contains several icons. Double-clicking an icon will open a property sheet, which contains Registry settings that can be altered.

- *Add-on utilities.* Several add-on utilities (such as Win Hacker and Power Toys) are available for changing Registry settings. Some functions of the Power Toy modules are discussed in later chapters.

■ *Property sheets of applications.* Some application programs store their settings in the Registry. You can update these settings by modifying the options in the appropriate application property sheet.

■ *REG and INF files.* These are discussed in Chapters 3 through 7.

■ *Install programs.* These are discussed briefly in Chapter 7.

6810×8850

1090-1170

This book brings together all the scattered details about the Registry and provides a comprehensive look at how it works and how you can use it. Fortunately, the concept of the

The Registry is the central database in Microsoft Windows 95 that stores and maintains configuration information and is thus one of the most interesting and important components of Windows 95. Until now, details about the Registry haven't been readily available, and developers, administrators, and end users have all faced the challenge of trying to find information about it.

CHAPTER THREE

Registering
Filename Extensions

When you double-click a filename in Microsoft Windows 95, the file opens in an application associated with that file type. For example, double-clicking a file with a DOC extension opens the file in Microsoft Word (assuming you have Word installed on your machine). The file is opened in the appropriate application because the file extension is stored in the Registry with an association to that application. This chapter describes the different ways to register new file types, extend the commands for registered file types, and delete unnecessary associations. But first, we'll discuss the *HKEY_CLASSES_ROOT* Registry structure.

The *HKEY_CLASSES_ROOT* Structure

File types and their associations to specific applications are stored in the Registry during the installation of new software. An application's setup program registers the file extension of the file type and the commands that are applied to this file type. All this information is stored in the branch *HKEY_CLASSES_ROOT*.

Each file type must have two keys in *HKEY_CLASSES_ROOT*. The first key defines the file extension and a name (*name_ID*) for this file type. This name is then used in a second key to define the commands for this file type. The structure follows:

```
HKEY_CLASSES_ROOT
    .ext = "name_ID"
    name_ID = <"Description">
        shell
            verb = <menu item text>
                command = command string
                ⋮
```

The text shown in brackets (< >) is optional. Since this structure probably looks a little bit too abstract, let's examine how this structure looks for the BAT file extension. A BAT file type is registered during the Windows 95 setup, creating two keys in the Registry: the *.bat* key and the *batfile* key. Figure 3-1 shows these keys.

Figure 3-1.
Keys for registering the BAT file type.

The *.bat* key defines the file extension (BAT) and the associated value (*name_ID*). This *name_ID* is set to the string *"batfile"*, which is the unique name identifier for the second key. (You can use any name that is valid for a key. For example, *"batchfile"* is also valid.)

Although the BAT extension is registered by the inclusion of the *.bat* key, Windows needs some additional information about what to do with a BAT file—in other words, some executable commands that enable the user to double-click and open the file. This is handled by the second key, *batfile* (shown in the lower part of Figure 3-1). The *Default* value shown in the lower right part of Figure 3-1 defines the description text, *"MS-DOS Batch File"*, for this file type. This description is what you see in Microsoft Explorer in the Type column and in the Registered File Types list on the File Types property page of the Options dialog box. The *EditFlags* value enables and disables the edit options in the Edit File Type dialog box (discussed further on pages 91–94 in this chapter). More interesting than the values of the *batfile* key are its subkeys.

The *DefaultIcon* Subkey

If you open a window (for example, the My Computer window or the Explorer window), each file is shown with an associated icon. Registered file types have their own symbols to simplify their identification. Information about each icon is defined in the *DefaultIcon* subkey. The *Default* value for this subkey is set to the path and filename that contains the icon. A BAT file value, for example, is set to the SHELL32.DLL file in the \Windows\System folder. Because this DLL file contains a collection of different icons, an index is required to select the appropriate icon. (The first icon has the index *0*.) The value for a BAT file, then, is set to something like this:

```
"C:\Windows\System\Shell32.dll,-153"
```

For other file types, this path might address other EXE or DLL files, such as this:

```
"C:\Windows\Notepad.exe, 1"
```

This string uses the Notepad icon as the default icon for a file type. (We will see further examples in the following chapters.) If the file contains only one icon, you can omit the comma and the index value following the filename.

> **NOTE:** Depending on the handler for the file type, you can omit the name of the icon file and use *"%1"* instead. This means that the Windows icon handler can use a different symbol for each instance of a file type. In this case, the *IconHandler* key must be added to the *shellex* key. In Chapter 5, I'll show how this can be used to customize the Windows shell.
>
> Another issue concerns the index number given for an icon. If the icon source (an EXE, DLL, or ICO file) contains more than one icon, you must specify an icon index. Icons are indexed with positive values starting from *0*. However, if you look at the *DefaultIcon* entry in the *batfile* key (see above), you will notice the index is a negative value (*-153*). In this case, the icon is designated using a resource contained in an EXE or DLL file. A negative value defines a resource identifier, so the *"C:\Windows\System\Shell32.dll,-153"* value means the resource defined with the identifier *-153* will be used for the icon. In order to use a resource as an icon source, you must know the resource identifier. Unfortunately, Windows 95 doesn't come with a tool to inspect resource identifiers; you need a resource construction tool found in software packages such as Microsoft Visual C++. Therefore I haven't used resource identifiers in this book.

The *shell* Subkey

The second subkey under the *batfile* key is called *shell* (as shown in Figure 3-1 on page 50). This subkey is important because Windows 95 retrieves information about what actions the shell (the Windows operating system) can perform on the BAT file type. For example, double-clicking a file of a registered file type executes commands: Files with the extensions BAT, COM, and EXE are executed, a TXT file is loaded into Notepad, and so on. Figure 3-2 shows how this shell information is stored in the Registry.

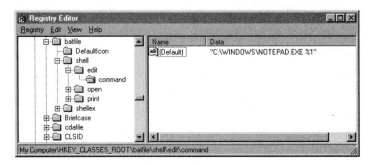

Figure 3-2.
Subkeys of the shell *key.*

The *shell* subkey contains other subkeys that define the actions that can be performed on the given file type—in this example, the BAT file type. (Sometimes these subkeys are called *verbs.*) In Figure 3-2, the subkeys (or verbs) *edit, open,* and *print* are shown. If you select a BAT file by right-clicking it, you will find the commands Edit, Open, and Print on the context menu. Double-clicking a BAT file invokes the *open* verb (which is the default).

Each verb subkey can contain a *command* subkey. This subkey contains the command string in the *Default* value entry. Figure 3-2 shows the *command* subkey for the *edit* verb. The subkeys *open* and *print* also contain *command* subkeys.

The *Default* value of the *command* subkey is set to a string with the name of the executable application. The command string for the *edit* verb in the *batfile* subkey looks like this:

```
"C:\WINDOWS\NOTEPAD.EXE %1"
```

This line is easy to understand—it contains the drive, path, and name of an application. The parameter *%1* is just a placeholder. When the user selects the Edit command from the context menu, the shell invokes the application and substitutes the *%1* placeholder with the path and name of the selected file. If the application needs some optional parameters, you can add these parameters into the command line. The following lines define a Play command for a file that runs in the CD Player application:

```
shell
    play
        command = "C:\WINDOWS\CDPLAYER.EXE /play %1"
```

The *shellex* Subkey

The third subkey in the *batfile* branch is named *shellex*. This key is optional and contains information about shell extensions that handle the BAT file type under Windows 95. Windows offers a special property sheet handler for these files.(See Figure 3-3.)

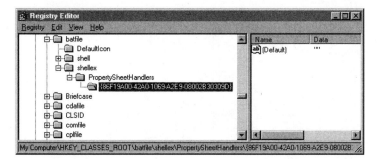

Figure 3-3.
The PropertySheetHandlers *subkey under the* shellex *subkey.*

The subkey under the property sheet handler is a bit cryptic, so here are short explanations of two of the more critical features:

- *PropertySheetHandlers* is a key containing a subkey that defines the Class ID for the new handler. (See Figure 3-3.)

- This Class ID (or CLSID) is a 16-byte value that identifies the ActiveX class of the handler. The value is set in curly brackets, or braces: *{86F19A00-42A0-1069-A2E9-08002B30309D}*. You can interpret this value like a phone number. In the same way that a single phone number corresponds to one person, the CLSID number stored in the Registry corresponds to a specific ActiveX module that contains this code. There can be only one module (ActiveX server) with this code, and it is invoked when you right-click the file and select Properties from the context menu. The module will handle the request and display the property sheet of the file type. BAT files have property sheets like the one shown in Figure 3-4 on the following page.

Comparing a BAT file property sheet and the property sheets of other file types—a TXT file, for example—reveals differences. The property sheet of a BAT file contains several pages with information about the file. The property sheet of a TXT file consists of only one page showing the general properties. TXT files use the default Windows 95 property sheet.

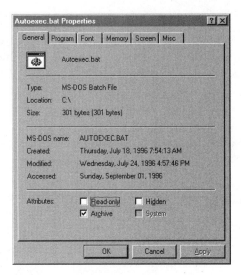

Figure 3-4.
A property sheet for a BAT file.

How Do You Retrieve the CLSID Code for a Module?

To register a new module (ActiveX server), you need a CLSID code that is unique worldwide—no other handler can use the same code because modules will collide. The solution comes from the world of networks, where the Open Software Foundation developed the unique identifiers for the Distributed Computing Environment (DCE) standard. If you are a programmer, you can use the GUIDGEN (Globally Unique Identifiers) or UUIDGEN (Universally Unique Identifiers) tools to create a unique code for the component class in order to identify your module as an ActiveX server. (More information about the registering of CLSID codes can be found in these books: Kraig Brockschmidt's *Inside ActiveX,* Charles Petzold's *Programming Windows 95,* Nancy Cluts's *Programming the Windows 95 User Interface,* and the *Programmer's Guide to Microsoft Windows 95.*) If you aren't a programmer, you must know an existing CLSID code to register an ActiveX module.

Combining Branches into a REG File

The previous sections explained how Windows 95 recognizes a registered file type. As we've seen, each file type has two entries: one that describes its extension and one that contains its properties. For the BAT file type, these definitions can be combined into a single REG file. In the following lines, I've exported both branches and merged them into one REG file:

```
REGEDIT4

[HKEY_CLASSES_ROOT\.bat]
@="batfile"

[HKEY_CLASSES_ROOT\batfile]
@="MS-DOS Batch File"
"EditFlags"=hex:d0,04,00,00

[HKEY_CLASSES_ROOT\batfile\shell]
@=""

[HKEY_CLASSES_ROOT\batfile\shell\open]
@=""
"EditFlags"=hex:00,00,00,00

[HKEY_CLASSES_ROOT\batfile\shell\open\command]
@="\"%1\" %*"

[HKEY_CLASSES_ROOT\batfile\shell\print]
@=""

[HKEY_CLASSES_ROOT\batfile\shell\print\command]
@="C:\\WINDOWS\\NOTEPAD.EXE /p %1"

[HKEY_CLASSES_ROOT\batfile\shell\edit]
@="&Edit"

[HKEY_CLASSES_ROOT\batfile\shell\edit\command]
@="C:\\WINDOWS\\NOTEPAD.EXE %1"

[HKEY_CLASSES_ROOT\batfile\shellex]
[HKEY_CLASSES_ROOT\batfile\shellex\PropertySheetHandlers]
```

(continued)

(continued)

```
[HKEY_CLASSES_ROOT\batfile\shellex\PropertySheetHandlers\{86F19A00-
42A0-1069-A2E9-08002B30309D}]
@=""

[HKEY_CLASSES_ROOT\batfile\DefaultIcon]
@="C:\\WINDOWS\\SYSTEM\\shell32.dll,-153"
```

> **N O T E :** This REG file contains all the information you need to register the default icon, the commands, and the shell extensions. We can use this REG file or parts of it as a template for registering other file types. The pitfalls of doing this will be shown later.

Registering New File Types and Modifying Existing Ones

Windows offers you several ways to register and modify file types: using the Open With dialog box, using the Windows Explorer, using the Registry Editor, and using a REG file.

We've examined the structure of the *HKEY_CLASSES_ROOT* branch, but we haven't really addressed what you can do with this knowledge. Registering a new file type allows you to manipulate how you access and enable functions, applications, and so on. For example, in Windows 95, all files with an EXE, COM, or BAT extension allow you to double-click them in order to execute them. When you double-click a data file, the associated application starts and the data file is loaded. Double-clicking a shortcut executes a Windows application. Right-clicking a file opens the context menu, allowing you to select a command.

Unfortunately, many files do not have a registered extension. For example, files downloaded from mailboxes can be simple text files with extensions like DIZ. These files can be opened with Notepad, but since DIZ isn't a file type registered with Notepad, double-clicking won't open the file in Notepad. (Try double-clicking the file README.DIZ in the \chapter3 folder of the down-loaded sample files.) Other documents are stored in files with the name README.1ST and so on. Programmers use file extensions such as C, BAS, or PAS. Wouldn't it be nice to have quick access to these files? All you have to do is register these extensions as new file types.

Using the Open With Dialog Box to Register a File Type

Before you start the Registry Editor and dig deeply into *HKEY_CLASSES_ROOT*, you should understand the simplest way to register a file type.

Let's register the file type 1ST as a new extension. If there is no 1ST file available, create a small TXT file with Notepad and rename it to README.1ST. The \chapter3 folder of the downloaded sample files also contains a test file with this name. You need this file to execute the next steps.

Before we continue, confirm first that the 1ST extension isn't already registered. You can get this information quickly by checking the right pane of the Explorer window (see Figure 3-5). The new file README.1ST is described in the Type column as *1ST File*. This is how Windows indicates unregistered file types—by listing the file type as the file extension in uppercase letters, followed by a blank and the appendix File. You know that the TXT file type is registered because *Text Document* has been assigned as the type. (See the file README.TXT in the \chapter3 folder of the downloaded sample files.) The icon in the first column also indicates whether a file type is registered. The standard Windows icon is assigned to files with unregistered types.

N O T E :   Files with the file type of "file extension File" (1ST File) aren't always unregistered file types. Entering a type name when registering a file is optional, so if no name is entered, the type remains the default. Along the same lines, registered files can still have the standard Windows icon. You could drive somebody crazy by assigning the standard icon to a registered file type. Also, Windows itself will sometimes assign the standard icon to registered file types.

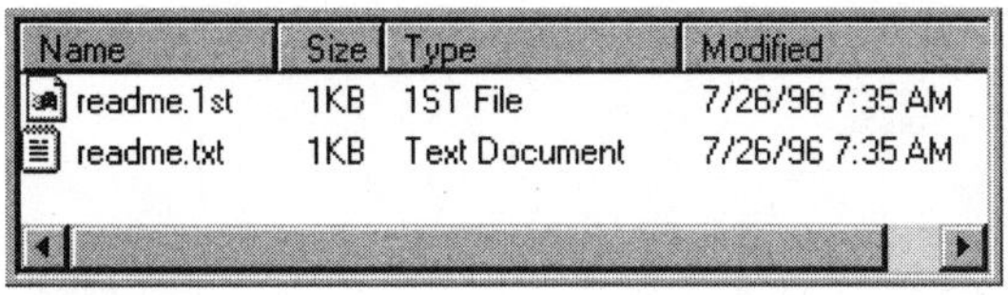

Name	Size	Type	Modified
readme.1st	1KB	1ST File	7/26/96 7:35 AM
readme.txt	1KB	Text Document	7/26/96 7:35 AM

Figure 3-5.
The right pane of the Explorer window with files.

Let's register the new 1ST file type. (Remember to back up your Registry before making any changes. See the section "Backing Up and Recovering Your Registry" on pages 35–42 of Chapter 2.)

1. Open the Explorer and double-click the README.1ST file. If the extension is unregistered (in our example, 1ST isn't registered), Windows 95 invokes the Open With dialog box (see Figure 3-6 on the following page).

2. Enter a short description in the text box. This description will be used in other places to inform the user about this file type, such as

in the Type column in the Explorer window. (See Figure 3-5; see also the Tip on the facing page to learn how to define this description text.)

3. Select NOTEPAD from the list box.

4. Activate the Always Use This Program To Open This File checkbox. This option is checked by default when you open the dialog box by double-clicking a file.

5. Close the dialog box by clicking OK. As Windows opens the README.1ST file with Notepad, the new file type is registered.

Figure 3-6.
The Open With dialog box.

You can confirm that the file type was registered by closing Notepad and looking at the Explorer window. The entry in the Type column is now set to *Textfile, open with Notepad* (or whatever you entered as the name). If this isn't the case, click in the right pane and press F5 to refresh the display. Double-click the README.1ST file again. The text file should be properly loaded into Notepad.

Verifying the Newly Registered File Type

Let's verify what happened in the Registry. Start the Registry Editor, expand the *HKEY_CLASSES_ROOT* branch, and search for the *.1st* entry. It should be at the top of the hierarchy. If you don't see it, click in the left pane and press F5. (The number *1* is always at the top of the hierarchy because numbers come before letters. See the Tip on the facing page.)

Figure 3-7 shows two Registry entries that are relevant for the registered file type 1ST. The first entry is the key *.1st.* The *Default* value for this key (which I called *name_ID* earlier in this chapter) is set to *1st_auto_file.* This value was automatically generated by the Open With dialog box in Windows, and it identifies the second key for the registered file type. The algorithm for creating this name is simple: Use the file extension (in our example, 1ST) and add "_auto_file".

You will find this second key in the middle of the *HKEY_CLASSES_ROOT* structure. This key contains the *shell* subkey, which contains the subkey *command* under the *open* verb. Figure 3-7 shows that the value of the *command* key is set to the path and name of the application. That's all you have to do—one keystroke can change your Registry.

Figure 3-7.
Registering the 1ST file type.

> **T I P :**   The file description you enter in the Open With dialog box (see the description I entered in Figure 3-6) is used for many purposes, including to comment the registered file type in the File Types property page of the Options dialog box in the Windows Explorer. These registered file types are sorted by comment line, first numerically and then alphabetically. When the registered file types list is huge, you will find it difficult to locate a desired file type unless you use a number as a prefix to your comment. For example, the description I entered in Figure 3-6 appears far down the list in Figure 3-8 (on page 62). If I had entered *1 Textfile, open with Notepad,* the file would have appeared at the top of the list. You should consider adding numerical prefixes to your descriptions to ensure that you can easily locate the files you define.

Changing the Associated Application of a Registered File Type

Occasionally you'll need to change the association between a certain file type and an application. Consider these scenarios: Suppose an install program overwrites the default file types of your favorite application. Or suppose you inadvertently register a file type with the wrong application. The Open With dialog box is a great feature of Windows 95 because it allows you to quickly register any new file type. There is a risk, however: If you select the wrong application in the Open With dialog box and click OK, the wrong application is registered for the file type and it is invoked whenever you double-click on that file type. How do you change an incorrect association? Don't start the Registry Editor and modify the *HKEY_CLASSES_ROOT* key! Use this process instead:

1. Click once on the desired file to activate it, and then hold down the Shift key and right-click. Select Open With from the context menu. This displays the Open With dialog box on the screen.

2. Select a new application. If the application program isn't available in the list, just click Other and search for the application's executable filename. Select the new application.

3. Place a check in the Always Use This Program To Open This Type Of File checkbox. This checkbox is always clear if the Open With dialog box is invoked as described in Step 1.

4. Click OK to close the dialog box.

Windows starts the selected application and opens the file. The entries in the Registry are updated, and the name of the new application is set for the Open command.

Disadvantages of Using the Open With Dialog Box

Although the Open With dialog box offers a quick way to register a new file type, there are the following disadvantages to using it as an all-purpose tool:

- The context menus of other registered file types allow additional commands, such as Print. The Open With dialog box does not offer you a way to define such optional commands for a file type.

- Each registered file type comes with its own icon. You cannot use the Open With dialog box to change the icon for the registered file type. If you associate a Windows application with the file type, the default icon of the EXE file (or the default data file icon) will be used. If the program does not contain an icon (let's assume it is a DOS file), Windows 95 sets a default icon (which can be the default icon associated with a DOS application or the default icon for unregistered file types). In the 1ST file example we looked at earlier, we can see the default icon for text files. (This icon is contained in NOTEPAD.EXE.)

▓ You can't define the name for the command shown on the context menu. The Open With dialog box always uses the name Open.

Using the Explorer to Change Registry Data for File Types

Given the disadvantages of using the Open With dialog box as an all-purpose tool, you need an alternative method for changing a registered file type. Now do we have to fire up the Registry Editor and jump into the Registry? Not so fast—before I lead you down the "highway to hell," I insist that you fasten your safety belt and consider using the Explorer instead.

Removing a Registered File Type

In the beginning of my Windows 95 days, a lot of garbage cluttered my Registry because I kept tampering with the Open With dialog box. My question was: How can I delete unnecessary entries in the Registry?

Windows can do this job for you. (Before you delete the key, create your backup as discussed in Chapter 2.) Follow these steps:

1. Start the Windows Explorer, and select Options from the View menu. The Explorer opens the Options property sheet.

2. Select the File Types property page, and search for the entry of the registered file type. Figure 3-8 on the following page shows the previously registered 1ST file type.

3. Be sure you have selected the correct entry! Click Remove.

4. Windows recognizes that you want to clean up the Registry and presents a message box asking you whether you're sure you want to remove the file type. Click Yes.

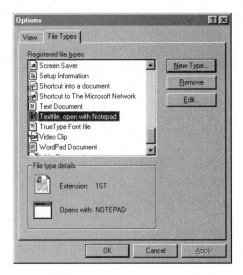

Figure 3-8.
A registered file type on the File Types property page.

Windows will remove from the Registry all keys for this registered file type, so be careful to select the right file type.

NOTE: If you have Internet access, then the installed software, such as Microsoft Internet Explorer, might have caused your File Types property page and its associated dialog boxes to look a little different from what you see here. Internet software will sometimes add display fields, such as Content Type, to your File Type property page and to the dialog boxes used to add and edit file types.

You will find the *Content Type* value with a *Default* value set to a text string such as *"audio/aiff"* in the key with the associated file extension (.*aif,* for example). Registry entries provided by third-party software are beyond the scope of this book.

Registering a New File Type

You can register a new file type by using the Windows Explorer rather than the Open With dialog box. Access the Options property sheet, select the File Types property page, and click New Type. The Explorer invokes the Add New File Type dialog box shown in Figure 3-9, where you can do nearly everything to register your file extension.

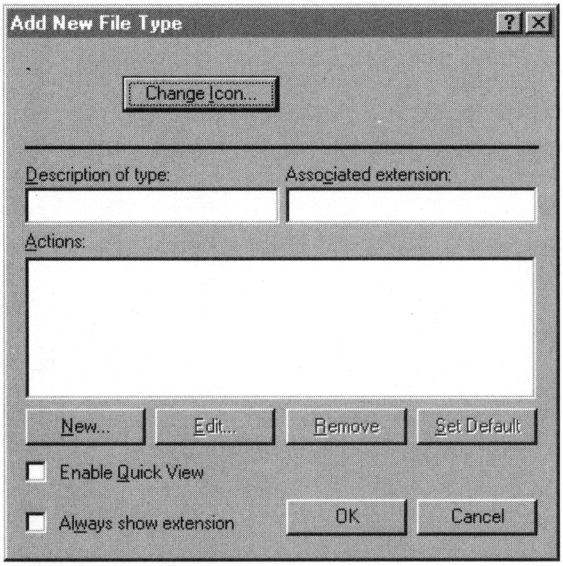

Add New File Type [?] [X]

Change Icon...

Description of type:

Associated extension:

Actions:

New...   Edit...   Remove   Set Default

☐ Enable Quick View

☐ Always show extension   OK   Cancel

Figure 3-9.
Registering a new file type.

You should enter the information about the new file type according to the
following steps:

Step 1: entering the description and extension   Enter a description for the
file type. A numerical prefix, or any other valid character that comes before
letters in a sorted list, ensures that your entry will be shown on the top of the
list. An underscore is one of these characters, so I chose the description _*Textfile*.

Now enter the file extension of your new file type; you do not need to
include the dot—for example, *1st*. The Explorer uses this extension in the
name of the first key inserted in the *HKEY_CLASSES_ROOT* branch but short-
ens the value of the *name_ID* to the file extension plus *file*. In our example, the
name_ID is set to *1stfile*, as shown in Figure 3-10.

Figure 3-10.
The .1st *key in the Registry.*

You must enter a unique, unregistered extension for the file type or you will get an error message and the Explorer will refuse to accept your input.

Step 2: defining a command for the file type   Now you need to assign a command to the file type so that when the user double-clicks the file, this command will be invoked.

1. Click New, which invokes the New Action dialog box shown in Figure 3-11.

2. Enter the name for the new command in the Action text box. I use *open* in this example, which will be shown on the context menu of this file type.

3. Click in the second text box, and fill in the path and the name of the application that will perform the command. (If you don't know the exact path, click Browse to browse the system in the Open With dialog box.) After the application name, append a space followed by *%1* as a placeholder for the filename. If you inspect other file types, you will see that many of the commands include this placeholder. However, if you forget the placeholder, the Explorer adds it to the value before storing the value in the Registry.

4. After defining the name and the application, click OK to close the New Action dialog box. (The Use DDE option will be examined later in this chapter on pages 70–71.)

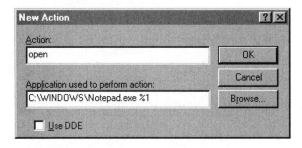

Figure 3-11.
You define a new action for a file type in the New Action dialog box.

Windows now knows a lot more about the file type, so the new command and associated icon are shown in the Add New File Type dialog box (see Figure 3-12). You can repeat these steps to define additional commands (Print, Edit, and so on).

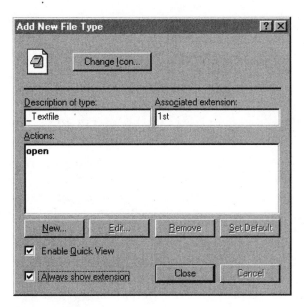

Figure 3-12.
The dialog box after you define the first command.

After you have defined all the commands you want, close the Add New File Type dialog box and the Explorer registers the new file type for you. The *open* verb is used as a subkey in the *HKEY_CLASSES_ROOT \ 1stfile\Shell* branch, and a second subkey, *command,* with the path and the application name is also added (Figure 3-13). You can inspect this key with the Registry Editor.

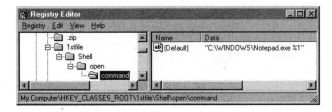

Figure 3-13.
The resulting structure in the Registry.

Step 3: setting the icon for the file type   To distinguish among file types, Windows associates an icon with each registered file type. When you defined the *.1st* key, the 1ST file type was automatically assigned the default icon for Notepad data files. If you desire a different icon, follow these steps:

1. From the File Types property sheet, select _Textfile, and click Edit to open the Edit File Type dialog box.

2. Click Change Icon to invoke the Change Icon dialog box (see Figure 3-14).

3. Select an icon shown in the Current Icon image list. Figure 3-14 shows the icons available in NOTEPAD.EXE. For an example, select the second icon.

4. If you want to use a different icon source, you can either change the entry in the File Name text box by entering the path and name of a new file or you can click the Browse button and select a new filename. Any icons this file contains will be displayed in the Current Icon image list.

5. Close the dialog box, and confirm your selection by clicking OK. Click Cancel to keep the old settings intact.

6. Close the Edit File Type dialog box to register the new icon.

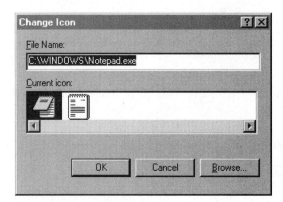

Figure 3-14.
The Change Icon dialog box.

How is this icon setting represented in the Registry? You will see the *DefaultIcon* key under *HKEY_CLASSES_ROOT\1stfile.* As discussed in the first section of this chapter, the value of the *DefaultIcon* key stores the path and name of the icon file. If you inspect this branch in the Registry Editor, you will find the path to *C:\WINDOWS\Notepad.Exe, 1*. This means that the second icon will be used for this file type. (The icon index is counted from zero.)

If you inspect other entries in *HKEY_CLASSES_ROOT*, you might not be able to find a *DefaultIcon* key. The Registry follows these rules:

- If you don't change the icon in the Add New File Type session, the Explorer won't generate a *DefaultIcon* entry in the Registry.

- If you click the Change Icon button and select a new icon, the *DefaultIcon* key is generated and the *Default* value will be set to the path and filename of the icon source.

- If there is no *DefaultIcon* key, Windows uses the first icon contained in the application's EXE file.

TIP: Where can you find icons for new file types? In many cases, the standard application has the right icon for your file type. If you prefer atypical icons, you can access other icon sources. Try, for example, the SHELL32.DLL file in the \Windows\System folder. This DLL is an excellent source for many icons. Try also the PIFMGR.DLL file in the \Windows\System folder, which contains icons for DOS applications. MORICONS.DLL in the \Windows folder is also another source. You can inspect the EXE and DLL files found on your computer. Most of these files contain one or more icons.

Step 4: enabling the Quick View command (optional)   If you open the context menu by right-clicking the symbol of a registered file type, sometimes you will see the Quick View command. Selecting this command opens the Quick View window, which shows the contents of the selected file. You can enable the Quick View command in the context menu by clicking the Enable Quick View checkbox in the Add New File Type or Edit File Type dialog box. (See Figure 3-12 on page 65.)

When you enable Quick View for the 1ST file type, the *1stfile* key in *HKEY_CLASSES_ROOT* will contain a *QuickView* subkey. The *Default* value of this subkey is set to *"*"*, which means that the default Quick Viewer should be used. (*HKEY_CLASSES_ROOT* contains its own *QuickView* key that contains subkeys with the installed Quick Viewers. The subkey * contains the default SCC [Systems Compatibility Corporation] viewer, which detects the right format automatically.)

Step 5: enabling the file extension (optional)   Windows hides the file extensions of registered file types by default. If you prefer to see the file extension (as an old DOS freak, I always like to see the extension), you must activate the Always Show Extension option in the Add New File Type or Edit File Type dialog box. If you check this option, the Explorer adds the name *AlwaysShowExt* as a value in the *1stfile* key (see Figure 3-15). The value for this name is set to an empty string. (Further aspects are discussed later.)

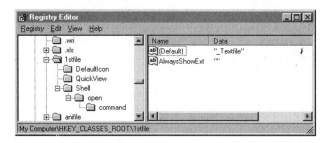

Figure 3-15.
The AlwaysShowExt *flag.*

Adding a Print Command to a Registered File Type

If you registered a new file type by using the Open With or Add New File Type dialog box, the Registry contains the required settings. But what if you want to change a setting or add a new command? When you right-click a TXT file and select the Print command from the context menu, Windows knows to open Notepad and print the contents of the file. But try to do this with the README.1ST file—you can't because the Print command isn't listed on the context menu. Obviously something is missing in the Registry. Let's try to add this missing Print command to the Registry:

1. Open the Explorer window, and select Options from the View menu.

2. Select the File Types property page from the Options property sheet.

3. Search for the _Textfile entry in the Registered File Types list, and select it. The extension 1ST is shown in the File Type Details section of the File Types property page (see the left-hand window in Figure 3-16).

4. Click the Edit button. The Edit File Type dialog box is invoked (Figure 3-16).

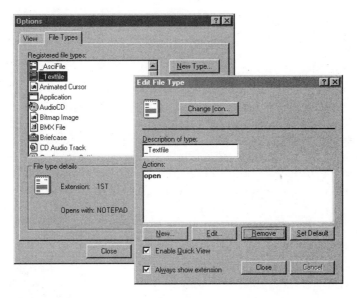

Figure 3-16.
The File Types property page and the Edit File Type dialog box.

5. Click the New button to define a new command for the file type.

6. Enter the print action in the New Action dialog box as shown in Figure 3-17.

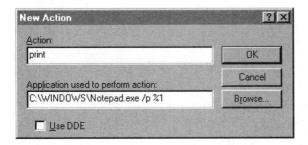

Figure 3-17.
The Print command is added to a registered file type in the New Action dialog box.

Notepad uses a simple /p switch in the command line to print the contents of a text file. I have appended this switch to the end of the application name. (Different applications require different methods of controlling internal functions. Some applications recognize switches; others are controlled by DDE messages. It is always a good idea to look and see how other registered file types use commands so that you can figure out how to start a program.) You should also append *%1* as a placeholder for the filename.

Windows will exchange the *%1* placeholder with the current filename if the command for this action is executed. (If you omit this placeholder, the Explorer appends *%1* to the command string before this string is stored in the Registry.) The new command is added into the Registry in the *\HKEY_ CLASSES_ROOT\1stfile\Shell\print\command* key, which you can examine with the Registry Editor. Now the new Print command is available from the context menu if you right-click to the README.1ST file.

Using the DDE Option in a Registered File Type

In the lower left corner of the New Action dialog box is a Use DDE checkbox (see Figure 3-17 on the preceding page). If an application accepts DDE commands, you can check this option. The Explorer expands the New Action dialog box with the following additional text boxes (see Figure 3-18).

- The DDE Message text box contains the command to start an action (open a file, create a new file, print a file, and so on).

- The Application text box contains the name of the DDE application. In Figure 3-18, this is Word for Windows.

- The DDE Application Not Running text box is optional. In it you can enter a command to start the application and execute an action (open a file, create a new file, print a file, and so on). This command will be executed if you select the action and the DDE application isn't already running on your PC.

- The last text box defines the Topic for the DDE conversion.

Your entries depend on the application used for the DDE conversion. Consult the application manuals to determine the necessary DDE commands.

NOTE: DDE commands entered in the dialog box are inserted in the Registry into the *HKEY_CLASSES_ROOT\...\shell* branch of this file type. For example, if you define a DDE command for *open* you will find two subkeys under *open: command* and *ddeexec*. The *command* subkey contains the path and name of the application. The *ddeexec* subkey contains a *Default* value with the DDE message. Depending on the other options you set in the New Action dialog box, the *ddeexec* subkey can contain other subkeys: *Application, Topic,* and *ifexec.* (The *ifexec* subkey contains the value entered in DDE Application Not Running.)

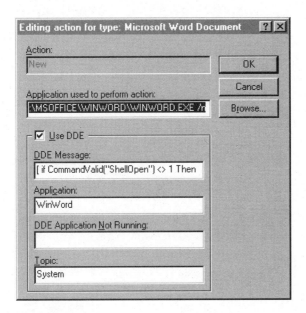

Figure 3-18.
DDE commands for a new action.

Using the Registry Editor to Register a File Type

We have examined several easy, efficient, and nearly foolproof ways to register new file types and define new commands for these file types without using the Registry Editor. These methods are real advantages if you like to do tasks quickly and want Windows to keep track of all modifications to the Registry. My suggestion is that you first try the Open With dialog box and the Explorer before turning to the Registry Editor. This will save you a lot of trouble and time. For all you masochists, here's how you register a new file type with the Registry Editor:

1. Start the Registry Editor, and expand the *HKEY_CLASSES_ROOT* branch.

2. Add a new subkey with the name of the file extension in *HKEY_CLASSES_ROOT.* (You must include the dot, as in *.1st.*)

71

3. Set the *Default* value of this key to the *name_ID*. (This is the name of the second key you need, to define the properties.)

4. Use the previously defined *name_ID* to add the second subkey in *HKEY_CLASSES_ROOT*. (We used the *name_ID 1stfile*, for example.)

5. Add the *shell* subkey, and expand this branch with the keys (verbs) for the required commands (Open, Print, etc.).

6. Add a *command* key to each verb key.

7. Add the command string (path and name of the executable) in the *Default* value.

8. Close the Registry Editor, and try to test the registered file type in the Explorer window.

Using a REG File to Register a New File Type

Defining a new file type using the Registry Editor can seem to be a pretty detailed process because you must manage every component of the process correctly. One alternative to manually adding keys and values to the Registry Editor is to import Registry settings from REG files; many programs come with REG files. All you do is double-click a REG file, and Windows 95 imports all the settings into the Registry. This method is preferable when registering a new file type for users other than yourself. Here is the REG file that adds the 1ST file type to your Registry:

```
REGEDIT4

[HKEY_CLASSES_ROOT\.1st]
@="1stfile"

[HKEY_CLASSES_ROOT\1stfile]
@="_Textfile"
"AlwaysShowExt"=""

[HKEY_CLASSES_ROOT\1stfile\Shell]
@=""

[HKEY_CLASSES_ROOT\1stfile\Shell\print]
@=""

[HKEY_CLASSES_ROOT\1stfile\Shell\print\command]
@="C:\\WINDOWS\\NOTEPAD.EXE /p %1"
```

(continued)

(continued)

```
[HKEY_CLASSES_ROOT\1stfile\Shell\open]
@=""

[HKEY_CLASSES_ROOT\1stfile\Shell\open\command]
@="C:\\WINDOWS\\Notepad.exe \"%1\""

[HKEY_CLASSES_ROOT\1stfile\QuickView]
@="*"

[HKEY_CLASSES_ROOT\1stfile\DefaultIcon]
@="C:\\WINDOWS\\Notepad.exe,1"
```

As discussed in Chapter 2, the keys are enclosed in brackets like this:

```
[HKEY_CLASSES_ROOT\.1st]
```

The @= stands for a *Default* value of a key. A name is set in quotes in the beginning of a line (such as *"EditFlags"=*). The equal sign (=) is always followed by a value (a string, DWORD, or binary value). String values are enclosed in quotation marks:

```
"C:\\WINDOWS\\Notepad.exe,1"
```

Path names in a string must follow unique naming conventions (for example, you must use a double backslash). Binary values are represented as a byte sequence:

```
"EditFlags"=hex:01,00,00,00
```

The command lines shown above contain the settings to register the file type 1ST with the commands Open and Print. Notepad is used to process these commands. (The 1ST.REG file is available from the \chapter3 folder of the downloaded sample files.)

If you plan to register a single file extension on more than one computer, you can use a REG file. You can customize the lines shown in the preceding code for a new file extension. For example, to register a DIZ file you must replace all instances of *1st* with *diz*.

Risks of Using a REG File

Double-clicking a REG file and receiving a message from Windows that the data contained in the REG file has been successfully stored in the Registry is misleading—unfortunately, Windows 95 doesn't use a smart algorithm to interpret the information in the REG file. To determine whether a file is valid,

Windows tests only the first line of the file. If this line contains the signature REGEDIT4, the rest of the file is read and the information is stored in the Registry. This is a source of many problems. Suppose, for example, you import the REG file but the action won't take effect. Let's investigate by looking at Figure 3-19.

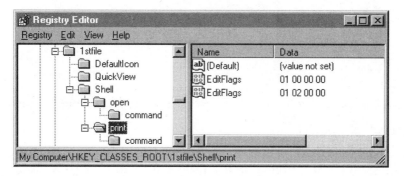

Figure 3-19.
Two entries with the same name?

Two entries with the same name but different values exist in the *print* key. In conformance with the Windows 95 specification, one key can have several values, but a single value name can occur only once in a particular key. However, Figure 3-19 reveals that the *print* key contains the name *EditFlags* twice. What has happened? To determine the problem, we must take a look at the REG file. The REG command that set the second occurrence of *EditFlags* in the *print* key of Figure 3-19 is shown below:

```
[HKEY_CLASSES_ROOT\1stfile\Shell\print]
"EditFlags "=hex:01,02,00,00
```

The second line contains the bug: A blank follows the name *EditFlags*. The name "EditFlags " in the REG file is different from the name "EditFlags" already contained in the Registry, so a new entry was generated for the value. In this scenario, your new setting would never be detected by Windows. All values must match the specification exactly, or your update will not provide the expected results. If your update fails, load the REG file into Notepad and compare each line for trailing blanks, misspelled keys, missing quotes, and so on. (Don't use Word for Windows or any word-processing system to change entries in a REG file. Word contains an option that allows you to unintentionally extend an inserted expression with blanks.)

The next problem can be even more difficult to solve. I came across this problem as I was translating Nancy Cluts's book, *Programming the Windows 95 User Interface.* The book comes with a CD-ROM containing sample programs and REG files. There was a simple line similar to this for registering a new Quick Viewer:

```
[HKEY_CLASSES_ROOT\1stfile\Shell\open\command]
@="C:\\WINDOWS\\Notepad.exe \"%1\""
```

Of course, Cluts's code was a little bit different because the intention was to register a viewer. (I'm using a simplified example to demonstrate the same effect.) After compiling the application and double-clicking the REG file, the viewer wouldn't run for the extension. I spent several hours finding the bug. The second line caused the problem.

What's wrong with the command *@="C:\\WINDOWS\\Notepad.exe\"%1\""*? At first glance, nothing. Care to take a second look? I guarantee you won't find anything wrong with the line itself, and it will work on 90 percent of the computers that are running Windows 95. Still—what explains the fact that some people run into serious trouble with this line?

The name of the Windows 95 folder is incorrect. The path above says that NOTEPAD.EXE is located in the \WINDOWS folder. But on one of my PCs, I run Windows 3.1 and Windows 95 in parallel, and on my other PC, I installed both a German and an English version of Windows 95. On both my PCs, then, I'm using two versions of Windows, so I'm unable to use WINDOWS as a name for each of the Windows folders. All users who try to import the REG file on a system that has a different name for the Windows folder will fail.

NOTE: It is also a risk to install one Windows version in the folder \WINDOWS and use a different folder name for the second version. If you boot with the second version, the paths in the Registry will still point to the \WINDOWS folder. If a command is executed, the library modules are loaded in \WINDOWS\SYSTEM. The result is a mix of different modules, which can cause problems.

You can solve this REG file problem in only one way: Omit the path to the application. The lines of our code example would be written like this:

```
[HKEY_CLASSES_ROOT\1stfile\Shell\open\command]
@="Notepad.exe \"%1\""
```

In this approach, Windows 95 would try to locate the application after you invoked the Open command. First the \Windows folder would be scanned, and if the file was not available, the \Windows\System folder would be scanned. If this search wasn't successful, Windows would then try to scan the folders set in the PATH environment variable (set in AUTOEXEC.BAT). Finally, Windows would check the following branch in the Registry: *\HKEY_LOCAL_ MACHINE\SOFTWARE\Microsoft\Windows\CurrentVersion*. This branch contains the paths to EXE and DLL files for certain applications. An application found in one of these folders would be loaded.

I don't recommend omitting path names from REG files, however, because all other entries in the Registry contain a path description. The next section shows how you can use Windows to get around this problem of hard-coded paths.

> TIP: Do you have to use a different name for the \Windows folder? Are you worried about always having to edit the Windows path in REG files obtained from other machines? I felt that way, too, until I began running Windows 95. Thanks to the ingenious Windows developers, I found a sneaky way to get around that mess. All you need to do is define a folder as a shortcut to your \Windows folder and name it WINDOWS. To do this, open the Windows Explorer, hold down the right mouse button, and drag the \Windows folder to the drive icon, release the mouse button, and select the command Create Shortcut(s) Here. Windows will create a shortcut to the \Windows folder. Rename this new folder to WINDOWS.
>
> If you use a REG file with \\WINDOWS\\ in a path, the shortcut will direct Windows to the correct folder. Don't forget to delete this shortcut before you boot another copy of Windows 95. This trick won't work if Windows needs data files in a directory (for example, for icons).

Using INF Files to Register a New File Type—A Better Solution than REG Files

The \Windows folder is not always named Windows—each user can change its name during installation. So what we need is a method that lets Windows itself assign the Windows path. Earlier I described how Windows can do this during run time, but you're better off to assign the path during the Registry update. Fortunately, Windows comes with the appropriate tool: the INF files. In an INF file, you can specify a placeholder for a path that will be determined during run time. The following lines, for example, will update the *open* verb for the 1ST file type in your Registry:

```
; File: 1ST.INF
; by Guenter Born
;
; Install script, register the 1ST file type
[version]
signature="$CHICAGO$"

[DefaultInstall]
AddReg = 1st.AddReg

[1st.AddReg]
HKCR,.1st,,,"1stfile"
HKCR,1stfile\Shell\open\command,,,%10%"\NOTEPAD.EXE %1"
; End ***
```

The most important commands are shown in the [1st.AddReg] section, which contains statements that add some Registry data. Each statement is defined with the following syntax:

```
root-key, [subkey], [value-name], [flag], [value]
```

A statement consists of five parameters separated by commas. Parameters that are shown in brackets are optional. These brackets are omitted in the INF file. The root key is identified by one of the following abbreviations:

HKCC	for *HKEY_CURRENT_CONFIG*
HKCR	for *HKEY_CLASSES_ROOT*
HKCU	for *HKEY_CURRENT_USER*
HKLM	for *HKEY_LOCAL_MACHINE*
HKU	for *HKEY_USERS*

The second parameter defines a subkey (in our example, these are the subkeys *.1st* and *1stfile*). The name for the value is omitted in the example because we're setting the *Default* value. The flag is also omitted here. The last parameter defines the value that should be updated in the Registry. If you inspect the second-to-last line in the INF file shown in the preceding code, you will see the *%10%* string. This is a placeholder for the Windows directory and will be filled with the name of the current Windows directory when the INF file is processed. The INF file above creates (or updates) the Registry entry:

```
HKEY_CLASSES_ROOT\1stfile\Shell\open\command
```

The *Default* value is set to:

```
"drive\windowsfolder\NOTEPAD.EXE %1"
```

This is all we need. To install this INF file, you right-click its name and select the Install command shown on the context menu. Additional information about INF files is provided on pages 258–279 in Chapter 7.

NOTE: You will find the file 1ST.INF in the \chapter3 folder of the downloaded sample files.

Techniques for Extending Registered File Types

Earlier in this chapter, I discussed the principles of registering file types. We have seen that we can accomplish a lot using the Explorer without ever having to examine the Registry. Now I want to show you how to apply these principles.

Using Several Applications for a Single File Type

Opening a file of a registered file type by double-clicking its file icon is handy. When you do this, Windows always registers one application for the Open command. (This command will be executed by default if you double-click a shell object in Windows 95. The exceptions are discussed later in this chapter in the section "Defining the Default Command for a Registered File Type" on page 88.) But there are situations when you need more than one application to load a file type. Here are a few typical situations:

- *Loading text files.* If you double-click a text file, Windows tries to load it in Notepad. If the file length exceeds 64 KB, Windows asks you to load the text file with WordPad. In the Explorer, you can see the file size and decide which application to use to load the file. Perhaps you have a "super-editor" that is able to load text files larger than 64 KB, or you want to start WordPad directly for larger files.

- *Graphics files.* Graphics files are often more conveniently opened with several applications (for example, with PaintShop or with PhotoFinish).

- *Files with the DOC extension.* These files might contain ASCII text or Word documents, so you need several applications to open them.

Typically, with these file types, you start the application and load the data file. In Windows 95, you can select the application with the following shortcut:

1. Click the file to select it.

2. Press the Shift key and right-click the file icon.

3. Select the Open With command from the context menu.

4. Select the application in the Open With dialog box.

If your favorite application isn't in the Open With list, you have to browse the system for the EXE file. Wouldn't it be nice to save yourself this trouble and have a second or third application available on the context menu with which to open a data file? You can extend the file type properties by using the File Types property page of the Explorer, the Registry Editor, or REG files.

First, we'll extend the 1ST file type properties. Currently, when you right-click a 1ST file, a context menu is shown with only the Open and Print commands (because we have defined only these commands in the Registry). Let's add a third command, Open1, which will start WordPad. The steps are easy:

1. Add a new *open1* subkey to *HKEY_CLASSES_ROOT\1stfile\Shell*.

2. Add a *command* subkey to *HKEY_CLASSES_ROOT\1stfile\Shell\open1*.

3. Set the *Default* value of the *open1* subkey to the application name.

You can do this using the Explorer or the Registry Editor. As an alternative, we'll add file type properties to our 1ST file type by using a REG file, which I exported from my Registry:

```
REGEDIT4

[HKEY_CLASSES_ROOT\.1st]
@="1stfile"

[HKEY_CLASSES_ROOT\1stfile]
@="_Textfile"
"AlwaysShowExt"=""

[HKEY_CLASSES_ROOT\1stfile\Shell]
@=""

[HKEY_CLASSES_ROOT\1stfile\Shell\print]
@=""

[HKEY_CLASSES_ROOT\1stfile\Shell\print\command]
@="C:\\WINDOWS\\NOTEPAD.EXE /p %1"

[HKEY_CLASSES_ROOT\1stfile\Shell\open]
@=""
```

(continued)

(continued)

```
[HKEY_CLASSES_ROOT\1stfile\Shell\open\command]
@="C:\\WINDOWS\\Notepad.exe \"%1\""

[HKEY_CLASSES_ROOT\1stfile\QuickView]
@="*"

[HKEY_CLASSES_ROOT\1stfile\DefaultIcon]
@="C:\\WINDOWS\\Notepad.exe,1"

[HKEY_CLASSES_ROOT\1stfile\Shell\open1]
@=""

[HKEY_CLASSES_ROOT\1stfile\Shell\open1\command]
@="C:\\Program Files\\Accessories\\Wordpad.exe \"%1\""
```

The last four lines define the new subkeys for the open1 command. Perhaps you recognized the \"%1\" string in the last line. You can add the %1 placeholder with or without quotation marks. If you decide to add the placeholder with quotation marks (″%1″), the quote will be recognized as the start or end signature of a string unless you enter each quotation mark in the text string with a preceding backslash (\), so ″%1″ is inserted as \"%1\" in the REG file.

After installing this REG file, the Registry contains a new *open1* subkey, as shown in Figure 3-20. (The complete key hierarchy for this value is shown in the status bar of the Registry Editor.)

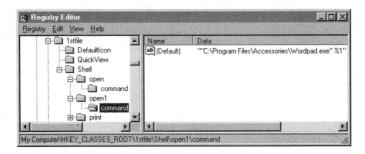

Figure 3-20.
The new open1 *verb in the Registry.*

We now have three commands in the *shell* branch. The *open1* verb defines WordPad as the application, and the context menu is extended with a new open1 command (see Figure 3-21). (You can view this by selecting the file

README.1ST in the \chapter3 folder of the downloaded sample files with a right mouse click.)

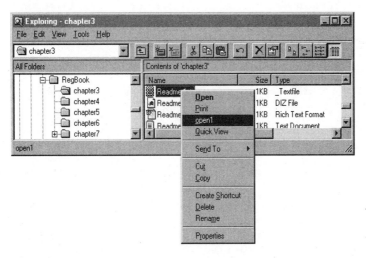

Figure 3-21.
The context menu with the new open1 command.

If you select the Open command, Windows uses Notepad to load the text file. Selecting the open1 command opens WordPad and loads the text file (without a warning that the file is too large for Notepad). If you choose Print, Notepad is used to print the text file. (You might consider extending the context menu with a print1 command that uses WordPad to print a large text file.) You can inspect the *\shell\print\command* branch of *Wordpad.Document.1* in the Registry to find out which parameters are necessary for printing a file in WordPad.

You can use this technique for all registered file extensions. I use this technique to open graphics files with the extensions TIF, PCX, BMP, and so on with different applications.

NOTE: The REG file shown on the preceding pages can be found as 1STA.REG in the \chapter3 folder of the downloaded sample files. You can install this REG file by double-clicking the file icon in the Explorer window. Your folders must have the same names as those defined in the REG file. Otherwise, you have to modify all path entries in this file before you import the file! The solution of using INF files to match path names, which we examined earlier, isn't possible because I haven't found any way to use a placeholder for the \Program Files\Accessories folder.

Defining the Command Name on the Context Menu

Did you notice a difference between the Open command names shown on the context menu in Figure 3-21? They are capitalized differently. If you compare the Registry entries shown in Figure 3-20 on page 80, the verbs *open* and *open1* are capitalized consistently in the *Shell* branch. Windows obviously uses the name of the verb (key) as an entry on the context menu, but why is the verb *open* shown with an initial capital in the context menu?

This is one of the secrets buried in the Windows architecture. The general syntax of a Registry entry for a context menu command shown in the shell is defined as:

```
HKEY_CLASSES_ROOT
    .ext = "name_ID"
    name_ID = "description"
        shell
            verb = "menu item text"
                command = "command string"
```

We have seen this structure many times. The *shell* key can contain several subkeys that describe verbs such as *open* and *print*. The syntax above indicates that we can set the value of the verb key to the menu item text, which is what you will see on the context menu. In the *open1* examples, I omitted this optional string to show you the side effects. Windows uses the following rules to build the entries for the context menu:

- If there is a menu item defined in the *Default* value of the verb, this string is used for the context menu entry.

- If the *Default* value is empty, the verb is used as the name for the context menu entry.

These rules imply that we should see the commands open, open1, print, etc., on the context menu, but we don't. That's because Windows follows these additional rules:

- Microsoft has defined some canonical verbs with a special meaning. If you use the names *open, print,* and *printto* as verbs in the *shell* key, Windows will insert predefined names for these canonical verbs into the context menu.

- The names depend on the localized Windows 95 version. The US version uses Open and Print in the context menu. The German version uses *Öffnen* and *Drucken*.

■ The canonical verb *printto* is never shown on the context menu. This verb is reserved for drag-and-drop operations (as we will see later).

With this knowledge, you can easily rename the context menu entries. You must insert the name of the context menu entry into the *Default* value of the verb. For our example, I prepared a short REG file that enables us to rename the context menu entries:

```
REGEDIT4

[HKEY_CLASSES_ROOT\.1st]
@="1stfile"

[HKEY_CLASSES_ROOT\1stfile]
@="_Textfile"
"AlwaysShowExt"=""

[HKEY_CLASSES_ROOT\1stfile\Shell]
@=""

[HKEY_CLASSES_ROOT\1stfile\Shell\print]
@="Print with Notepad"

[HKEY_CLASSES_ROOT\1stfile\Shell\print\command]
@="C:\\WINDOWS\\NOTEPAD.EXE /p %1"

[HKEY_CLASSES_ROOT\1stfile\Shell\open]
@="Edit with Notepad"

[HKEY_CLASSES_ROOT\1stfile\Shell\open\command]
@="C:\\WINDOWS\\Notepad.exe \"%1\""

[HKEY_CLASSES_ROOT\1stfile\Shell\open1]
@="Edit with Wordpad"

[HKEY_CLASSES_ROOT\1stfile\Shell\open1\command]
@="C:\\Program Files\\Accessories\\Wordpad.exe \"%1\""

[HKEY_CLASSES_ROOT\1stfile\QuickView]
@="*"

[HKEY_CLASSES_ROOT\1stfile\DefaultIcon]
@="C:\\WINDOWS\\Notepad.exe,1"
```

If you remove any existing Registry entries for the 1ST file type and import this REG file into the Registry, the context menu will look like Figure 3-22. The Open command is gone; instead you will find more descriptive names for the commands.

Figure 3-22.
New names on the context menu.

NOTE: The preceding REG file is named 1STB.REG and is located in the \chapter3 folder of the downloaded sample files. You can install this REG file by double-clicking the file icon in the Explorer window. You have to name your folders as defined in the REG file. Otherwise, you have to modify all path entries in this file before you import it.

Defining Accelerator Keys for Commands

Now we have a few options for opening a 1ST file and new names on the context menu. Unfortunately, in the process, we've lost the ability to select a command with a keystroke. On the context menu shown in Figure 3-21 on page 81, notice that certain letters in the command names are underlined. These underlined characters define accelerator keys for these commands. For example, on the context menu shown, you can press the *P* key on the keyboard to invoke the Print command and print the selected file.

How can we define accelerator keys? Figure 3-21 should give us a few ideas. The *o* in the command open1 is underlined. By default, Windows uses the first character of a verb as the accelerator key if no menu name has been defined. Hmm, that's strange—if we don't set a menu name, we'll get the verb name and an accelerator key on the context menu. Maybe we could use keys such as *Edit with Notepad* and *Edit with WordPad* instead of *open1*. Well, we could do that, but then two commands would each have the letter *E* as an accelerator key.

My preferences for creating accelerator keys are simple:

■ Use short verbs such as *open, edit, print,* and *show* as key names.

■ Define different strings for the context menu entries (as I have shown in the previous section).

When I came across this problem a year ago, I couldn't believe that Microsoft hadn't provided a solution. After playing a little bit with the Registry, I figured it out. The solution actually is buried in the Registry and is fairly simple. Let's take a look at the Registry value for the *edit* key in *HKEY_CLASSES_ROOT\batfile\shell* (see Figure 3-23). This part of the Registry is set up during the Windows installation. The *Default* value for the verb *edit* is defined as *"&Edit"*, but if you select a BAT file with a right-click, the E̲dit command is shown. The ampersand character (&) preceding a character creates an accelerator character on a menu, so in this example, the *E* in Edit is the accelerator key. If you used the string *"E&dit"* for the command, the key *d* would be defined as the accelerator key and the command would be shown as Ed̲it in the context menu. This method also works when naming verbs, not just context menu names. So you could produce the same result by naming the verb *E&dit* rather than *edit*.

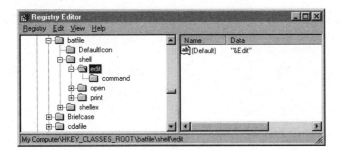

Figure 3-23.
Defining an accelerator key in a command.

The following rules for defining accelerator keys for menu commands are a little bit complicated:

■ When a verb is defined without a *Default* value set and without an ampersand in the key name, Windows 95 defaults to displaying the verb on the context menu and underlining the first character. (Keep in mind that we have exceptions for the canonical verbs *open* and *print*, which are shown as <u>O</u>pen and <u>P</u>rint).

■ You can use the ampersand in a verb to identify an accelerator character. For example, the verb *Ope&n1* would be shown as Open<u>1</u> on the context menu. Be careful not to interfere with the Windows accelerator keys used in other commands. If two entries used the same accelerator key, a keystroke would select only the first command with that key; you would need a second keystroke to invoke the second command.

■ If you add *&* to the canonical verbs *open* and *print*, the verbs would no longer be canonical. For example, the verb *ope&n* would be shown as ope<u>n</u> on the context menu.

■ If the *Default* value of a verb is set, this string will be used for the context menu entry. If this string does not contain an ampersand, the first character of the string is used as the accelerator key. This character is not shown underlined on the context menu.

■ If you want an accelerator key to be any character other than the first for a verb with a *Default* value, the character in the string must be preceded by an *&*. The string *Open with &WordPad* will be shown on the context menu as *Open with <u>W</u>ordPad*.

A defined name in the *Default* value always has a higher priority than the key name. If you define accelerator keys, avoid duplicating other accelerators defined in Windows. (The context menu might have other commands such as Cut, Paste, Delete, Send To, and Property). Following is the revised REG file, which defines the extensions with accelerators in the context menu.

```
REGEDIT4

[HKEY_CLASSES_ROOT\.1st]
@="1stfile"

[HKEY_CLASSES_ROOT\1stfile]
@="_Textfile"
"AlwaysShowExt"=""

[HKEY_CLASSES_ROOT\1stfile\Shell]
@=""
```

(continued)

continued

```
[HKEY_CLASSES_ROOT\1stfile\Shell\print]
@="&Print with Notepad"

[HKEY_CLASSES_ROOT\1stfile\Shell\print\command]
@="C:\\WINDOWS\\NOTEPAD.EXE /p %1"

[HKEY_CLASSES_ROOT\1stfile\Shell\open]
@="Edit with &Notepad"

[HKEY_CLASSES_ROOT\1stfile\Shell\open\command]
@="C:\\WINDOWS\\Notepad.exe \"%1\""

[HKEY_CLASSES_ROOT\1stfile\Shell\open1]
@="Edit with &Wordpad"

[HKEY_CLASSES_ROOT\1stfile\Shell\open1\command]
@="C:\\Program Files\\Accessories\\Wordpad.exe \"%1\""

[HKEY_CLASSES_ROOT\1stfile\QuickView]
@="*"

[HKEY_CLASSES_ROOT\1stfile\DefaultIcon]
@="C:\\WINDOWS\\Notepad.exe,1"
```

If you import this REG file, the context menu shown in Figure 3-24 will be available. This is a step toward building a customized user shell. (We will see other examples in Chapter 4.)

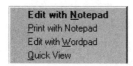

Figure 3-24.
Extended context menu with accelerator keys.

> **N O T E :**   The preceding REG file is named 1STC.REG and is lo-
> cated in the \chapter3 folder of the downloaded sample files. You
> can install this REG file by double-clicking the file icon in the Ex-
> plorer window. Remember to use the names for your folders as
> defined in the REG file.

Defining the Default Command for a Registered File Type

One command in the context menu is shown in boldface (see Figure 3-24). This boldface command is the default command, which is activated by double-clicking the file. You can select which command will be the default if you modify the entries of the context menu. At this point, we have not set any parameter that prevents Windows from selecting the default command, so Windows is free to make its own choice. The rules are pretty simple:

■ If you use one of the canonical verbs (*open*, *print*) as a key name, one of these verbs will be selected. If both verbs are available, *open* is the first priority; *print* is selected next.

■ If none of these canonical verbs are used in the *shell* subkeys, Windows will use the first entry in the *shell* branch as the default command in the context menu.

Sometimes you'll want to select alternative default commands. (For example, a BAT file is executed if you double-click it, but perhaps you want to open the file in Notepad instead.) The Set Default button in the Edit File Type dialog box allows you to change the default (see Figure 3-16 on page 69). The default command is always shown in the dialog box in boldface. To change the default, select another command in the dialog box and click the Set Default button; this new command will be shown in boldface, and the context menu for this file type will use that command as the default when the file is double-clicked.

Inspecting the Registry after you have set the default command for the context menu through the File Types property page will give you an idea about how to set the default command using the Registry. The verb of the command is inserted as the *Default* value of the *shell* key. Figure 3-25 shows this for the registered 1ST file type, where the open1 command is used as the default.

If you want to use a REG file to set the default command, use the following lines:

```
REGEDIT4
```

```
[HKEY_CLASSES_ROOT\1stfile\Shell]
@="open1"
```

You will find the 1STD.REG file with these instructions in the \chapter3 folder of the downloaded sample files. If there is a *1stfile* key already in the Registry, you can import the new REG file by double-clicking it.

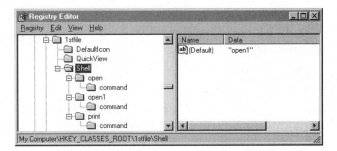

Figure 3-25.
Defining the default command in the Registry.

If you run this REG file, two things change on the context menu: the Edit With WordPad entry is shown in boldface since it is now the default; and the default command, Edit With WordPad, moves to the top of the context menu. This is a nice benefit of setting the default command. (We will use it in the next section.)

Sequencing the Context Menu Commands

Windows displays the commands on the context menu in the same order that the keys appear in the Registry. (The one exception is the default command, which is always shown at the top of the context menu.) When you're defining many commands for a particular registered file type, consider grouping related entries on the context menu. (For example, you might want to list all the Open commands together, then the Print command, and so on.) Because the Registry Editor offers no way to move a branch in the hierarchy—you can only delete a branch and append it to the end of a node—reordering the commands on the context menu would appear to be a hassle.

Fortunately, the Windows developers offer us an easy way to do this with the user-defined entries. You just specify the names of the verbs in the *Default* value of the *shell* key. The verbs must be separated by commas. For the registered 1ST file type, the *Default* value of the *shell* key must be set to the following in order to sequence the commands as suggested above:

```
"open, open1, print"
```

The following lines have the same effect. (This file is available as 1STE.REG in the \chapter3 folder of the downloaded sample files.)

```
REGEDIT4

[HKEY_CLASSES_ROOT\1stfile\Shell]
@="open, open1, print"
```

89

NOTE: This ordering technique for context menu entries has one small disadvantage. If you open the File Types property page, the Open With information is missing.

Defining a *printto* Command Key

Some registered file types come with a *printto* key in the *shell* branch. If you right-click one of these registered files, however, a Print To command isn't available from the context menu. The reason for the *printto* key in the Registry has to do with the Windows 95 drag-and-drop functionality: Dragging a data file (with a registered extension) over a printer icon and releasing the mouse button causes Windows to start the associated application, load the dropped data file, and direct the output to the printer.

If a registered file type supports this feature, a *printto* key is required in the *shell* branch of the Registry. The Registry branch for registering *printto* for WORDPAD.EXE has the following structure:

```
shell
    printto
        command = C:\Progra~1\Access~1\Wordpad.exe /pt "%1" "%2" "%3" "%4"
```

The /pt switch enables WordPad to direct to a selected printer, and the other parameters are placeholders. The placeholders function as follows:

- %*1* is used for the name of the data file.

- %*2* is used for the name of the printer.

- %*3* enables WordPad to find the name of the printer driver.

- %*4* contains the printer port.

The parameters in %*3* and %*4* are superfluous because printer names are unique in Windows 95.

NOTE: You will find the value above in the following branch of the Registry: *HKEY_CLASSES_ROOT\Wordpad.Document.1\shell\printto\ command.*

Fixing Problems with the File Type Association

Sometimes I experience problems with registered file types, and I've discovered a couple of fairly simple ways to approach them. One way is to delete the Registry data altogether (on the Explorer's File Types property page, for example) and then reenter the definition. (You can export the Registry branch of that file type before you delete the key.)

Another approach is to inspect the *HKEY_LOCAL_MACHINE\SOFTWARE\ Microsoft\Windows\CurrentVersion\Extensions* branch. As shown in Figure 3-26, additional information about the file type association exists here. These entries must be appropriately set to the associations found in the *HKEY_ CLASSES_ROOT* key.

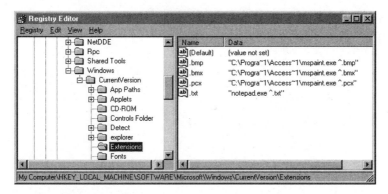

Figure 3-26.
File type associations.

Using *EditFlags* to Protect Registered File Types

We have used the Edit File Type dialog box to customize the settings of a registered file type. The process is straightforward until, in the course of modifying these settings, necessary data is accidentally deleted. The results could be disastrous. So system administrators must protect these settings from inadvertent modification. One obvious way would be to delete the Registry Editor from each local system—except that we have seen how easily the user can change settings with the Edit File Type dialog box available in the Explorer. So it would be more secure to have methods that disable the buttons (Edit, Remove, and so on) or lock the access to all settings of a registered file type.

How can we do this? Well, we need the Registry Editor, or we need to use a REG or INF file.

Perhaps you have noticed the *EditFlags* value in some keys. This flag is a "gatekeeper" that either allows or prevents a user from changing the settings of a registered file type in the Edit File Type dialog box. If this flag is omitted, the user has access to all options on the File Types property page and in the Edit File Type dialog box. To restrict access, you must insert the *EditFlags* value into the keys of a registered file type. This value is set as a binary value in the format *xx xx 00 00*, where *xx xx* stands for two bytes.

To hide the name of the registered file type on the File Types property sheet, you must insert the following into the main key of the registered file type:

```
EditFlags = 01 00 00 00
```

For our example, the main key is the *1stfile* key. (See Figure 3-27.)

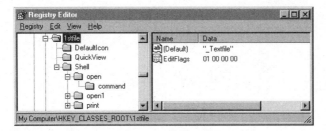

Figure 3-27.
The EditFlags *value.*

The flag value *01* hides the registered file type (_Textfile) in this list; if this entry isn't visible, the user can't modify it. Inspecting the Registry will reveal several items with this flag value. Take a look at *dllfile*, for example.

Other values also enable and disable several options on the File Types property page and the Edit File Type dialog box. To disable the Remove button, you can use this value:

```
EditFlags = 10 00 00 00
```

If you want to protect the properties of registered file types, use this:

```
EditFlags= 08 00 00 00
```

You can combine these values in a bitwise OR operation. This means that *EditFlags* is a bit array that has 16 bits to enable and disable several options. Table 3-1 shows the coding of these bits.

Table 3-1 defines only the least significant 16 bits of a DWORD (or of a binary value sequence, if you prefer this notation). Note also that the Registry Editor will display the hex byte sequence. The value *0x00000001* (this value will hide the file type—see Table 3-1) will be displayed in the Registry Editor as *01 00 00 00*.

Coding of the *EditFlags* Value

Bit	Coding
0000 0000 0000 0001	Hide the description in the Registered File Types list.
0000 0000 0000 0010	N/A
0000 0000 0000 0100	N/A
0000 0000 0000 1000	Disable the Edit button on the File Types property page.
0000 0000 0001 0000	Disable the Remove button on the File Types property page.
0000 0000 0010 0000	Disable the New button in the Edit File Type dialog box.
0000 0000 0100 0000	Disable the Edit button in the Edit File Type dialog box.
0000 0000 1000 0000	Disable the Remove button in the Edit File Type dialog box.
0000 0001 0000 0000	Disable the Description Of Type edit box in the Edit File Type dialog box.
0000 0010 0000 0000	Disable the Change Icon button in the Edit File Type dialog box.
0000 0100 0000 0000	Disable the Set Default button in the Edit File Type dialog box.

Table 3-1.
The entries shown in the Bit column are given as binary values (a value
0000 0000 0000 0001 *is equivalent to the hex value* 00 01 *).*

Let's try one example. You want to disable the Remove button on the File Types property sheet and the Edit and Remove buttons in the Edit File Type dialog box. You can calculate the *EditFlags* value as shown below:

```
0000 0000 0001 0000 disable Remove on the File Types property page

0000 0000 0100 0000 disable Edit in the Edit File Type dialog box
0000 0000 1000 0000 disable Remove in the Edit File Type dialog box
_____

0000 0000 1101 0000 result
```

The result is the binary value *0000 0000 1101 0000*, or *0x00D0* in hex notation. You must enter this value as *D0 00 00 00* in the Registry Editor.

NOTE: If you change the *EditFlags* value in the Registry, you must close the File Types property page and reopen it before you will see the effect.

Hiding and Showing File Extensions

The View property page controls how the shell (including Explorer) shows the files and their extensions. This property page is shown in Figure 3-28.

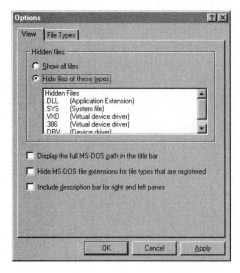

Figure 3-28.
The View property page.

If you activate the Hide MS-DOS File Extensions For File Types That Are Registered checkbox, all registered file type extensions are omitted. Why, then, do you sometimes find a registered file type extension in the Explorer window?

The Always Show Extension checkbox in the Edit File Type dialog box has a higher priority than the Hide MS-DOS File Extensions setting, so if you check the Always Show Extension option, the file extension will be shown. Sometimes the extension of a file type is never visible (regardless of what you set on the View property page). This is controlled inside the Registry by two entries in the main key of the registered file type. Here's how it works:

■ If the value named *NeverShowExt* is present in this key, Windows always hides the extension in the shell. In Figure 3-29, you see this value shown for *1stfile*. The value of this name is set to an empty string.

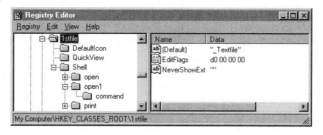

Figure 3-29.
The NeverShowExt *flag.*

■ If the value named *AlwaysShowExt* is present in this key, Windows always shows the extension in the shell. In Figure 3-30, this entry is shown for *1stfile*. The value of this name is set to an empty string.

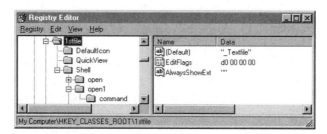

Figure 3-30.
The AlwaysShowExt *flag.*

You can use these values to overwrite the global settings in the Windows shell to hide or show the extension of a registered file type.

NOTE: If you add one of these names in the Registry Editor, it might take a few seconds to flush the new value onto the disk. Close the Explorer window and reopen it to ensure that the new options will be used.

In Chapter 4, I show how Windows stores the Hide MS-DOS File Extensions For File Types That Are Registered option in the Registry.

Registering a Quick Viewer for a File Type

As mentioned in the first part of this chapter, you can register a Quick Viewer for a selected file type. This can be done in the Edit File Type dialog box by activating the Enable Quick View checkbox. The Explorer adds into the Registry the *QuickView* subkey with the *Default* value set to *"*"* (see Figure 3-31).

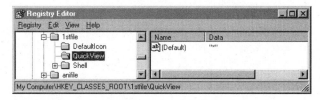

Figure 3-31.
The QuickView *entry in the Registry.*

The Viewer installed in Windows 95 (SCC viewer) detects the file format and shows the contents of the file. The text used on the context menu depends on the localized Windows version.

You can extend properties of each file type with a QuickView command, enabling you to right-click the file, select Quick View on the context menu, and get the Quick View display of the file contents on the screen. Figure 3-32 shows the Quick View window with the contents of a REG file.

There is no default Quick Viewer for REG files registered in Windows 95, but you can use the following lines to extend the REG file type properties. (This file is available as REG1.REG in the \chapter3 folder of the downloaded sample files.)

```
REGEDIT4

[HKEY_CLASSES_ROOT\regfile\QuickView]
@="*"
```

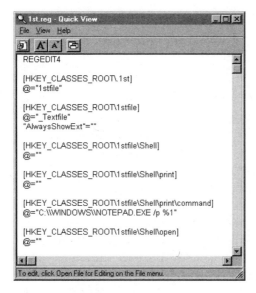

Figure 3-32.
Quick View window with the contents of a REG file.

Whenever you right-click a REG file, the Quick View context menu entry will appear.

Defining a Standard *QuickView* Property

After inspecting other branches in the Registry, I did find it curious that, for example, I couldn't find a *QuickView* key entry in *HKEY_CLASSES_ROOT\ rtffile\.* (See Figure 3-33.)

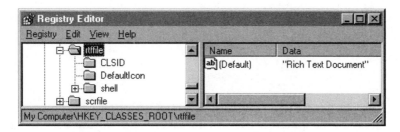

Figure 3-33.
The keys for the RTF file type.

The RTF format is widely supported under Windows 95, so I wondered why this key was missing. A short test reveals that right-clicking an RTF file opens the context menu with a Quick View entry. (Try right-clicking the file README.RTF in the \chapter3 folder of the downloaded sample files.)

How could Windows 95 know that the context menu should contain a Quick View command? Other file extensions have no *QuickView* key and also no such command on the context menu. The answer can be found in the *HKEY_CLASSES_ROOT* branch, in which a key named *QuickView* defines the properties of the Quick View function. The branch contains the extensions of all registered file types for which the Quick Viewer is available.

Figure 3-34 shows part of this structure. Each file type can be registered by its extension, which is used as the key name. The child of this "extension" uses the Class ID (CLSID) code value of the Quick Viewer as a key name. Windows uses this CLSID value to define the ActiveX server, which will be invoked as a Quick Viewer. Figure 3-34 shows the CLSID of the default Windows 95 Quick Viewer. You can also insert the CLSID of a third-party viewer. The *QuickView* branch contains the file extensions for many file types used in Windows 95, so for those file types there is no need to add a *QuickView* subkey to the file type main key.

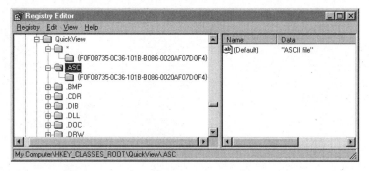

Figure 3-34.
The QuickView *branch in* HKEY_CLASSES_ROOT.

You can verify this for the REG file type. This file type has no default *QuickView* property. Earlier, we registered the *QuickView* key in the *regfile* branch. If you delete this key, you can try to register a *QuickView* property for

REG files in the *HKEY_CLASSES_ROOT\QuickView* branch. You can use the following commands for this purpose:

```
REGEDIT4

[HKEY_CLASSES_ROOT\QuickView\.REG]

[HKEY_CLASSES_ROOT\QuickView\.REG\{F0F08735-0C36-101B-B086-
0020AF07D0F4}]
@="Born's Quick View Test"
```

After importing this file, the REG file type should have a Quick View property. (This file is available as REG2.REG in the \chapter3 folder of the downloaded sample files.)

Information About Viewer Modules

Windows 95 keeps the files for the viewers in the subfolder named \Windows\System\Viewers. Information about the SCC viewer modules can be found in the Registry in this branch:

HKEY_LOCAL_MACHINE\ SOFTWARE\SCC\ViewerTechnology

By default, this Registry branch contains an *MS1* subkey containing two subkeys (*Engine List, Filter List*) with internal viewer data. The settings for the Quick View windows can be found in the key *HKEY_USERS\ xxxx\Software\SCC\QuickViewer\1.00*. The characters *xxxx* stand for a user name (or for the default). Entries exist for the fonts (*CurrentFontCharset, CurrentFontName, CurrentFontSize*), for the options (*Orientation, PageView, Statusbar, Toolbar*), and for the *UseOEMCharSet* flag.

Information about how to write a viewer may be found in Nancy Cluts's book *Programming the Windows 95 User Interface*.

Using an Application as a Viewer

Would you like to use another application as a Quick Viewer? You can add a *quickview* verb in the *shell* key, name it *QuickView*, and set the *command* key *Default* value to the application (for example, *"C:\tools\hexview.exe %1"*).

You can also use the QUIKVIEW.EXE file to open a file. For example, if you want to view the contents of a 1ST file with Quick View, use the following REG structure:

```
REGEDIT4

[HKEY_CLASSES_ROOT\1stfile\Shell\view]

[HKEY_CLASSES_ROOT\1stfile\Shell\view\command]
@="C:\\WINDOWS\\SYSTEM\\VIEWERS\\quikview.EXE %1"
```

This REG file, available as 1STF.REG in the \chapter3 folder of the downloaded sample files, requires that you have already registered the 1ST file type. After importing this REG file, you will see the view command on the context menu if you right-click a 1ST file.

NOTE: If you open the context menu and select the view command, and a message box that tells you that viewers aren't registered for this file type is invoked, then Windows started the Quick Viewer and couldn't find registration information in the Registry. To suppress this message box you must register the *QuickView* property using the techniques discussed earlier.

Registering a Command for All File Types

In the previous sections, we have seen how to register a selected file type and its properties (context menu commands, for example). But suppose you want to register a command for all file types. Perhaps you have a hex editor (available as shareware or freeware) that you want to use to show the internals of a selected file. It's pretty time-consuming to add a command to each registered file type to load this hex editor:

```
shell
    openhex
        command = "C:\TOOLS\HEXEDIT.EXE %1"
```

Fortunately, a key in *HKEY_CLASSES_ROOT* for wildcard (*) extensions is available (as shown in Figure 3-35). If you enter a command in this subkey, this command is valid for all registered file types.

Figure 3-35.
*The * branch for wildcard extensions.*

In Figure 3-35, only shell extensions are registered, but we can extend the * key with a *shell* subkey. Within the *shell* branch you can use your own verbs to extend the properties of all file types.

Let's have a look at Figure 3-36. There I have defined a verb *view* with the *Default* value set to *"&View"*.

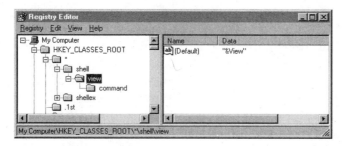

Figure 3-36.
Defining a new command for all file types.

The *command* key is set to the following:

"C:\WINDOWS\SYSTEM\VIEWERS\quikview.exe %1"

The whole structure to register this extension is shown in the following REG file:

```
REGEDIT4

[HKEY_CLASSES_ROOT\*\shell]

[HKEY_CLASSES_ROOT\*\shell\view]
@="&View"

[HKEY_CLASSES_ROOT\*\shell\view\command]
@="C:\\WINDOWS\\SYSTEM\\VIEWERS\\quikview.EXE %1"
```

If your system uses a different folder to store the Quick Viewer, you must edit the last line of the path. You can also exchange QUIKVIEW.EXE with the name of another application. (This REG file is available as ALL1.REG in the \chapter3 folder of the downloaded sample files.)

Now if you select a file and right-click, the context menu contains the new View entry (see Figure 3-37 on the following page). Until now, the default entry shown in boldface was at the top of the context menu. In Figure 3-37, notice that the View entry is at the top of the menu. This ordering relates to how Windows 95 scans the Registry.

Figure 3-37.
Extending the context menu with a View command.

First, the wildcard (*) branch is checked by Windows 95—it detects that we have extended this branch with a new command. This command is shown as the top entry on the context menu. Next, Windows 95 scans the Registry for the entry matching the file extension. All verbs in the *shell* branch are appended to the context menu. These entries are sorted. (See the section "Sequencing the Context Menu Commands" earlier in this chapter for an explanation.) Then the *QuickView* property for this file type is analyzed, and if the command is available, it is appended on the context menu. After these steps, other entries (Send To, Copy, and so on) are added to the context menu. In Chapter 4, I discuss several examples of extending the context menu with new functions.

Getting Your Hands on Unregistered Files

If you double-click an unregistered file, the Open With dialog box opens. Right-clicking the file shows the Open With entry on the context menu. That is all you can do with an unregistered file type. Many unregistered files contain only ASCII text, so it would be helpful to use Notepad to open these files (or to use Quick View to display the contents). One place to add commands to unregistered files is *HKEY_CLASSES_ROOT**, but any command you enter will be shown for all file types. If you want to display a command for only unregistered file types, you should use the branch found in *HKEY_CLASSES_ROOT\Unknown\shell*. This key contains a subkey *openas*, which is set as shown in Figure 3-38.

The subkey *openas* is another canonical verb defined in Windows 95. This verb will be shown as Open With on the context menu. You can examine the *Default* value of the *command* key to find out how RUNDLL32.EXE is called to invoke the Open With dialog box.

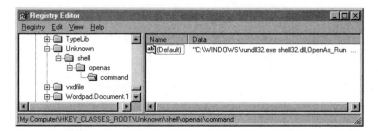

Figure 3-38.
The Unknown *branch in* HKEY_CLASSES_ROOT.

How can you use the *Unknown* branch? Because there is a *shell* key, all you need to do is add a new verb and define a *command* key using a command string. The following REG file contains the command to register NOTEPAD.EXE as the application for opening unregistered file types. Be sure your system uses the same path as shown in the preceding REG file.

```
REGEDIT4

[HKEY_CLASSES_ROOT\Unknown\shell\open1]
@="Notepad"

[HKEY_CLASSES_ROOT\Unknown\shell\open1\command]
@="C:\\Windows\\Notepad.exe %1"
```

After importing the REG file by double-clicking, you can open an unregistered file type by right-clicking it and selecting Notepad. (This REG file is available as UNKNOWN1.REG in the \chapter 3 folder of the downloaded sample files.)

For unregistered file types, the context menu contains the Notepad entry (see Figure 3-39 on the following page). If you select this entry, the file will be loaded into Notepad. Also note the Open With entry, which is used to register an application for this file type, and the View command, which is shown in bold. This command was registered in *HKEY_CLASSES_ROOT*\shell.* View has become the default command for the unregistered file type. View is shown in bold only if you select an unknown file type, where the commands registered in the wildcard branch will be used as the default.

Figure 3-39.
Extended context menu for unregistered file types.

Conclusion

In this chapter, I showed you how to register file types in Windows 95. Now you can fix some problems in your Registry and extend the shell with several new commands. Don't forget to use the easy way to register and modify the file type properties—the Explorer's File Types property page is a smart tool for changing the settings. In Chapter 4, I will show how to extend the shell further with new commands.

CHAPTER FOUR

Customizing the Desktop, Start Menu, and Control Panel Properties

Microsoft Windows 95 uses a shell, of which the Explorer is a significant feature, to handle all user interface tasks. If you use the Start menu or change something on the desktop, the Explorer is involved. As we have seen in Chapter 3, you can easily register a new file type or change the default icon of a file type, but these are only two ways in which you can customize the Windows 95 shell. You can also do the following:

- Rename title text for desktop icons
- Change the icons themselves
- Change Start menu entries
- Customize the Explorer commands

In this chapter, I show several techniques for customizing the desktop, the Start menu, and the Control Panel properties, and discuss how these changes affect the Registry.

Customizing the Open With List

On a freshly installed Windows 95 system, the program list in the Open With dialog box contains only a few entries. After you install additional application programs, this list grows, but it's often incomplete.

When I started working with Windows 95, I wondered why some application programs never appeared in the Open With dialog box and why others were completely nonsensical. For example, the list on my system contains install programs, HTML wizards, and so on—unnecessary entries left on my system by application setup programs that violate the rules of good Windows-based programming. A good setup program should delete entries in the Registry that are used only for installation purposes and should also offer an option to uninstall the files that will clean these entries, but the world is full of unfriendly programs.

If you've worked with Windows 95 for a while, you'll probably find that your Open With dialog box contains a huge list of application names that aren't helpful anymore. Some entries remain even if you have deleted the application. And while you've got too many applications you don't need, you don't have a list of the ones that you do need: Some programs (especially shareware) are shipped only as EXE files, and because setup programs aren't necessary, these programs are never added to the Open With list. The Other button is your only option for accessing these applications. Needless to say, this frustrating situation forced me to think about a solution. Wouldn't it be nice to find a way to add your favorite applications to the Open With list and delete unnecessary entries?

How the Shell Inserts Applications in the Open With List

Before I dig into the details, we have to find out what information is needed in order to add or remove entries from the Open With list. It took me a long time to find out how Windows 95 manages this list, but the answer is fairly simple. If you look back at Chapter 3, you'll find an explanation of the canonical verbs used to register a command for a new file type. Windows 95 uses those verbs to determine which applications to include in the Open With list. Whenever a user invokes the Open With dialog box, Windows 95 scans the *HKEY_CLASSES_ROOT* key in the Registry. Any application that is defined in the *command* subkey of the *open* verb of a registered file type is added by Windows to the Open With list. If the application contains its own icon, this icon will be shown. The text for the entry is taken from the name of the EXE file or from the *Default* value of the file extension key.

So it's easy to add your favorite application to the Open With list—all you need to do is register a file type with this application. To remove an entry, delete the *open* verb for the registered file type using this application. The following sections explain in detail how to add and delete applications from the Open With list.

Adding an Application to the Open With List

First let's register an application for the Open With dialog box. To simulate a typical situation, I'll use a new, unregistered file type and application. Here's our situation:

- The new file extension is set to ASC because many ASCII text files have this extension. You can easily register this file type, as we saw in Chapter 3. (Look at the README.ASC file in the \chapter4 folder of the downloaded sample files.)

- We'll open our ASCII text file with the MS-DOS program EDIT.COM, which is shipped with Windows 95. (You'll find this application in the \Windows\Command subfolder.) We could also open our ASCII text file with Notepad, but NOTEPAD.EXE is already registered for the Open With dialog box.

Registering the ASC file type with the EDIT.COM application adds the application to the Open With list. (You might prefer to register some other application available on your computer. I have chosen to register EDIT.COM on my system because it allows me to show and modify MS-DOS–based files containing the OEM character set. With Notepad, you can't edit files containing line-drawn characters and umlauts.) Once EDIT.COM (or another editor) is added to the Open With list, you can use this program to load the file instead of using Notepad. You can add an application to the Open With list by using the Open With dialog box or a REG file.

Using the Open With Dialog Box

To add EDIT.COM to the Open With dialog box permanently, we have to register an *open* key for the new file type in *HKEY_CLASSES_ROOT* and enter the command that invokes EDIT.COM in the *command* subkey. Following is the simplest method for adding EDIT.COM to the Open With dialog box:

1. Right-click the unregistered README.ASC file and select Open With from the context menu. Windows 95 opens the Open With dialog box. The Always Use This Program To Open This Type Of File checkbox must contain a check mark to ensure that the Registry is updated.

2. Enter a description in the Description Of '.Asc' Files text box. (See the Tip on page 59 in Chapter 3 for tips on creating a description.)

3. Click the Other button to invoke another dialog box—the Open With file dialog box. Select All Files (*.*) in the Files Of Type section, and browse the Windows\Command subfolder.

4. Select EDIT.COM and click Open. Click OK to close the Open With dialog box.

Windows registers the new ASC file type with an *open* verb and the EDIT.COM command and opens the MS-DOS Editor. Close the Editor, select the README.ASC file in the Explorer, press the Shift key, and right-click the file. Select the Open With command from the context menu to invoke another Open With dialog box (see Figure 4-1). As you can see, the Edit entry is now available in the Open With list. Since EDIT.COM is an MS-DOS application, the default icon for EXE files is used for this entry. The text following the icon is built from the application's filename.

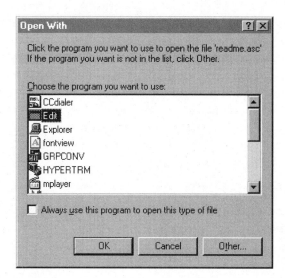

Figure 4-1.
Open With dialog box with the new Edit entry.

Using a REG File
The second way to add EDIT.COM to the Open With list is to use a REG file to extend the Registry with the necessary entries. Following are the lines necessary to register the ASC file type and use EDIT.COM as an associated application:

```
REGEDIT4

[HKEY_CLASSES_ROOT\.asc]
@="ascfile"

[HKEY_CLASSES_ROOT\ascfile]
@="_AsciFile"

[HKEY_CLASSES_ROOT\ascfile\Shell]
@=""

[HKEY_CLASSES_ROOT\ascfile\Shell\open]
@="DOS-Edit"

[HKEY_CLASSES_ROOT\ascfile\Shell\open\command]
@="C:\\WINDOWS\\Command\\Edit.com \"%1\""

[HKEY_CLASSES_ROOT\ascfile\DefaultIcon]
@="C:\\WINDOWS\\Notepad.exe,1"
```

All commands in the ASC.REG file are contained in the \chapter4 folder of the downloaded sample files. If you double-click this file, all settings are added to the Registry. I used \WINDOWS as the standard name for the \Windows folder, so if you use a different name, you have to modify the preceding code lines to map the right path to EDIT.COM—before you double-click the REG file.

> N O T E : If you plan to ship your application with an installation script, don't use a REG file. If you aren't using a setup program, try to install the application and update the Registry with an INF file. I've discussed this topic in Chapter 3 and will show the details of constructing such an INF file in Chapters 5 and 7.

Removing an Application from the Open With List

Removing a superfluous entry from the list can be a simple task, but you should be aware of the potential problems. Following are techniques for removing items from the list.

Removing a Phantom Entry

If you have deleted software from your PC (maybe the package was installed only for test purposes), the Registry could contain the entries for registering the associated file types. Because uninstall features often are either nonexistent or don't work properly, many unused entries can remain in the Registry. Selecting one of these entries in the Open With dialog box invokes the Program Not Found dialog box (see Figure 4-2 on the following page), which indicates that the application isn't available, or at least not in the specified folder—which also indicates that it's time to clean your Registry. You can handle this in several different ways.

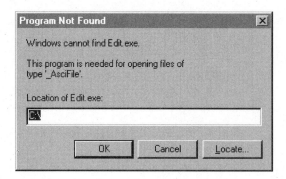

Figure 4-2.
The Program Not Found dialog box.

The most radical solution would be to start the Registry Editor and delete the entries for this application. You would have to remove two keys in *HKEY_CLASSES_ROOT*: one that specified the file extension (in our previous example, this was the *.asc* key) and one that defined the commands for this file type (the *ascfile* key). If you knew which entries had to be modified, this would be the best method. (I have used this approach many times.)

If you're feeling more cautious, you can use a different approach: redirecting the Open With dialog box to use one of the other installed applications. For example, you could register the ASC file type to use Notepad. (You could use a different application program as well, depending on your situation.) To remove the phantom entry and register another application for this file type, follow these steps:

1. Press the Shift key and right-click the file type. Select the Open With command from the context menu to open the dialog box.

2. Activate the Always Use This Program To Open This Type Of File checkbox.

3. Select the application that you want to register for this file type. (You can select an application from the list or click Other to display additional applications.)

4. Click OK to close the dialog box.

Windows 95 overwrites the value defined in the *command* subkey with the selected application's name and path. Double-clicking the file type opens the new application, and if you open the Open With dialog box again, the old (phantom) entry will be gone, assuming no other registered file types use that application. If you clicked Other to select a new application, you'll see the new entry. Even if several file types are registered for a single application, the application will appear only once in the list.

> **T I P :** This trick is handy if the application you're removing had overwritten registered file types of other applications. For example, if the BMP extension was overwritten by a graphics application, you could use the above steps to reset this extension to open with the Microsoft Paint application.

Using the Explorer to Remove an Open With List Entry

Suppose you need to remove some rarely used entries, but you have no idea which file types the Open command is registered under. The application you want to remove could support several file types (for example, WordPad supports DOC, RTF, and TXT file extensions). So if you delete an entire branch for a given file type in the Registry, you will probably disable other functions. (Perhaps you'd lose the ability to print with drag-and-drop, or you'd lose the Quick View feature for a file type.)

You could inspect the *HKEY_CLASSES_ROOT* branch with the Registry Editor and remove all unused entries, but that's time-consuming and you might inadvertently remove or change the wrong keys. Fortunately, there is a less risky way to alter the Registry and find out what you need to change. If you want to remove an entry from the Open With list but you're not sure which file types are responsible for the entry, perform the following steps:

1. Open the Explorer window, click the View menu, and select Options to open the Options property sheet.

2. Select the File Types property page, and click an entry in the Registered File Types list. Windows shows the entry's file type and the associated application in the File Type Details section (see Figure 4-3 on the following page).

3. If the Registry contains an *open* verb for this file type, you'll see the icon and the application name in the Opens With line. In Figure 4-3, I chose the *_AsciFile* entry (which I registered earlier). The ASC file extension is associated with the Edit application (see Figure 4-3).

4. Click the Edit button to open the Edit File Type dialog box, and check the commands registered for this file type. Here you can select open in the Actions box and then click Edit to bring up the Editing Action For Type dialog box. In this dialog box, you can confirm that the application used for the open action is the one you want to remove. If it is, close the Editing Action For Type dialog box, be sure the open action is still highlighted, and click Remove.

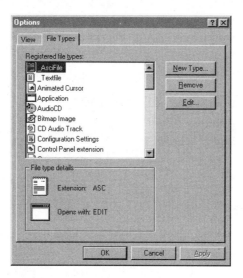

Figure 4-3.
The File Types property page.

You can continue to look for entries on the File Types property page to determine whether other file types exist that contain open actions for this application. You must delete all entries that contain the application's name in the Opens With line on the File Types property page.

This process will work fine as long as you don't need the application to be associated with the registered file types anymore. A problem arises if you want to remove the application's name from the Open With list but still keep the file types registered with that application. In this case, you can't simply delete the *open* verbs in the Action box of the Edit File Type window—you must rename them. I will explain how to do this in the next section.

Using the Registry Editor to Remove an Open With Entry

Sometimes you don't want to delete a registered file type's *open* verb and its command, because you need this command for that file type. So how do you force Windows to prevent the application's name from appearing in the Open

With list? As I mentioned earlier, the *open* verb is a canonical verb and is used to build the Open With list. In Chapter 3, I discussed several ways to register a file type without using a canonical verb, such as renaming the *open* verb to *open1*. This prevents the application from being added to the Open With list.

Unfortunately, you can't change an entry in the Action box of the Edit File Type dialog box. In this case, you can use the Registry Editor to solve the problem. Follow these steps:

1. Create a Registry backup so that you can recover the old settings if you fail to alter the Open With list correctly. (See pages 35–42 in Chapter 2 for backup procedures.)

2. Search *HKEY_CLASSES_ROOT* for all *open* keys associated with the application that will be removed from the Open With list. (If you don't know the file types, you can identify them by using the File Types property page, as explained in the previous section.)

3. Right-click the *open* key in the left pane, select Rename from the context menu, and change the key's name to *open1*. Enter the name you want displayed in the context menu in the *Default* value of this key (right pane). In Figure 4-4 I've used *DOS-Edit*, but you can also use *Open*.

4. Select the *Shell* key (the parent of the *open1* key) of this branch, and set the *Default* value in the right pane to *open1*. This assures that the command will be used when you double-click the file.

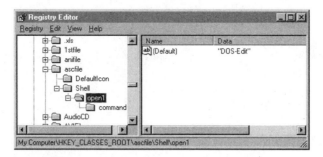

Figure 4-4.
Modified Registry branch.

If the application is registered for several file types, you must repeat these steps for each *open* key of each of these file types. After changing all entries, you should run a test to determine whether the system is still functioning properly (for example, perhaps an application relies on the *open* verb). If all *open* keys for file types associated with the specified application are renamed properly, the application's name will be removed from the Open With dialog box.

NOTE: Be careful when removing or renaming system-specific entries such as folders, drives, and so on in the Registry. These entries are used by the system, and unpredictable events could occur if their settings are damaged. (The most serious event would be that Windows wouldn't boot up anymore.) Also be careful deleting entries in *HKEY_CLASSES_ROOT*. Always create a Registry backup before you remove or modify an entry so that you can recover the previous settings.

HKEY_CLASSES_ROOT and HKEY_LOCAL_MACHINE\SOFTWARE\Classes

In Chapter 3, I discussed how to register a file type in *HKEY_CLASSES_ROOT*. The sole purpose of *HKEY_CLASSES_ROOT* is to provide compatibility with the Microsoft Windows 3.1 registration database. If an old 16-bit application inserts entries in the [Extension] section of the WIN.INI file, these entries will also be stored in the Registry in *HKEY_CLASSES_ROOT*. These entries are available the next time you start Windows 95.

The *HKEY_LOCAL_MACHINE\SOFTWARE\Classes* branch contains the entries for the registered file types. *HKEY_CLASSES_ROOT* always keeps the same data as the key *HKEY_LOCAL_MACHINE\SOFTWARE\Classes*. If you change something in one branch, all modifications are automatically applied to the other branch. I prefer to use only *HKEY_CLASSES_ROOT* to register new file types (as I have shown here in this book).

Another key defined in the Registry with the name *HKEY_LOCAL_MACHINE\SOFTWARE\Microsoft\Windows\CurrentVersion\Extensions* contains entries in the WIN.INI [Extensions] style. The *CurrentVersion* subkey contains information about software that supports services built into Windows. As I mentioned in Chapter 3, you must be careful that the settings in the *Extensions* subkey don't contradict the settings defined in *HKEY_CLASSES_ROOT*.

Modifying the Desktop Items

The desktop contains both user-defined and predefined, or system-specific, items. User-defined items, such as a shortcut to an application, can be modified easily. A typical user can change an icon and its title, for example, or delete the item altogether.

The system-specific items, however, which include My Computer, Network Neighborhood, Inbox, Briefcase, and Recycle Bin, are much more difficult to modify. A typical user can change the text associated with a particular icon (for example, the user could change the icon title from My Computer to Danny's Computer), but it's unlikely that the typical user would be able to modify or hide the physical icon itself without knowing important details about the Registry. In this section, I show you how to modify the system-specific desktop elements.

Modifying the My Computer Components

The My Computer item is always shown by default in the upper left corner of the desktop. The only attributes you can change directly on the desktop are the text below the icon and the icon position. If you know where to edit in the Registry, you can also change the icon or hide the displayed drive symbols in the My Computer window.

Changing the My Computer Icon

Where should you edit in the Registry? You might already know the way because this trick has appeared in many books, magazines, and World Wide Web sites, but I want to discuss the details and also point out the problems.

The Windows 95 shell is built as a combination of several ActiveX components. Shell parts, such as the Recycle Bin, have their own modules. The handlers for all ActiveX modules are registered in the *HKEY_CLASSES_ROOT\ CLSID* branch. (See the second bullet on page 53 and the sidebar on page 54 in Chapter 3 for more information about the CLSID code.) Figure 4-5 on the following page shows the *CLSID* branch in the Registry Editor window.

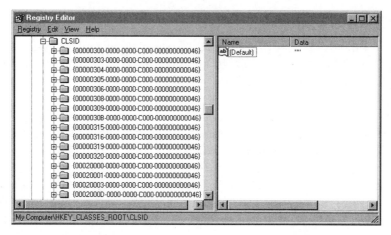

Figure 4-5.
The HKEY_CLASSES_ROOT\CLSID *entries in the Registry Editor.*

Finding the entry for My Computer   After starting the Registry Editor, search the *HKEY_CLASSES_ROOT\CLSID* branch for the ActiveX component entry that handles the My Computer icon. Use the Find function, accessible from the Edit menu, to find the entry. Add a check mark to the Keys, Values, and Data options. The Match Whole String Only checkbox can be checked or unchecked.

Which string should you enter in the Find What text box? The simplest solution is to enter the icon's title, My Computer. Unfortunately, this procedure doesn't work in all cases. The reasons are simple but not well-documented. Here's what I found out:

- You must enter the exact string of the icon's title. If your desktop displays My Computer, the search string is *My Computer*. If the icon title is set to Danny's Computer, you must enter the string *Danny's Computer*. This is important, because if you use a localized Windows 95 version, you have to enter the localized title.

- Sometimes the Find function will fail even if you use the correct string—you will get the message that there is no match in the Registry. This happens when Windows 95 is newly installed and the original title, My Computer, is still used. Even if Windows 95 has been installed for some time, if you have never changed the name of My Computer, the Registry contains no My Computer entry.

So rather than enter the icon title in the Find What textbox, enter the key's name as the search string. The key for the ActiveX component of My Computer is always (as far as I know) named this: *{20D04FE0-3AEA-1069-A2D8-08002B30309D}*. If you enter this key name, the Registry Editor will find the correct entry in the *HKEY_CLASSES_ROOT\CLSID* branch. It is, however, a rather large number, and the likelihood of entering a wrong digit is high (in which case the Registry Editor would fail to find the entry).

So rename the title of the My Computer icon to something else, and then, if you want, set the name back to My Computer. The effect is fairly simple: The name you entered will be added in the *Default* value of this key—*HKEY_CLASSES_ROOT\CLSID\{20D04FE0-3AEA-1069-A2D8-08002B30309D}*. Future searches in the Registry Editor will result in a pattern match. (It took me more than a year to figure this out. Most people try to change the icon's title first and then dive into the Registry. This might be the reason that tips on this topic don't mention this problem.)

OK, let's wrap this up. If you follow my advice, the Registry Editor will find the *CLSID* entry for My Computer. This branch contains several subkeys that define the properties of the ActiveX component (see Figure 4-6). The *InProcServer32* key contains two entries, one defining the ActiveX server module and the other defining the Threading model. (You can find additional information about this topic in Nancy Cluts's book *Programming the Windows 95 User Interface*.) The *shell* subkey defines the *find* command for the shell.

Figure 4-6.
Subkeys for My Computer.

Modifying the *DefaultIcon* value   The interesting part of the *My Computer* branch is the *DefaultIcon* key. The *Default* value of this key is set to the icon source used in the ActiveX component. If you inspect this key with the Registry Editor, you will find an entry like this:

C:\WINDOWS\Explorer.exe,0

The *DefaultIcon* key is used in many places to define the icon source of an entry. (We have seen this in Chapter 3.) For My Computer, the first icon in EXPLORER.EXE is used (because the Explorer is part of the shell). To change the icon of My Computer, you must alter the *Default* value of the *DefaultIcon* key. Set the *Default* value to *C:\WINDOWS\Explorer.exe, 1*. After entering this value in the Registry Editor, click a free space on the desktop and press the F5 key to refresh the display and show the new icon for My Computer (see Figure 4-7).

My Computer

Figure 4-7.
A new icon for My Computer.

> NOTE: You can also use other files as sources for icons. For example, all Windows 95 applications come with built-in icons. As well, some DLL files, such as SHELL32.DLL, contain icons. (If you have installed Microsoft Plus!, you will probably see many *DefaultIcon* entries that use COOL.DLL.) You can also create your own ICO file and associate it with My Computer. You will find some additional information about the requirements for new icons in Chapter 5, in the section "Changing the Shell Icons" on pages 204–210. This information is important if you use different screen resolutions and color resolutions.

Hiding the Drive Symbols in the My Computer Window

Double-clicking the desktop's My Computer icon opens a window that contains the Printers and Control Panel folders as well as the symbols for all drives and associated network devices. Figure 4-8 shows the My Computer window on my computer.

As you can see, the symbol for the floppy drive A: isn't visible, even though my computer has a floppy disk drive. Obviously, you have the option to hide or show individual drive symbols in this window. Why would you want to hide them?

Sometimes you'll need to hide drive symbols for an individual user in order to customize the desktop for special user groups. Suppose, for example, you needed to limit user access to certain drives: A manager might want access to all drives but needs to prevent his assistant from accessing the CD-ROM drive. Let's take a look at how this is accomplished.

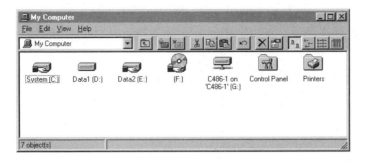

Figure 4-8.
My Computer window, missing the floppy disk drive symbol.

First, in order for the hide and show options to work, the user profiles must be enabled. (Further information on user profiles can be found in the section "The System Policy Editor" on pages 42–46 in Chapter 2.) Then, to activate the hide option, follow these steps:

1. Log on to the system and start the System Policy Editor.

2. Open the local Registry by clicking on the File menu and selecting the Open Registry entry.

3. Double-click the Local User icon in the System Policy Editor window.

4. Select the Shell\Restrictions path on the Policies property page (see Figure 4-9 on the following page).

5. Check the Hide Drives In 'My Computer' option.

6. Click OK and save the settings.

7. Open the My Computer window. (If the window is already open, click the window and press F5 to refresh the display.)

All drive symbols are hidden, and you will see only two folder symbols: Printers and Control Panel. Keep in mind that this option is valid only for the current user. If you log on again under a new user name, the drive symbols will still be visible.

> **NOTE:** You can use the System Policy Editor to hide the drive symbols for other users or user groups. (This feature is beyond the scope of this book. You should consult the *Windows 95 Resource Kit* for further details about the System Policy Editor.)

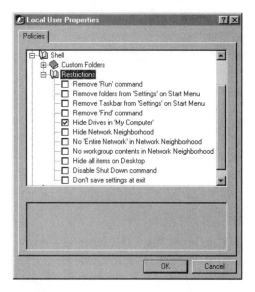

Figure 4-9.
Using the System Policy Editor to hide the drive symbols in My Computer.

So what does all this have to do with the Registry? Windows 95 keeps all information about the system in the Registry key ...\ *Software\Microsoft\Windows\ CurrentVersion.* Settings global to the local computer are held in the *HKEY_LOCAL_MACHINE* branch. User-specific settings of the current system can be found in the *HKEY_CURRENT_USER* branch (and also a copy in *HKEY_USERS*). If you use the System Policy Editor to hide the drives in My Computer, the following key is updated:

HKEY_CURRENT_USER\Software\Microsoft\Windows\CurrentVersion\Policies\Explorer

The System Policy Editor adds a *NoDrives* value (DWORD) to this key. This value will be set to *NoDrives = 0x03ffffff.*

If this value is found, Windows hides all drive symbols in the Explorer windows. If the user invokes the My Computer window or the Explorer window, no drive symbols are displayed (and the desktop shows the My Computer symbol, which contains only the Printers and Control Panel folders).

While this is an excellent method to customize the Windows 95 shell and prevent the user from accessing a drive, the System Policy Editor is the wrong tool for fine-tuning these settings. Instead, you should use the Registry Editor to alter the *NoDrives* value. The DWORD is coded as a bit flag, so the value *0x03ffffff* stands for 26 bits. Each of these bits corresponds to one of the 26 possible drive names. Bit *0* corresponds to drive A:, Bit *1* corresponds to drive B:, and so on. I set the *NoDrives* value to *00000001* to get the results shown in Figure 4-8 on page 119. In this case, the first drive (which is always the floppy disk A:) is hidden. A bit set to *1* hides the corresponding drive symbol. The trick is to translate the bit pattern into a hex value.

> T I P : You can save the *NoDrives* value in a REG file and create a short-cut to the REG file in the user's Startup folder. Each time the user logs on, this REG file will be imported into the Registry. There is only one disadvantage: The drive containing the REG file remains visible, independent of the *NoDrives* settings. The file NODRIVES.REG is in the \chapter4 folder of the downloaded sample files.

> To show all drives, you should delete the *NoDrives* value. To do this you can use the Registry Editor, or you can use the System Policy Editor and uncheck the option shown in Figure 4-9.

Hiding All Desktop Items

If you take a closer look at Figure 4-9, you'll find the Hide All Items On Desktop option. All you have to do to hide desktop items is activate the corresponding checkbox, close the Policies property page by clicking OK, and then save the settings (File, Save) in the Registry. The next time you log on, all items on the desktop will be hidden. Only the taskbar and the Start menu are accessible.

As we've seen, Windows 95 stores the information about the desktop elements in the following Registry branch because shell items are user-specific:

HKEY_CURRENT_USER\Software\Microsoft\Windows\CurrentVersion\Policies\Explorer

If you select the Hide All Items On Desktop option, the *NoDesktop* entry is added in the above branch and the DWORD value is set to *00000001*. The next time you log on, Windows will detect this flag and hide all desktop symbols. If the flag is not available or the value is set to *00000000*, the desktop symbols remain visible.

> N O T E : You can disable the Registry Editor for a user (by following this path: System Policy Editor, Local User, System, Restrictions; and then selecting the Disable Registry Editing Tools option) so that . the user can't go in and change the *NoDesktop* and *NoDrives* entries that you set to limit user access, but that user can still import a REG file to change the Registry settings. So an experienced user can bypass your settings by creating and running a simple REG file. We look at a strategy for preventing this later in this chapter in the "Restricting Access to the Registry Editing Tools" sidebar on page 164.

Changing the Network Items

If the network services are installed on the local computer, the Network Neighborhood icon is shown on the desktop. You can easily change the title and position of this icon, change the icon itself, and control the icon's features.

Changing the Network Neighborhood Icon

You change the icon for the Network Neighborhood in the same way that you change the My Computer icon: using the Find function (see page 116). In the Find What text box, you can set the search string to one of three values: to *Network Neighborhood* (if the icon title is set to this name); to the icon's title that is shown on the desktop; or to *{208D2C60-3AEA-1069-A2D7-08002B30309D}*. A successful match reveals this key:

HKEY_CLASSES_ROOT\CLSID\{208D2C60-3AEA-1069-A2D7-08002B30309D}

The structure of this branch is similar to the structure of the *CLSID* branch for My Computer. The only difference is that you might have a *shellex* key, which defines a context menu handler for the Network Neighborhood. The icon source is defined in the *Default* value of the *DefaultIcon* key. The default value for this entry is set to the following: *C:\WINDOWS\SYSTEM\ shell32.dll,17*. The Network Neighborhood uses the 18th icon stored in the SHELL32.DLL file (icon indexes are counted from zero). You can then change this entry to *C:\WINDOWS\Explorer.exe,1*, for example, which is the icon shown in Figure 4-7 on page118. If the icon didn't change when you modified the Registry, click anywhere on the desktop and press F5 to refresh the screen.

> NOTE: You can use different files (DLL, EXE, ICO) as icon sources. The icons contained in SHELL32.DLL are shown in Appendix A beginning on page 281. You can also use your own ICO file, which is discussed later in this chapter.

Hiding the Network Neighborhood Icon

If you run a local computer without a network card, the Network Neighborhood icon is hidden. On a network computer, the icon is visible by default, but you have the option to hide it for the current user. You do this with the System Policy Editor.

1. Log on to the system with the user's name and password, and start the System Policy Editor.

2. Open the local Registry (File, Open Registry).

3. Double-click the Local User icon in the System Policy Editor window.

4. Select the Shell\Restrictions path on the Policies property page.

5. Check the Hide Network Neighborhood option and click OK.

6. Save the settings in the Registry and exit the System Policy Editor.

After the next logon, the Network Neighborhood icon is hidden. The information about the visibility of this icon is kept in this Registry key:

HKEY_CURRENT_USER\Software\Microsoft\Windows\CurrentVersion\Policies\Explorer

The System Policy Editor adds the *NoNetHood = 0x00000001* DWORD value to this key to hide the icon. If you delete this entry or set the value to *0x00000000,* the icon will be shown after the next logon.

> T I P : The Tweak UI utility (contained in Microsoft's Power Toys) allows you to hide and view the Network Neighborhood icon. Start Tweak UI by double-clicking its icon in the Control Panel, and then select the Desktop property page and check the Network Neighborhood option (see Figure 4-15 on page 132). Click OK. Tweak UI will change the Registry settings and inform you that you need to log off and then log back on to make the settings take effect.

Hiding the Icons in Network Neighborhood

When you double-click the Network Neighborhood icon, Windows shows the Entire Network icon and the icons of the current user's workgroup computers (see Figure 4-10).

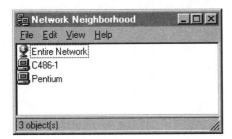

Figure 4-10.
The Network Neighborhood window.

You can hide these symbols for the current user by using the System Policy Editor. Start the System Policy Editor and load the local Registry, and then perform the steps on the following page.

1. Select the Shell\Restrictions path on the Policies property page.

2. Check the No 'Entire Network' In Network Neighborhood option to hide the icon.

3. If you want to hide all workgroup computer icons belonging to the user's workgroup, check the No Workgroup Contents In Network Neighborhood option.

4. Close the property page by clicking OK, and save the settings.

When you open the Network Neighborhood window, the icons you specified are hidden.

Windows keeps the information about the visibility of these icons in the following Registry key:

HKEY_CURRENT_USER\Software\Microsoft\Windows\CurrentVersion\Policies\Network

The *NoEntireNetwork* entry, shown in Figure 4-11, controls the visibility of the Entire Network icon. If this flag is set to the following DWORD value, the icon is hidden: *NoEntireNetwork = 0x00000001*. Deleting this entry or setting the value to *0x00000000* will display the icon again the next time the screen is refreshed. The second entry in Figure 4-11, *NoWorkgroupContents*, hides or shows the icons of the workgroup computers within the network. If this flag is set to the DWORD value *NoWorkgroupContents = 0x00000001*, all icons are hidden. Deleting this entry or setting the value to *0x00000000* will show the icons the next time the screen is refreshed.

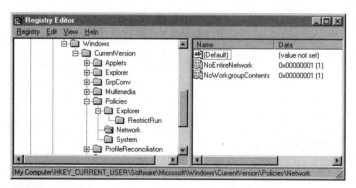

Figure 4-11.
The Network *key.*

Modifying the Recycle Bin Settings

The Recycle Bin is shown as an icon on the desktop and in the directory structure of each drive (that is, in the shell and Explorer windows). As with the other desktop items, you can rename it, choose a different icon, and hide it.

Renaming the Recycle Bin

Have you ever tried to rename the Recycle Bin? Right-clicking the desktop icon opens a context menu, but the Rename command is missing. So you have to go into the Registry, select the proper key, and change its *Default* value.

The way Windows handles the Recycle Bin is similar to the way it handles other desktop components: The Recycle Bin is an ActiveX component that is registered in the *HKEY_CLASSES_ROOT\CLSID* branch of the Registry. To change anything, you must inspect the key in the *CLSID* branch by accessing the Find dialog box in the Registry Editor and entering one of two search patterns:

■ Enter the name of the Recycle Bin as it appears on your desktop, and check only the Data and Values checkboxes.

■ Enter the key name *{645FF040-5081-101B-9F08-00AA002F954E}* for the ActiveX Server, which identifies the Recycle Bin entry in the *CLSID* branch.

A successful search reveals the branch shown in Figure 4-12 on the following page. The subkeys shown in this figure define the properties of the Recycle Bin:

■ The *DefaultIcon* key sets the icons used by the Recycle Bin handlers.

■ The *InProcServer32* key contains the definition for the server (SHELL32.DLL) and the Threading model (*Apartment*). (Further information about this topic may be found in Nancy Cluts's book, *Programming the Windows 95 User Interface*, and in Charles Petzold's book, *Programming Windows 95*.)

■ The *shellex* key contains two entries. One entry, called *ContextMenu-Handlers*, defines separate context menu handlers, which is the reason you don't see the common context menu that includes the Rename entry. Instead this handler defines commands appropriate for the Recycle Bin (such as Empty Recycle Bin). The second entry, called *PropertySheetHandlers*, defines separate property sheet handlers for the Recycle Bin; these contain the options for configuring the Recycle Bin.

■ The *ShellFolder* key contains the *Attributes* value, which defines the attribute bits for the folder that the Recycle Bin uses to temporarily store deleted files.

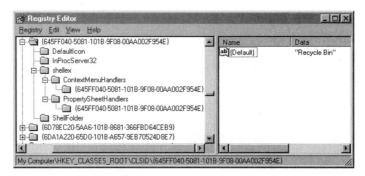

Figure 4-12.
CLSID *entry for the Recycle Bin.*

To rename the Recycle Bin, select the *CLSID* key *{645FF040-5081-101B-9F08-00AA002F954E}* and change its *Default* value to any name you want (to *Trash*, for example).

After changing the value, click the desktop and press F5 to refresh the screen and view the new icon name. When you rename the Recycle Bin, you should also customize the *Tips* entries in the *HKEY_LOCAL_MACHINE* branch to reflect the new name.

NOTE: Changing the name of the Recycle Bin does not affect what you see in the Explorer. You will still see the name Recycle Bin, because this is the name of a folder that keeps deleted files.

The other key that contains the *Recycle Bin* value is *\explorer\ Desktop\NameSpace\{645FF040-5081-101B-9F08-00AA002F954E}* in the *HKEY_LOCAL_MACHINE\SOFTWARE\Microsoft\Windows\CurrentVersion* branch. Modifications to this value don't affect what you see on the desktop (because this value is used like a comment—refer to the section titled "Hiding and Showing the Recycle Bin Icon" on page 132).

Changing the Recycle Bin Icons

The Recycle Bin uses two icons indicating its status as empty or full. The entries used to define these icons are located in the following key:

HKEY_CLASSES_ROOT\CLSID\{645FF040-5081-101B-9F08-00AA002F954E}\ DefaultIcon

We know that the *DefaultIcon* key typically contains one entry pointing to the icon source. For the Recycle Bin, however, *DefaultIcon* contains three values, as shown in Figure 4-13.

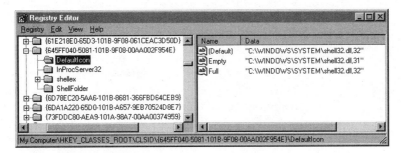

Figure 4-13.
The DefaultIcon *key for the Recycle Bin, which contains three values.*

The handler for the Recycle Bin uses these values to reflect the status of the Recycle Bin:

- The *Default* value always points to the icon source that indicates the status of the Recycle Bin. If the user empties the Recycle Bin, the *Empty* value is copied into the *Default* value. Each time a file is deleted (which means that the file is moved into the Recycle Bin), the Recycle Bin handler copies the *Full* value into the *Default* value. The *Default* value is also updated when you double-click the desktop's Recycle Bin icon, empty the Recycle Bin or insert a file, and then close the window.

- The *Empty* value points to the icon source that defines the symbol for an empty bin. The default for the empty bin symbol is the 32nd icon in SHELL32.DLL. The value, then, is set to *C:\WINDOWS\SYSTEM\shell32.dll,31*.

- The *Full* value points to the icon source that represents a Recycle Bin containing at least one entry. This value is set to *C:\WINDOWS\SYSTEM\shell32.dll,32*.

To change the icons for the Recycle Bin, you have to point the values for *Full* and *Empty* to new icon sources. The file SHELL32.DLL contains additional icons (positions 52 and 53, for example) for the Recycle Bin. (The next chapter addresses the icons stored in SHELL32.DLL in more detail.)

You can also use other icon sources, such as EXE or DLL files. In theory, you could also use pure ICO files as icon sources, but this is problematic: Windows 95 does not reliably refresh the icons taken from ICO files.

TIP: Do you want to inspect the icons contained in the file SHELL32.DLL? Create a shortcut to an application on the desktop, and invoke the icon's property sheet. (Right-click the icon and select Properties.) Select the Shortcut property page and click Change Icon. This invokes the Change Icon dialog box. Click Browse, and search for the SHELL32.DLL file in the Windows\System subfolder. Open the file and review the icons.

If you cannot find the SHELL32.DLL file in the Change Icon dialog box, open the Explorer window and select Options from the View menu. Select the Show All Files option in the Hidden Files section of the View property page, click the Apply button, and then try finding the file again.

Changing the Recycle Bin with a REG File

If you like to change the icons of your Recycle Bin frequently (some people like to change their icons every day), consider using a REG file. The simplest way to do this is to use the Registry Editor and export the following key, which contains the settings for the Recycle Bin icons:

HKEY_CLASSES_ROOT\CLSID\{645FF040-5081-101B-9F08-00AA002F954E}\DefaultIcon

Then set the entries for the *Full* and *Empty* values to new icon sources. Following is a REG file containing the statements to redefine the Recycle Bin icons:

```
REGEDIT4

[HKEY_CLASSES_ROOT\CLSID\{645FF040-5081-101B-9F08-00AA002F954E}\
DefaultIcon]
@="C:\\WINDOWS\\SYSTEM\\shell32.dll,31"
"Empty"="C:\\WINDOWS\\SYSTEM\\shell32.dll,31"
"Full"="C:\\WINDOWS\\SYSTEM\\shell32.dll,53"
```

This REG file sets a full Recycle Bin to the 54th icon of SHELL32.DLL and leaves the icon for the empty Recycle Bin set to the original system default values. Before you try to use this REG file, let me point out one problem. Let's assume the Recycle Bin is empty during the export of the Registry branch. If you export the *DefaultIcon* key, the REG file contains the following line:

```
@="C:\\WINDOWS\\SYSTEM\\shell32.dll,31"
```

This line defines the *Default* value for the icon that represents the current status of the Recycle Bin (in our example the Recycle Bin is empty). So when the Recycle Bin is full later on (it contains at least one file), and you try to import the REG file, the *Default* value is set to an empty Recycle Bin icon. Refreshing the screen reveals an empty bin even though the Recycle Bin is full! After deleting the next file (or opening and closing the Recycle Bin window), the icon is set to the correct value, but this unexpected result can confuse the user. To avoid this, delete the *Default* entry in the REG file. The resulting file contains the following lines:

```
REGEDIT4

[HKEY_CLASSES_ROOT\CLSID\{645FF040-5081-101B-9F08-00AA002F954E}\
DefaultIcon]
"Empty"="C:\\WINDOWS\\SYSTEM\\shell32.dll,31"
"Full"="C:\\WINDOWS\\SYSTEM\\shell32.dll,53"
```

This REG file leaves the Default setting intact and imports only the new values for *Full* and *Empty* into the Registry, ensuring that an icon representing the current Recycle Bin state is always displayed. This Reg file, called RECYCLE1.REG, is in the \chapter4 folder of the downloaded sample files.

> **N O T E :** If your Windows folder is named WINDOWS, you can double-click this REG file and it will run correctly. After you import the file, you can refresh the Recycle Bin symbol. The appropriate symbol should be displayed. To return to the original system default settings, you can use the RECYCLE0.REG file in the \chapter4 folder of the downloaded sample files. I created both RECYCLE0 and RE-CYCLE1 to demonstrate how to customize the Recycle Bin icons.

Customizing the Recycle Bin with INF Files

To avoid the path problems inherent in using REG files, consider using INF files to set the Registry entries. (I used this technique in Chapter 3 to update the Registry.) The following lines of an INF file set the Recycle Bin Full icon to the 54th icon of SHELL32.DLL.

```
; File: Recycle1.INF
; By Guenter Born
;
; Set the Recycle Bin Full icon to a new symbol
[version]
signature="$CHICAGO$"

[DefaultInstall]
AddReg = Recycle.AddReg
```

(continued)

continued

```
[Recycle.AddReg]
; Use HKEY_CLASSES_ROOT\CLSID
; Set "Full" to icon number 54 in shell32.dll
HKCR,CLSID\{645FF040-5081-101B-9F08-00AA002F954E}\DefaultIcon,Empty,,
"%11%\\shell32.dll,31"
HKCR,CLSID\{645FF040-5081-101B-9F08-00AA002F954E}\DefaultIcon,Full,,
"%11%\\shell32.dll,53"

; End ***
```

The meat of this code is in the [Recycle.AddReg] section. The lines beginning with HKCR, CLSID define the key. The name of the value is defined in the third parameter; the last parameter defines the value itself. The placeholder for the Windows System folder is *%11%*.

To import these settings into the Registry, right-click the INF file and select the Import command from the context menu. (Further details concerning the structure of an INF file are discussed in later chapters.) To help you out, I provided two INF files available in the \chapter4 folder of the downloaded sample files. The file RECYCLE1.INF contains the lines shown above. The RECYCLE0.INF file resets the original system default settings for the Full and Empty icons.

Using the Recycle Bin Properties
Property Sheet to Modify Settings

You can change settings for the Recycle Bin using the Recycle Bin Properties property sheet, shown in Figure 4-14. This sheet allows you to establish global settings for all drives or define independent values (such as the maximum size of the Recycle Bin) for a particular drive. This property sheet is accessible by right-clicking the Recycle Bin icon and selecting the Property command from the context menu.

The information established on this property sheet is stored in the Registry branch *HKEY_LOCAL_MACHINE\SOFTWARE\Microsoft\Windows\CurrentVersion\explorer*. Once you have opened the Recycle Bin Properties property sheet at least once and clicked OK, the above branch contains a subkey with the name *BitBucket*. The *Default* value of this key isn't set, but the *PurgeInfo* value contains a byte sequence with the Recycle Bin property settings. Table 4-1 contains a brief description of the entries contained in *PurgeInfo*.

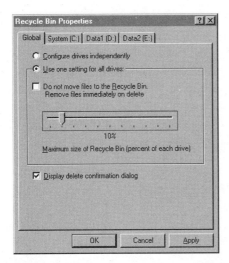

Figure 4-14.
The Recycle Bin Properties property sheet with the Global property page.

Coding of the *PurgeInfo* Value in *BitBucket*

Bytes	Description
4	The value *48 00 00 00*.
4	The flag defining global or individual settings, which is set by selecting one of the two option boxes on the Global property page of the Recycle Bin Properties property sheet (see Figure 4-14). The possible values in the first byte are: *00* Configure drives independently. *01* Use one setting for all entries.
2 * 28	28 entries that each define the maximum size of the Recycle Bin in terms of a percent of the drive's size. This value is set with the slider control contained on each property page. The first entry corresponds to drive A:, the second to drive B:, and so on. Entries for floppy disks are left empty. The 28th entry contains the value for the global settings (if one global value is used for all drives).
4	Bit field. The bits are set if the Do Not Move Files To Recycle Bin checkbox is activated on the property sheet for a particular drive. Each bit correspondents to a drive (Bit 0 = drive A:, Bit 1 = drive B:, and so on). Bit 27 corresponds to the checkbox on the Global property sheet.
4	The values in the last four bytes vary from machine to machine and will not be discussed here.

Table 4-1.
These values are a breakdown of the PurgeInfo *value for the Recycle Bin subkey* BitBucket.

The value for the Display Delete Confirmation Dialog checkbox located on the Global property sheet is stored in a curious way. You will find this value in the *HKEY_USERS\xxxx\Software\Microsoft\Windows\CurrentVersion\Explorer* key.

The characters *xxxx* are used here as a placeholder for the name of the current user. The key has a value named *ShellState*. The fifth byte is defined as a flag, with Bit 2 (counting starts with Bit 0) of this flag corresponding to the Display Delete Confirmation Dialog checkbox. If this option is checked, the bit is set to *1*. (Remember that the values are displayed in the Registry as hex values.)

Hiding and Showing the Recycle Bin Icon

Sometimes you'll want to hide the Recycle Bin icon on the desktop. Windows 95 doesn't offer a feature for hiding the icon, but you can get around that limitation by using Power Toys, which is a collection of tools for customizing Windows 95. For example, you can use the Tweak UI module of Power Toys to modify desktop icons. After you install Tweak UI, you can access it through the Control Panel.

Using Tweak UI You'll find the options for customizing the Windows 95 desktop on the Desktop property page of the Tweak UI property sheet (see Figure 4-15).

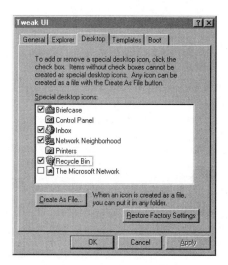

Figure 4-15.
The Tweak UI Property Sheet.

To hide or show the Recycle Bin icon, follow these steps:

1. From the Control Panel, double-click the Tweak UI icon.

2. Select the Desktop tab on the Tweak UI property sheet, which is shown in Figure 4-15.

3. Check (to show) or uncheck (to hide) the checkbox next to the Recycle Bin entry.

4. Click Apply.

After a few seconds, the icon will be either hidden or displayed, depending on your selection.

> **NOTE:**   If the Recycle Bin icon is hidden and you change the state to visible, the icon will be displayed in a predefined position on the desktop (on the left border). The current position of the icon is stored in *HKEY_CURRENT_USER\Software\Microsoft\Windows\ CurrentVersion\Explorer\Streams.*
>
> One subkey under *Streams* contains the settings for the Desktop folder, but these values are updated dynamically. Therefore I can't determine which byte is used for the Recycle Bin position. There is a shareware tool, EzDesk, written by Melissa Nguyen, which stores and restores the positions of all desktop elements. EzDesk uses separate keys to store the desktop icon positions. This tool is available at ftp://users.aol.com/EzDesk95/ezdesk17.zip.

Using Tweak UI to hide or show the Recycle Bin icon modifies the Registry. This "behind the scenes" business is pretty interesting because it shows how the Windows architecture handles extensions of the shell's namespace (a collection of symbols used to organize the shell's objects). The shell's namespace is discussed in Nancy Cluts's book, *Programming the Windows 95 User Interface.*

Using the Registry Editor   I mentioned earlier that the key *HKEY_LOCAL_ MACHINE\SOFTWARE\Microsoft\Windows\CurrentVersion* contains information about current Windows settings. Properties of the shell (comprising the desktop, taskbar, and so on) are available through the Explorer, so you will find the ...\explorer\Desktop\NameSpace subkey in this branch. This subkey contains several entries, each of which is a key containing the CLSID code of an ActiveX component (see Figure 4-16). The code for an entry is the same as in *HKEY_CLASSES_ROOT\CLSID*. The Windows shell checks the *NameSpace* key for additional subkeys. If a subkey with a CLSID code is found, the icon for this ActiveX component is shown on the desktop.

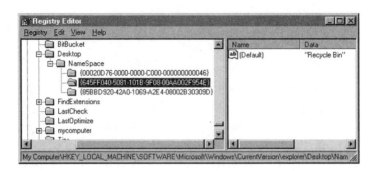

Figure 4-16.
Entries in NameSpace.

The *Default* value of each key contains a string with the component's name. (This name allows you to identify the correct key and is used in the same way as a comment.) To hide the Recycle Bin icon on the desktop, you must remove the subkey *{645FF040-5081-101B-9F08-00AA002F954E}* from the *\Desktop\ NameSpace* branch by using the Registry Editor. The next time you refresh the desktop, the icon will be hidden.

Using an INF file to delete the Recycle Bin icon   If you don't want to use the Registry Editor, you can create an INF file to do this job for you. The following lines will remove the Recycle Bin icon from the desktop:

```
; File: DelBin.INF
; By Guenter Born
;
; Remove Recycle Bin icon from desktop
[version]
signature="$CHICAGO$"

[DefaultInstall]
DelReg = BinIcon.DelReg

[BinIcon.DelReg]
; Use HKEY_LOCAL_MACHINE\SOFTWARE\Microsoft\Windows\CurrentVersion\explorer
```

```
; Remove the key {645FF040-5081-101B-9F08-00AA002F954E} from
; \Desktop\NameSpace

HKLM,"SOFTWARE\Microsoft\Windows\CurrentVersion\explorer\Desktop\NameSpace\
{645FF040-5081-101B-9F08-00AA002F954E}"

; End ***
```

You will find these statements in the DELBIN.INF file located in the \chapter4 folder of the downloaded sample files. To hide the Recycle Bin icon, right-click this file and select the Install command from the context menu. After refreshing the desktop, the icon will be hidden.

To show the Recycle Bin icon again, you must add the previously deleted key into *NameSpace*. This can be done with the following REG file:

```
REGEDIT4

[HKEY_LOCAL_MACHINE\SOFTWARE\Microsoft\Windows\CurrentVersion\explorer\
Desktop\NameSpace\{645FF040-5081-101B-9F08-00AA002F954E}]
@="Recycle Bin"
```

This file, ADDBIN.REG, is also located in the \chapter4 folder of the downloaded sample files.

Hiding and Showing the Briefcase and Inbox Icons

To hide or show the Briefcase or Inbox icon, follow these steps:

1. From the Control Panel, double-click the Tweak UI icon.

2. Select the Desktop tab on the Tweak UI property sheet.

3. Check (to show) or uncheck (to hide) the checkbox next to the Briefcase or Inbox entry. (If either of these entries isn't displayed, the application isn't installed.)

4. Click Apply.

After a few seconds, the icon will be either hidden or displayed, depending on your selection.

NOTE: The positions of the Briefcase and Inbox icons are predefined, so they will always appear in the same location on the desktop. See the Note on page 133 for details.

Windows uses the same Registry branch for both the Briefcase and Inbox icons: *HKEY_LOCAL_MACHINE\SOFTWARE\Microsoft\Windows\CurrentVersion\ explorer\Desktop\NameSpace*. The CLSID code of the Briefcase ActiveX component is the *{85BBD920-42A0-1069-A2E4-08002B30309D}* key, whereas the Inbox ActiveX component is the *{00020D75-0000-0000-C000-000000000046}* key. If the Registry branch contains these keys, the Briefcase and Inbox icons are displayed. To hide the icons, you must delete these keys.

NOTE: The CLSID for the Briefcase exists in the *NameSpace* key only if you have used Tweak UI as described in the preceding instructions for hiding or showing the entry. If you have not used Tweak UI, the Inbox entry will be in the *NameSpace* key, but the Briefcase entry won't. The Briefcase is defined in *HKEY_CLASSES_ ROOT\CLSID* and miscellaneous other places throughout the Registry. Manually adding to the *NameSpace* key the CLSID for the Briefcase will put the Briefcase icon on the desktop, but the icon will not be functional.

The \chapter 4 folder of the downloaded sample files contains the BRIEFON.REG and INBOXON.REG files. Importing these files restores the original system default settings for the Briefcase and Inbox icons, respectively, in the *NameSpace* key of the Registry. Both the Briefcase and Inbox options must be installed before you import these REG files.

TIP: To create a Briefcase icon, you can also right-click anywhere on the desktop and select New, then Briefcase, from the context menu. No entry is made in the *NameSpace* key; the Briefcase is created as a simple file in the \Windows\Profiles\username\desktop folder. The ability to create the Briefcase as a file is also available as an option in the Tweak UI module.

Adding the Control Panel Folder to the Desktop

By default, the Control Panel folder is located in the Settings section of the Start menu and in the My Computer window, but you have the option to add the Control Panel folder icon to the desktop. You can do this by creating a new folder that is recognized by the shell as the Control Panel.

Creating a Folder Using the Desktop Context Menu

To create a new Control Panel folder, follow these steps:

1. Right-click an empty place on the desktop, and select Folder from the New option in the context menu.

2. Enter the following folder name exactly:

   Control Panel.{21EC2020-3AEA-1069-A2DD-08002B30309D}

   This is the CLSID code of the Control Panel ActiveX module.

3. Click outside of the name box of this folder.

The shell creates a new folder with the Control Panel icon and the contents of the Control Panel. If you use this method to create the folder, be sure to enter the correct CLSID code for the Control Panel. The dot in front of this CLSID code is important (see the explanation in "System Icons as Folders" below). The name Control Panel can be set to any string (for example, to *Born's Control Panel.{21EC2020-3AEA-1069-A2DD-08002B30309D}*). This information is not stored in the Registry. The new Control Panel settings are stored in \Windows\Profiles\username\Desktop.

System Icons as Folders

The technique of creating a Control Panel folder by creating a new folder that is recognized by the shell as the Control Panel is rather interesting, because you begin to see some of the tricky methods used in Windows 95. If you create a new folder by using the context menu, the shell inspects the name assigned to this folder. The name of a folder follows the file-naming conventions: A filename consists of the name and an extension; these two components are separated by a dot. Although the extension is rarely used for folder names, you can define such an extension. If the name of the new folder contains an extension (the string after the dot), the shell inspects this extension. If the extension corresponds to a CLSID code of an ActiveX component, the shell tries to assign the properties of this component to this folder. In the naming procedure described above, the CLSID code for

(continued)

System Icons as Folders *continued*

the Control Panel was used to create the extension in the folder's name. The result is obvious: The shell shows the first part of the folder's name (Control Panel) and uses the extension to identify the ActiveX component. If the ActiveX component exists (and if the arrangement makes sense), the icon for this component is shown as the folder's icon.

This technique is not limited to the Control Panel. You can also add many different icons (such as the Printer folder, Inbox, and Briefcase icons) as new folders to the desktop. (The ActiveX codes are given in different sections of this chapter, and in the CLSID.TXT file in the \chapter4 folder of the downloaded sample files.)

What is the advantage of this approach? If you've ever tried to move a desktop item such as My Computer, the Briefcase, or the Inbox into a folder, you've likely received a message that you can't do it and that you can create only a shortcut instead. A shortcut provides the same functionality as the folder, but a shortcut is only a reference and the icon of the parent component still remains on the desktop. If you create a folder instead, this folder can be moved into other folders—no icon remains on the desktop. This functionality to transfer desktop items into files is also available by using the Tweak UI utility. Select the Desktop property page, select an item, and then click Create As File. Tweak UI removes the original icon and creates a file instead.

Adding the Printers Folder to the Desktop

By default, the Printers folder icon is located in the Settings section of the Start menu and in the My Computer window, but you can add a Printers folder to the desktop. The simplest way to do this is to create a shortcut to the Printers folder, which is contained in My Computer. The alternative is to create a new folder and assign the following name to it:

Printers.{2227A280-3AEA-1069-A2DE-08002B30309D}

(The steps are discussed in detail on page 137.)

Adding a Recycle Bin Icon to the My Computer Window

By default, the My Computer window comes without the Recycle Bin icon, and you can't drag the icon into the window. To add the Recycle Bin to the My

Computer window, then, you must extend the shell's namespace. This must be done in the following key: *HKEY_LOCAL_MACHINE\SOFTWARE\Microsoft\ Windows\CurrentVersion\explorer.* We can't use the *\Desktop\NameSpace* subkey because this only affects the desktop entries, so we'll use a second subkey with the name *\mycomputer\NameSpace* instead. To add the Recycle Bin to the My Computer window, add a new subkey with the name *{645FF040-5081-101B- 9F08-00AA002F954E}* into the Registry, using the following REG statements:

```
REGEDIT4

[HKEY_LOCAL_MACHINE\SOFTWARE\Microsoft\Windows\CurrentVersion\explorer\
mycomputer\NameSpace\{645FF040-5081-101B-9F08-00AA002F954E}]
@="My Computer Recycle Bin"
```

The string set in the *Default* value is just a comment for the user modifying the Registry. After you have imported the REG file, the My Computer window will show the Recycle Bin icon. To remove this icon, you must delete the *{645FF040-5081-101B-9F08-00AA002F954E}* key in the *NameSpace* branch. This can be done within the Registry Editor, but it is safer to use an INF file with the following commands:

```
; File: DelBin1.INF
; By Guenter Born
;
; Remove the Recycle Bin icon from the My Computer window
[version]
signature="$CHICAGO$"

[DefaultInstall]
DelReg = BinIcon.DelReg

[BinIcon.DelReg]
; Use HKEY_LOCAL_MACHINE\SOFTWARE\Microsoft\Windows\CurrentVersion\explorer
; Remove the key {645FF040-5081-101B-9F08-00AA002F954E} from
; \mycomputer\NameSpace

HKLM,"SOFTWARE\Microsoft\Windows\CurrentVersion\explorer\mycomputer\
NameSpace\{645FF040-5081-101B-9F08-00AA002F954E}"

; End ***
```

In this case, you can right-click the INF file and select the Install command from the context menu.

NOTE: The MYCOMBIN.REG file is located in the \chapter4 folder of the downloaded sample files. This file will add the Recycle Bin to My Computer. The DELBIN1.INF file in the same folder removes the entry from the Registry. The technique just described can be used to add other components, such as the Inbox, to My Computer.

Modifying Miscellaneous Desktop and Shell Settings

Settings for Windows elements (colors, backgrounds, cursors, and so on) are stored in different places in the Registry. Many settings can be controlled through the Display Properties property sheet. Others can be modified using the System Policy Editor or the property sheets available through the Control Panel. This section describes how to modify miscellaneous settings within the Registry.

Windows Metrics

The metrics for desktop elements such as icons, fonts, borders, scrollbars, and menus are user-specific and can be controlled through the Control Panel's Display Properties property sheet. You can search for these related parameters in the *HKEY_CURRENT_USER\Control Panel* branch, which contains the *\desktop\WindowMetrics* key. This key contains the settings for the Windows metrics. Table 4-2 briefly describes the values found in this key.

Values for Windows Metrics

Value	Description
BorderWidth	Border width of windows shown on the desktop
CaptionFont	Font used in captions
CaptionHeight	Font height of a caption
CaptionWidth	Width of a caption
IconFont	Font used for the icon title
IconSpacing	Horizontal spacing between desktop icons
IconSpacingFactor	Factor used to calculate the icon spacing
IconVerticalSpacing	Vertical spacing between desktop icons
MenuFont	Font parameters (typeface, font name, etc.) used within menu lines
MenuHeight	Height of a character cell used in a menu line

Table 4-2. *(continued)*
Entries in the WindowMetrics *key, which is located in* HKEY_CURRENT_USER\Control Panel\desktop.

Table 4-2 *continued*

Value	Description
MenuWidth	Width of a character cell used in a menu line
MessageFont	Font used in a message box
ScrollHeight	Height of a horizontal scrollbar
ScrollWidth	Width of a vertical scrollbar
ShellIconSize	Size of the icons shown on the desktop (and in the large mode in an Explorer window)
SmCaptionFont	Font used in small captions
SmCaptionHeight	Height of a character cell in a small caption
SmCaptionWidth	Width of a character cell in a small caption
StatusFont	Font used in the status bar of a window

Each font description consists of a byte sequence containing the font name and several flags (which define the font type, boldface and italic options, and so on). You can modify these options on the Appearance property page shown in Figure 4-17. (Right-click an empty space on the desktop, and select the Properties entry from the context menu). This property page allows you to view your modifications.

Figure 4-17.
The Appearance property page of the Display Properties property sheet allows you to make and view your metrics modifications.

Can I Disable the Animated Minimize Feature?

Windows animates the process of minimizing windows; you see a sequence of collapsing windows. This can be problematical on a system with a slow video card. To disable this feature, insert the following value in the key *HKEY_CURRENT_USER\ControlPanel\Desktop\WindowMetrics*:

    MinAnimate = "0"

The next time you start the system, the animation feature will be turned off.

Color Schemes and Custom Colors

Windows 95 maintains a palette of 48 basic colors that can be changed through the Color dialog box. Clicking the Color button on the Appearance property page of the Display Properties property sheet opens a panel with 20 of the basic colors available in Windows 95. Clicking the Other button in this panel opens the standard Windows Color dialog box, which reveals all 48 Windows colors. You can redefine these colors, as well as define 16 custom colors.

The colors used in Windows 95 are stored in schemes. These schemes can be altered on the Appearance property page shown in Figure 4-17 on the preceding page. Each time you modify a parameter (Font, Size, Color) for an item (Active Title Bar, ToolTip, and so on), this parameter is stored in the active scheme. You can save the active color scheme under a new name by using Save As. All these color schemes are stored in the Registry in the following key: *HKEY_CURRENT_ USER\Control Panel\Appearance\Schemes.*

Within this key you will find the names of all schemes defined on your system. Each scheme is stored as a byte sequence that contains the parameters accessible through the Appearance property page. The settings for the custom colors are stored in the *CustomColors* value of the *HKEY_CURRENT_USER\ Control Panel\Appearance* key. Each color is defined by 4 bytes. (The last byte of each color is always *00.*) The first 3 bytes define the red, green, and blue parts of the color. The values of a byte can be from *00* through *FF* (hexadecimal). A value of *FF* means 100 percent of the basic color will be used (for example, *FF 00 00 00* creates a pure red color).

Colors for Windows Elements

You can change the colors of some Windows elements (such as buttons, button text, inactive title bars, active title bars, and ToolTips) on the Appearance property page of the Display Properties property sheet. The element names are shown in the Item list box, and you can alter a color using the Color button to the right of the Item list box (see Figure 4-17 on page 141). The colors defined for each Windows element are stored as values in the *HKEY_CURRENT_USER\Control Panel\Colors* key. Each element is defined by its name (*ActiveBorder, ActiveTitle, ButtonFace, GrayText,* and so on) and a string value defining its color. The names of these values are self-explanatory. A color value is a combination of the basic colors red, green, and blue. The values can be from *0* through *255,* which means 0 through 100 percent. Unlike the *CustomColors* value, the colors within the *Colors* key are stored as decimal numbers in strings.

Cursor Schemes

The Pointers property page (accessible by clicking the Mouse icon in the Control Panel, which invokes the Mouse Properties property sheet) allows you to define several cursor schemes. Cursor schemes are the related symbols that represent specific actions, such as Normal Select, Help Select, Busy, and Text Select. Each scheme consists of 14 different cursor symbols, one symbol for each action. Windows has 14 predefined cursor symbols for the standard actions, but you can redefine the cursor symbol for each action and store it in a scheme under a unique name.

The cursor schemes are kept in the *HKEY_CURRENT_USER\Control Panel\Cursors\Schemes* key. Each item within this key consists of the scheme's name (the name defined by the user) and a string containing 14 entries. Each entry in a string corresponds to a cursor symbol, and the entries are separated by commas. An entry in the string defines the path to a cursor file (CUR or ANI). An entry can also be empty, in which case the default cursor symbol defined for the action would be used. The standard cursor definition consists of the Windows Standard name and the string set to *",,,,,,,,,,,,,,"*. If a user-defined scheme is available in the *Schemes* subkey, the name of the active scheme is found in the *Default* value of the *\Cursors* parent key.

Mouse and Cursor Parameters

The other mouse/cursor parameters (*MouseSpeed, Threshold,* and so on) are changed in the Mouse Properties property sheet (available through the Control Panel). The parameters are stored under the name of the current user in the key *HKEY_USERS\xxxx\ControlPanel\Mouse.* (The user's name is identified by *xxxx.*) The *Mouse* key can contain any of the values described in Table 4-3 on the following page.

Mouse Parameters

Value	Description
MouseSpeed	Defines how the mouse movement is transformed into a cursor movement. The transform factor is not always 1. When one of the *Threshold* values (*MouseThreshold1*, *MouseThreshold2*) is reached, Windows increases the cursor speed. The values for *MouseSpeed* can be set to the following: *0* Don't increase the cursor speed. *1* Double the cursor speed if *MouseThreshold1* is reached. *2* Double the cursor speed if *MouseThreshold1* is reached; quadruple the cursor speed if *MouseThreshold2* is reached. Both *MouseThreshold* values are established when the user moves the slider control for Pointer Speed on the Motion property page of the Mouse Properties property sheet.
MouseThreshold1	Defines a threshold for the allowable mouse movement (in pixels) between two mouse interrupts.
MouseThreshold2	Defines the second threshold for the mouse movement.
SwapMouseButtons	The values are as follows: *0* Use the original button scheme (right-handed). *1* Swap the left and right mouse button functionality (left-handed).
DoubleClickSpeed	Defines the interval (in milliseconds) between two mouse clicks, which is perceived as a double-click.
DoubleClickHeight, *DoubleClickWidth*	Defines the double-click sensitivity. The values set the height and width limits for mouse movement within a double-click. Two mouse clicks with movement outside these limits will not be accepted as a double-click.

Table 4-3.

This table describes mouse/cursor parameters in the Registry, which are stored under the name of the current user in the HKEY_USERS\xxxx\Control Panel\Mouse *key (where* xxxx *represents the user).*

The *MouseTrails* value, which controls the mouse pointer trail, can be altered on the Motion property page of the Mouse Properties property sheet and is stored in the Registry key *HKEY_CURRENT_CONFIGURATION\Display\Settings*. If this key contains the *MouseTrails* flag, a mouse pointer trail will be shown. The length of the mouse pointer trail is defined in the value of this flag (*0* through *7*). This key also contains the following:

- The current screen resolution (the value is *Resolution*)

- The *BitsPerPixel* value for the color resolution (a value of *4* means 16 colors, for example)

- The *DPILogicalX, DPILogicalY, DPIPhysicalX, DPIPhysicalY* parameters (which define the logical and physical screen resolution)

- The font files (fixed font, OEM font) used in the MS-DOS window (and in older Windows 2.*x* applications)

N O T E :   If you use a Logitech mouse with three buttons, you can activate the middle button by inserting this key: *HKEY_CURRENT_USER\Software\Logitech\Version*. Change the double-click value from *0* to *1* and restart Windows.

This key is an example of a key you would use for third-party entries in the Registry. Besides the *\Software\Microsoft* branch, the basic keys can also have *\Software\vendor name* entries. The contents of these branches are vendor-specific.

Background and Screen Saver Options

You can change the settings for the desktop background (pattern and wallpaper) and screen saver on the Background property page and Screen Saver property page, respectively, of the Display Properties property sheet. All these parameters are user-specific and are stored in the following Registry key:

HKEY_CURRENT_USER\Control Panel\Desktop

Each entry consists of a name and a value, which defines the parameter. Table 4-4 describes the Registry entries for the Background and the Screen Saver options.

Values for the Desktop Background and Screen Saver

Value	Description
Pattern	This entry is available when a pattern is used for the desktop background. The pattern is defined as a string value containing 8 byte values. This defines a pattern of 8 × 8 pixels.
ScreenSave_Data	This entry contains the encrypted screen saver password as a byte sequence.
ScreenSaveActive	The string value for an active screen saver is set to *1* (which means that the saver is activated when the wait time is over). You must select and apply a screen saver in order to create this entry.
ScreenSaveLowPowerActive	Is set to *1* when the monitor supports the energy saving feature and the Low-Power Standby option is set on the Screen Saver property page.
ScreenSaveLowPowerTimeout	The time-out is set in seconds. You can change the value using the Low-Power Standby option on the Screen Saver property page.
ScreenSavePowerOffActive	Is set to *1* when the monitor supports the energy saving feature and the Shut Off Monitor option is set on the Screen Saver property page.
ScreenSavePowerOffTimeout	The time-out is in seconds. You can change the value using the Shut Off Monitor option on the Screen Saver property page.
ScreenSaveTimeout	The time-out is set in seconds. You can change the value using the Wait control on the Screen Saver property page.
ScreenSaveUsePassword	This flag indicates whether the screen saver requires a password. The flag is set to *1* for an active password.
TileWallpaper	This entry defines whether a wallpaper is tiled (value is set to *1*) or centered (value is set to *0*). You can set the value on the Background property page of the Display Properties property sheet.
Wallpaper	This entry contains the path to the file with the wallpaper. This file must be a bitmap file. If no wallpaper is defined, the entry is empty (*""*).

Table 4-4.
This table describes possible entries in the Desktop *key.*

International Settings

International settings are set on the Regional Settings Properties property sheet, which you can access by clicking the Regional Settings icon in the Control Panel. For example, on the Regional Settings property page the user can define the region (country code), which will affect how information in many applications is displayed. This country code will be stored in various places in the Registry. The key *HKEY_CURRENT_USER\Control Panel\Desktop\ ResourceLocale*, for example, contains the country code used for international settings in system resources that require this setting, such as the default keyboard setting (referring to the Windows 95 country code, which is different from the country codes used under MS-DOS and previous Windows versions). You can modify the settings for international parameters (number, currency, time, date, and so on) on the various tabs, or property pages, of the Regional Settings Properties property sheet. These parameters are stored in the Registry key *HKEY_CURRENT_USER\Control Panel\International*.

This key contains at least one value with the name *Locale*. This value defines the country code for the selected international setting (*409* for the USA). When you use the standard settings for a selected country, the key contains only the *Locale* value. All settings are predefined for this country. If you change a predefined value on the Regional Settings Properties property sheet, a new value and name will be stored in the *International* key. Appendix B briefly describes the values used to control international settings.

Settings for the time zone, clock adjustments, locale, and code page can be found in the *HKEY_CURRENT_USER* and *HKEY_LOCAL_MACHINE* root keys. Specifically, the default settings for the time zone are located in the *HKEY_ LOCAL_MACHINE\SOFTWARE\Microsoft\Windows\CurrentVersion\Time Zones* key. The *Default* value of this key contains the current time zone of the user (Pacific Standard Time, for example). The *Time Zones* key contains subkeys with the default settings for all other time zones (Eastern Standard Time, for example). The entries in each subkey of the *Time Zones* key define the display string for the Time Zone property page on the Date/Time Properties property sheet (*Display*), the daylight name (*Dlt*), and the Standard Time (*Std*). The *MapID* value defines the time-zone mapping, and *TZI* (which stands for Time Zone Information) contains the default settings for *Time Zones*. To define user-specific settings, don't modify the *TZI* content; instead, use the keys for the international settings (*HKEY_CURRENT_USER\Control Panel\International*).

The *TimeZoneInformation* key of the *HKEY_LOCAL_MACHINE\System\ CurrentControlSet\control* branch contains international settings that control *Bias* values, clock adjustments (*DisableAutoDaylightTimeSet*), and so on. The value *DisableAutoDaylightTimeSet* = *0x00000001* prevents Windows from automatically switching to daylight saving time. (This option is available on the Time Zone property page of the Date/Time Properties property sheet, which is invoked by double-clicking the time shown in the right corner of the taskbar.) The value *StandardStart* contains a byte sequence representing several entries. The third byte in *StandardStart* defines the month that Windows changes to standard time. A byte set to *0A* defines the end of October for this change. The byte at offset 7 defines the month that Windows switches to daylight saving time (*5* = May).

Locale options are contained in the *HKEY_LOCAL_MACHINE\System\ CurrentControlSet\control\Nls* key. (This key exists only if you have set an option whose value is stored there.) The *Locale* subkey contains entries whose names are locale codes; the value is set to a string with the corresponding country's name. The *Default* value of the *Locale* subkey contains the code of the current setting. For example, *"00000409"* is the code for the United States. The *CodePage* subkey contains a list of the Windows code-page numbers and their mappings to optional NLS files.

Restricting Access to Display Properties

The System Policy Editor provides several options for restricting access to the Display Properties property sheet. (Right-clicking the desktop and selecting the Properties command from the context menu displays the Display Properties property sheet. This property sheet is also available via the Display icon in the Control Panel.) These access options are located on the Local Users Properties property page of the System Policy Editor when you open a user's *Control Panel\Display* key. These options are placed as values in the Registry in the following key:

HKEY_CURRENT_USER\Software\Microsoft\Windows\CurrentVersion\Policies\System

This key exists only if you have set an option whose value is stored in this key.

Table 4-5 shows the values available in this key that restrict access to the display properties. A value set to *0x00000001* disables the access. Deleting this entry or setting the value to *0* enables access.

Values Restricting Access to Display Properties

Name	Description
NoDispCPL	Disable Display Control Panel. If the value is set to *1*, the Display Properties property sheet is not accessible.
NoDispBackgroundPage	Hide Background Page. If the value is set to *1*, the Background property page on the Display Properties property sheet is hidden.
NoDispScrSavPage	Hide Screen Saver Page. If the value is set to *1*, the Screen Saver property page on the Display Properties property sheet is hidden.
NoDispAppearancePage	Hide Appearance Page. If the value is set to *1*, the Appearance property page on the Display Properties property sheet is hidden.
NoDispSettingsPage	Hide Settings Page. If the value is set to *1*, the Settings property page on the Display Properties property sheet is hidden.

Table 4-5.
These options can be altered with the System Policy Editor. For each table entry, the first phrase in the Description column is the option shown in the System Policy Editor.

Restricting Access to Network Properties

The Network property sheet is available via the Network icon in the Control Panel. Within the System Policy Editor, you can restrict the access to this property sheet. You'll find these options on the Policies property page of the System Policy Editor by opening the *Control Panel\Network* key of a particular user. Network options are placed as values in the Registry in the following key:

HKEY_CURRENT_USER\Software\Microsoft\Windows\CurrentVersion\Policies\Network

Table 4-6 on the following page shows the values that are available in this key to restrict access to the network properties. A value set to *0x00000001* disables access; deleting the value or setting the value to *0* enables access.

Values for Restricting Access to Network Properties

Name	Description
NoNetSetup	Disable Network Control Panel. If the value is set to *1*, the Network property sheet is not accessible.
NoNetSetupIDPage	Hide Identification Page. If the value is set to *1*, the Identification property page is hidden on the Network property sheet.
NoNetSetupSecurityPage	Hide Access Control Page. If the value is set to *1*, the Access Control property page is hidden on the property sheet.

Table 4-6.
Use the System Policy Editor to change these options. The first phrase in the Description column is the option shown in the System Policy Editor.

Restricting Access to Password Properties

From within the System Policy Editor, you can restrict the access to the Passwords Properties property sheet, which is available via the Passwords icon in the Control Panel. The restriction options are located on the Policies property page of the System Policy Editor, in the *Control Panel\Passwords* branch. Options to restrict access to password properties are placed in the Registry in the *HKEY_CURRENT_USER\Software\Microsoft\Windows\CurrentVersion\Policies\System* key.

Table 4-7 shows the values that are available in this key to restrict access to the password properties. A value set to *0x00000001* disables access; deleting the value or setting the value to *0* enables access.

Values for Restricting Access to Password Properties

Name	Description
NoSecCPL	Disable Passwords Control Panel. If the value is set to *1*, the Passwords Properties property sheet is not accessible.
NoPwdPage	Hide Change Passwords Page. If the value is set to *1*, the Change Passwords property page on the Passwords Properties property sheet is hidden.

Table 4-7.   *(continued)*
These options can be altered with the System Policy Editor. For each table entry, the first phrase in the Description column is the option shown in the System Policy Editor.

Table 4-7 *continued*

Name	Description
NoAdminPage	Hide Remote Administration Page. If the value is set to *1*, the Remote Administration property page on the property sheet is hidden.
NoProfilePage	Hide User Profiles Page. If the value is set to *1*, the Profile property page on the property sheet is hidden.

Restricting Access to Printer Properties

The System Policy Editor allows you to restrict access to the Properties property sheets of each printer. These options are located on the Policy property page of the System Policy Editor in the *Control Panel\Printers* branch. The options are stored in the Registry in the *HKEY_CURRENT_USER\Software\Microsoft\Windows\CurrentVersion\Policies\Explorer* key.

Table 4-8 shows the values that are available in this key to restrict access to the printers properties. A value set to *0x00000001* disables access; deleting the value or setting the value to *0* enables access.

Values for Restricting Access to Printer Properties

Name	Description
NoPrinterTabs	Hide General and Details Pages. If the value is set to *1*, the pages are hidden on the Printer Properties property sheet.
NoDeletePrinter	Disable Deletion of Printers. If the value is set to *1*, the Delete Printer function is disabled.
NoAddPrinter	Disable Addition of Printers. If the value is set to *1*, the Add Printer function is disabled.

Table 4-8.
Set these options in the System Policy Editor.

Restricting Access to System Properties

The System Policy Editor allows you to restrict access to the System Properties property sheet. These options for restricting access are located on the Policies property page of the System Policy Editor in the *Control Panel\System* branch. The options are stored in the Registry in the *HKEY_CURRENT_USER\Software\Microsoft\Windows\CurrentVersion\Policies\System* key. Table 4-9 on the following page shows the values that are available in this key to restrict access to the system properties. A value set to *0x00000001* disables access; deleting the value or setting the value to *0* enables access.

Values for Restricting Access to System Properties

Name	Description
NoDevMgrPage	Hide Device Manager Page. If the value is set to *1*, the page on the System Properties property sheet is hidden.
NoConfigPage	Hide Hardware Profiles Page. If the value is set to *1*, the page on the System Properties property sheet is hidden.
NoFileSysPage	Hide File System Button. If the value is set to *1*, the File System button on the Performance property page on the System Properties property sheet is hidden.
NoVirtMemPage	Hide Virtual Memory Button. If the value is set to *1*, the Virtual Memory button on the Performance property page on the System Properties property sheet is hidden.

Table 4-9.
Set these options in the System Policy Editor.

NOTE: The contents of the Control Panel folder are built during each system startup. Windows stores the entries in the Registry key *HKEY_LOCAL_MACHINE\SOFTWARE\Microsoft\Windows\CurrentVersion\ ControlsFolder.* This key contains a record of binary data that points to CPL files found in the Windows\System subfolder.

Altering the Tip List

When you start Windows, the Welcome dialog box opens with a tip of the day (see Figure 4-18). Each time WELCOME.EXE is invoked, the tip contents change. You can deactivate the Welcome window by removing the check from the Welcome Screen option. You can also use the Next Tip button to skip through the tip list.

All information provided in the tip list is maintained in the Registry. The *HKEY_CURRENT_USER\Software\Microsoft\Windows\CurrentVersion\Explorer\Tips* key contains two entries that control the Welcome window:

■ *Show.* This is a flag that contains a binary value. If this value is set to *01 00 00 00*, the Welcome window will be shown after each Windows startup. Resetting this value to *00 00 00 00* disables the Welcome function.

■ *Next.* This entry contains an index that defines the next tip to be displayed. The number *14 00*, for example, is equal to 20 decimal, and since indexing begins with 0, this value defines tip number 21.

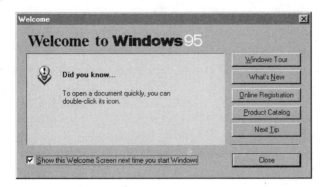

Figure 4-18.
The Welcome window.

Both settings are user-specific, as indicated by their location in the *HKEY_ CURRENT_USER* branch. The list with the tip text itself is defined as global for the computer and is stored in the *HKEY_LOCAL_MACHINE\ SOFTWARE\ Microsoft\Windows\CurrentVersion\explorer\Tips* key. This is the same key that contains the *Show* entry, *Next* entry, and tip text; only the root keys are different. The tip text is defined as a string value; the name of a value is the index number in the list (see Figure 4-19). Windows comes with a predefined list of 48 tips. You can alter the text inside the list and customize it for your own purposes.

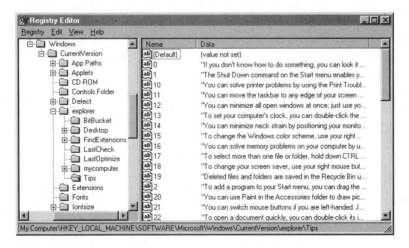

Figure 4-19.
The tip list in the Registry.

TIP: You can use the *Tips* entries in *HKEY_CURRENT_USER* to reset the tip list during each Windows startup. Set the *Next* item to a fixed value (*00*, for example, points to the first tip text string), and export this branch into a REG file. If you create a shortcut from the Startup folder (\Start Menu) to this REG file, the tip list is reset each time the user logs on. You can also export the *Tips* entries with the tip text from the *HKEY_LOCAL_MACHINE* branch, modify the tip text of the REG file using Notepad, save the new version, and then create a shortcut from the Startup folder to the REG file. After each Windows startup, the tip list is updated to the contents of the REG file.

Changing the Start Menu Options

The Start menu and the taskbar are also parts of the Windows 95 shell. Customizing the options for these items requires different tools. In this section, I discuss the customization options, the required tools, and the behind-the-scenes functionality.

Adding a Cascading Control Panel Menu to the Start Menu

Typically, you open the Control Panel window by selecting Control Panel from the Settings option of the Start menu. Often after opening the Control Panel and clicking an icon, you end up with a series of windows on top of one another and on top of any other open Windows-based applications. Wouldn't it be less cumbersome to see a cascading Control Panel menu in the Start menu that closes automatically after you select an option?

Unfortunately, it doesn't do any good to open the My Computer window and drag the Control Panel icon onto the Start button of the taskbar—all that does is create a shortcut to the Control Panel. The Control Panel window will still occupy space on the screen when it is opened, and you save only one mouse click opening it. My solution is based on the technique I used to create a Control Panel folder on the desktop. To add a cascading Control Panel to the Start menu, follow these steps:

1. Right-click the Start button and select the Open command from the context menu. The Start Menu folder window opens.

2. Create a new folder in the Start Menu window and name it this: Control Panel.{21EC2020-3AEA-1069-A2DD-08002B30309D}. Enter the code following the dot carefully; it defines the CLSID code of the Control Panel ActiveX component.

When you click outside of the name box, the shell detects the new definition, Windows changes the folder symbol to the Control Panel icon, and the title is set to Control Panel. (If this didn't happen, you entered the name incorrectly.)

3. Close the Start Menu window.

4. Click Start on the taskbar. Control Panel is now an option available directly from the Start menu. When you click this option, you will get the cascading menu shown in Figure 4-20. This menu allows direct access to each entry in the Control Panel.

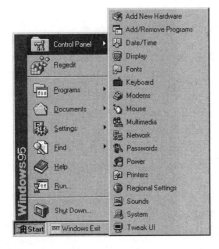

Figure 4-20.
A cascading Control Panel menu.

Adding a Cascading Printers Menu to the Start Menu

Accessing the Printers folder is as cumbersome as accessing Control Panel options. You have to open the My Computer window, or you have to click the Start menu, then Settings, then Printers to open the Printers folder. To access the printer icons directly from the Start menu, follow these steps:

1. Open the Start Menu window. (Right-click the Start button and select Open from the context menu.)

2. Create a new folder in the Start Menu folder and name it this: Printers.{2227A280-3AEA-1069-A2DE-08002B30309D}.

The Printers folder icon should appear. When you open the Start menu, the Printers entry will show a cascading menu.

NOTE: To remove the Printers folder or the Control Panel folder from the Start menu, open the Start Menu window and delete the associated icon.

TIP: If you created a Printers folder or Control Panel folder following the steps in the preceding procedure, you can copy or move this folder into other subfolders of the Start Menu folder. This creates a cascading submenu that reflects these additional Start menu levels.

Removing Entries from the Start Menu's Settings Branch

Clicking the Start button and selecting Settings from the Start menu reveals a cascading submenu with the Control Panel, Printers, and Taskbar entries. These entries allow you to customize your shell. They are user-specific and are customized using the System Policy Editor.

If you want to change the settings for users other than the current user, you must open a profile and select the user or user group. The procedures for defining a user policy are in the *Windows 95 Resource Kit*. The advantage of the System Policy Editor over other methods of modifying the Registry is that it can modify the entries for one or more users at one time. In the next procedure, we're going to hide a few entries in the Settings branch of the Start menu for the current user of the system. So start the System Policy Editor, select File, then Open Registry, and then click the Local User option.

1. Open the Shell\Restrictions branch on the Local User Properties property page (see Figure 4-21).

2. To hide the Control Panel and Printers folders, check the Remove Folders From Settings On Start Menu option.

3. To hide the Taskbar option from the Settings submenu, check the Remove Taskbar From Settings On Start Menu option.

4. Close the property page by clicking OK, and save the settings.

The next time the system is started, all System Policy Editor entries you checked above will be hidden in the Settings submenu. If you check both options (as shown in Figure 4-21), the Settings entry itself will be hidden.

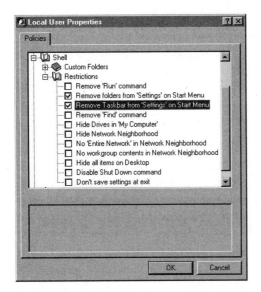

Figure 4-21.
The Shell\Restrictions branch of the System Policy Editor.

Because the options for hiding and showing the Settings submenu entries are user-specific, and because all desktop elements—including the Start menu and the Explorer—belong to the Windows shell, we can search the Registry entries for these options in the *HKEY_CURRENT_USER* branch. We also know that the current settings are always stored in the following key: *\Software\Microsoft\Windows\CurrentVersion*. And finally, because the entries have something to do with the Explorer and user policies, we can guess in which Registry branch the options set in the System Policy Editor will be stored. That's right—it's the *HKEY_CURRENT_USER\Software\Microsoft\Windows\CurrentVersion\Policies\Explorer* branch, which contains a bunch of values for customizing the Start menu. Table 4-10 describes the entries that hide and show the options under Settings.

Values for Hiding and Showing Settings Submenu Entries

Name	Description
NoSetFolders	Hides the symbols for Printers and Control Panel folders in the Settings submenu when the value is set to *0x00000001*. Deleting the value or setting it to *0x00000000* shows the folders in the Settings submenu.

Table 4-10.   *(continued)*
These values are contained in the Explorer *subkey.*

Table 4-10 *continued*

Name	Description
NoSetFolders (continued)	If the value is set to *0x00000001*, the Control Panel and Printers folders are also hidden in My Computer. This flag will have no effect on Printers and Control Panel folders that are defined as files or shell extensions. (See pages 138–139 to find out how to define a folder symbol on the desktop and pages 154–156 to find out how to define a cascading submenu in the Start menu.)
NoSetTaskbar	Hides the Taskbar entry in the Settings submenu when the value is set to *0x00000001*. Deleting the value or setting it to *0x00000000* shows the entry in the Settings submenu.

If both flags are available and set to *0x00000001*, the Settings item in the Start menu will be hidden after the next system startup.

Disabling the Run Entry in the Start Menu

You can start any application program by using the Run entry on the Start menu and entering the name of the executable file. The System Policy Editor has a user-specific option to disable (hide) this entry in the Start menu. To hide or show the Run entry in the Start menu, follow these steps:

1. Open the *Shell\Restrictions* branch on the Policies property page.

2. Check (to hide) or uncheck (to show) the Remove 'Run' Command option. Close the property page by clicking OK, and save the settings.

Your selection takes effect after the next system startup.

The flag to remove the Run entry from the Start menu is stored in the *NoRun* value of the following Registry branch:

HKEY_CURRENT_USER\Software\Microsoft\Windows\CurrentVersion\Policies\Explorer

If this value is set to *0x00000001*, the Run command is removed from the Start menu after the next system startup. Deleting the *NoRun* value or setting the value to *0x00000000* brings the Run entry back to the Start menu.

Resetting the Shell Without Rebooting

Newly selected options take effect after the next system startup because during the startup process the Registry is reorganized—some entries are copied from *HKEY_USERS* to *HKEY_CURRENT_USER*, and other branches are rebuilt to reflect the current state. A complete reboot, however, takes a long time. So if you alter shell options, you can reset the shell without a complete reboot by following these steps:

1. Press Ctrl-Alt-Del. This invokes the Close Program dialog box, which has a list of all active tasks.

2. Click the Explorer entry, and close the dialog box by clicking the End Task button. Windows notifies the Explorer about this user request, and since the Explorer is an essential part of Windows, the Shut Down Windows dialog box with the shutdown options is displayed.

3. Click No to close this dialog box without shutting down Windows, which prevents the Explorer from shutting down, too. Windows detects this after a few seconds and displays the Explorer message box notifying you that the program is not responding.

4. Close the Explorer message box by clicking End Task.

N O T E : It takes a few moments for the Explorer message box to appear. If you don't click No in the Shut Down Windows dialog box right away, the Explorer message box will appear anyway. Click End Task, and the Explorer message box and the Shut Down Windows dialog box will both close, shutting down the Explorer and invoking your new settings without shutting down Windows.

Clicking End Task drops the Explorer out of memory. Windows then immediately loads a new copy of the Explorer to re-create the shell (with the taskbar and the desktop). All previous Registry settings are replaced with any modifications you made.

NOTE: You might wonder why you can disable some options by either setting the flag value to *0x00000000* or deleting the flag altogether. You will appreciate this feature if you want to alter the settings with a REG file. You cannot remove an entry from the Registry using a REG file, so if you set the *NoRun* flag once so that it exists in the Registry, you cannot remove it to disable the option. But since you can toggle the value between *0* and *1*, you can still disable the option with the REG file.

Disabling the Find Command

The Windows shell offers you the ability to search for computers, folders, or files. This function is available through the Find command, which is accessed from the Start menu; through the Explorer window (Tools menu); or from a context menu when you select a folder, computer, or drive icon. You can disable this Find function by using the System Policy Editor. To enable or disable the Find command, follow these steps:

1. Open the *Shell\Restrictions* branch on the Local User Properties property sheet.

2. Check (to hide) or uncheck (to show) the Remove Find Command option. Close the property sheet by clicking OK, and save the settings.

After the next system startup, if the item in the System Policy Editor was checked, the Find command will be removed from the Start menu, the Explorer Tools menu, and the context menu.

The flag to disable the Find function is stored in the *NoFind* value of the Registry branch *HKEY_CURRENT_USER\Software\Microsoft\Windows\CurrentVersion\Policies\Explorer*. Setting the value to *0x00000001* disables the Find command after the next system startup. Deleting the *NoFind* value or setting it to *0x00000000* brings the Find function back to the menus.

Disabling the Shut Down Command

You can shut down Windows in two ways:

■ Using the Shut Down command from the Start menu.

■ Invoking the Close Program dialog box by pressing Ctrl-Alt-Del and clicking the Shut Down button.

Windows allows you to disable this Shut Down feature for the current user. The option for disabling Shut Down is available in the System Policy Editor. To enable or disable the Shut Down command, follow these steps:

1. Open the *Shell\Restrictions* branch on the Policies property page.

2. Check (to hide) or uncheck (to show) the Disable Shut Down Command option. Close the property page by clicking OK, and save the settings.

The Shut Down command is either disabled or enabled immediately after you save the settings in the Registry. Although the Shut Down entry in the Start menu is still available, the user cannot activate it: Windows displays a message box explaining that the operation has been canceled for this computer. (The Shut Down entry in the Start menu will be removed or inserted after the next reboot of the shell.) If the user invokes the Close Program dialog box (by pressing Ctrl-Alt-Del) while the Shut Down function is disabled, the Shut Down button becomes disabled (grayed out).

The flag to disable the Shut Down command is stored in the *NoClose* value of the Registry branch *HKEY_CURRENT_USER\Software\Microsoft\Windows\ CurrentVersion\Policies\Explorer*. A value set to *0x00000001* disables the Shut Down command immediately. Deleting the *NoClose* value or setting it to *0x00000000* brings the Shut Down function back to the shell.

> **WARNING :** The *NoClose* flag affects only the Shut Down command provided by the shell. An individual program can still notify Windows about a restart request—many tools allow a "quick Windows exit." (In some of my screen shots, you will see the Exit button on the taskbar. This button belongs to a tool I developed to exit Windows with a mouse click.) You can't block a Shut Down function provided by such a tool by using the *NoClose* flag.

Restricting the Executable Application Programs

By default, the user can start any application under Windows by selecting the Run command from the Start menu; by selecting an application from the Start menu submenus; or by double-clicking a shortcut, document, or application icon on the desktop or in a folder window. Sometimes you'll want to restrict access to a group of selected applications. For example, you might want your office manager to use only Microsoft Word for Windows and Microsoft Excel but allow the system administrator to access all other applications, including the Explorer. A system administrator can define these restrictions using the System Policy Editor. Following are the steps to set restrictions for a single user:

1. Start the System Policy Editor, load the (local) Registry, and select the user whose access rights will be restricted. (For example, you can double-click Local User.)

2. Expand the \System\Restrictions branch in the Policies property page. This branch contains several options that restrict user access to the system (see Figure 4-22).

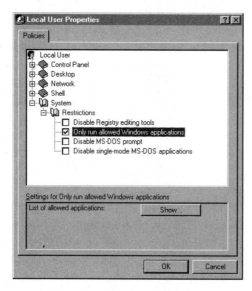

Figure 4-22.
Entries in the System\Restrictions branch.

3. Check the Only Run Allowed Windows Applications option on the Policies property page. You have to set the allowed applications manually, so click Show to display your options.

4. The Show Contents dialog box opens with a list of all allowed applications (see Figure 4-23). Edit this list using the Add and Remove options.

5. Close the open dialog boxes by clicking OK, and save the settings in the Registry.

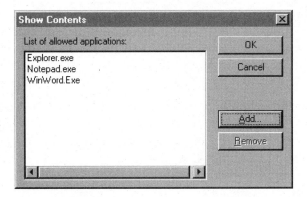

Figure 4-23.
List of applications that you can restrict access to.

After these steps, the Windows shell allows the current user to access only the specified applications. These restrictions are valid for all shell components (shortcuts on the desktop, icons in the Explorer window, the Run command on the Start menu, submenu entries on the Start menu, and so on). The new restrictions take effect the next time the system is reset.

These access-restriction settings are stored in the Registry in the branch *HKEY_CURRENT_USER\Software\Microsoft\Windows\CurrentVersion\Policies\ Explorer.* If the access to applications is restricted for the current user, the key contains the value *RestrictRun*, which is set to *0x00000001*. The names of the applications that can be accessed by this user are stored in the *RestrictRun* subkey. The entries in this subkey are numbered from *1* through *n*, and the values are strings containing the paths (optional) and names of the applications (see Figure 4-24). Only applications found in the *RestrictRun* subkey are accessible by the user.

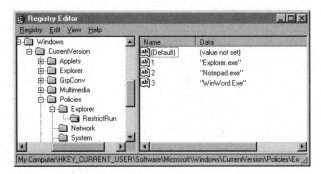

Figure 4-24.
Registry entries for RestrictRun.

To enable access, remove the *RestrictRun* value from the *Explorer* key or set the value for *RestrictRun* to *0x00000000*. The latter option is preferable if you use REG files to modify the Registry. (See the RESRUNOF.REG file in the \chapter 4 folder of the downloaded sample files.)

> WARNING: Be careful if you use this option. If you restrict access to several modules and only one profile for all users is enabled, you can't restart the System Policy Editor to alter the *RestrictRun* settings. You would have to edit the Registry with the Real Mode version of the Registry Editor and reset the *RestrictRun* option.

On network systems, you can use the System Policy Editor to set access rights for different user groups. Consult the *Windows 95 Resource Kit* to learn how to create and set remote system and user policies.

Restricting Access to the Registry Editing Tools

To prevent an experienced user from resetting Registry settings, set the Disable Registry Editing Tools option, which is available in the LocalUser\System\Restrictions branch of the System Policy Editor (see Figure 4-22 on page 162), and store it in the Registry. The entry *DisableRegistryTools* is then inserted in *HKEY_CURRENT_USER\Software\ Microsoft\Windows\CurrentVersion\Policies\System*. If this flag is set to *0x00000001*, the user can't launch the Registry Editor but the System Policy Editor is still executable.

It might seem advantageous to remove both the Registry Editor and the System Policy Editor from the local computer, but an experienced user can create a simple REG file and import it into the Registry with a double-click. Surprisingly, a user can reset many Registry entries. (In Microsoft Windows NT, additional access privileges are required to access system components.) The *RestrictRun* feature offers you a way to construct a second barrier against users who try to use REG files to change the Registry. If the Registry Editor isn't included in the list of accessible applications, the user can't import a REG file by double-clicking the file's icon. The only way to change the Registry would be to use a boot disk containing the Registry Editor and alter the values in Real Mode. If you accidentally lock yourself out, you can use this backdoor method to reset the Registry. (The better approach, however, is to recover the Registry with your backup copy, which you created—we hope—before you modified the Registry.)

Disabling the MS-DOS Prompt
and the Single-Mode MS-DOS Feature

Windows lets you invoke an MS-DOS window and execute old MS-DOS applications. This command is available from the Programs submenu of the Start menu, or you can create a shortcut to the MS-DOS command window on the desktop. You can disable the MS-DOS command prompt for the current user (or for a user group) by using the System Policy Editor. To disable the MS-DOS prompt from the Windows shell, follow these steps:

1. Start the System Policy Editor, load the (local) Registry, and select the user whose access rights will be restricted (for example, the Local User).

2. Expand the *\System\Restrictions* branch on the Policies property page, and check the Disable MS-DOS Prompt option.

3. Close the open dialog box by clicking OK, and save the settings in the Registry.

The settings for disabling the MS-DOS command prompt are stored in the Registry in the branch *HKEY_CURRENT_USER\Software\Microsoft\Windows\ CurrentVersion\Policies\WinOldApp.* (This key will not exist until you set an option whose value is stored there.) If the MS-DOS command prompt is disabled, this key contains an entry with the name *Disabled,* and the value is set to *0x00000001.* Removing this value or setting it to *0x00000000* enables the MS-DOS command prompt again.

The other option you can disable with the System Policy Editor is the single-mode MS-DOS feature, which is available as an option in the Shut Down Windows dialog box. (To access this dialog box, click the Start menu, then Shut Down). To disable this mode under Windows 95, follow these steps:

1. Start the System Policy Editor, load the (local) Registry, and select the user whose access rights will be restricted (the Local User, for example).

2. Expand the *\System\Restrictions* branch on the Policies property page, and check the Disable Single-Mode MS-DOS Applications option.

3. Close the open dialog box by clicking OK, and save the settings in the Registry.

After these steps are executed, the Restart The Computer In MS-DOS Mode option in the Shut Down Windows dialog box is hidden.

The settings for disabling the single-mode MS-DOS feature are stored in the *HKEY_CURRENT_USER\Software\Microsoft\Windows\CurrentVersion\Policies\ WinOldApp* Registry branch. When the single-mode MS-DOS feature is disabled, this key contains the *NoRealMode* entry, and the value is set to *0x00000001*. Removing this value or setting it to *0x00000000* enables the single-mode MS-DOS option again.

> **N O T E :**   You can enter single-mode MS-DOS—despite the Registry settings—by rebooting the system and entering the MS-DOS mode or using a boot disk.

Enabling and Disabling the Click Here To Begin Start Banner

When Windows starts, if the taskbar is empty, an animated banner with the message Click Here To Begin is displayed (see Figure 4-25). If there is an entry in the Startup folder that starts an application, there will be a button on the taskbar (in addition to the Start button), so this banner won't be shown.

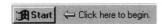

Figure 4-25.
The Click Here To Begin banner.

Windows does not offer a property page option that enables and disables this animated banner, but you can use the Tweak UI tool or the Registry Editor to change the Registry settings. In Tweak UI, select the Explorer property page and uncheck the Animated Click Here To Begin (If Room) option to suppress this banner. The flag to suppress this banner is user-specific and is stored in the *HKEY_CURRENT_USER\Software\Microsoft\Windows\CurrentVersion\Explorer* Registry branch. (Did you notice that the branch contains no *\Policy\Explorer* expression? This option is not available in the System Policy Editor.) By default, this key contains a value with the name *NoStartBanner* set to *00 00 00 00* (or *NoStartBanner* not present), which allows Windows to show the animated banner if room is available on the taskbar. Changing this value to *01 00 00 00* disables the animated banner for all subsequent restarts.

Changing the Menu Delay

Clicking a menu item often invokes a pop-up or pull-down submenu. You can increase or decrease the speed with which Windows shows and hides those submenus. The value is stored in the Registry key *HKEY_CURRENT_USER\ Control Panel\desktop.* If this value is set, there will be a value in the key named

MenuShowDelay that can be set from *1* through *10*. A value of *1* represents the fastest response to a mouse click; a value of *10* sets the slowest speed. After restarting the system, the modification takes effect.

Changing the Update Mode

If you are connected to a network, policies for the local computer can be downloaded from the network when you log on. You can enable this feature using the System Policy Editor. Open the Policies property page for the Local Computer. Select the *Network\Update* branch and click the Remote Update option. Here you can set the Update Mode to either Automatic (Use Default Path) or Manual (Use Specific Path). If you select Manual, you must fill in the Path For Manual Update text box with the path containing the policy (POL) file from which you want the policies loaded. The update mode is stored in the Registry in the key *HKEY_LOCAL_MACHINE\System\CurrentControlSet\ control\Update* in the *UpdateMode* value. *UpdateMode* can contain the values *0* (no update), *1* (automatic update), or *2* (manual update). The *NetworkPath* value in the same key contains the path to the policy file for manual updates.

Resetting the Run MRU List

Windows maintains lists of the most recently used (MRU) files or commands for several shell functions. One list contains the last commands executed by the Run command from the Start menu; you can display it by clicking the open list arrow (see Figure 4-26).

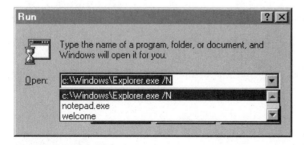

Figure 4-26.
The MRU list for the Run command.

This list is called the Run MRU list, and it is maintained in the following Registry branch: *HKEY_CURRENT_USER\Software\Microsoft\Windows\ CurrentVersion\Explorer\RunMRU*. The structure of the entries contained in this key is shown in Figure 4-27 on the following page. The entries define the order of the commands shown in the list box and the commands themselves (see Figure 4-26).

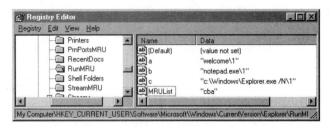

Figure 4-27.
The structure of the Run MRU list in the Registry.

Here are the attributes of the Run MRU list:

- The *MRUList* value contains a string defining the order of the other entries in the list. In the example shown in Figure 4-27, the entry *c* indicates the first item to be shown in the Run list (see also Figure 4-26 on the preceding page).

- The commands themselves are stored as strings (terminated with the characters *\1*) in values with the names *a*, *b*, *c*, and so on. Twenty-six entries are possible.

This structure is used in several MRU lists. You can revise this list by using a REG file to reset the values to empty strings. (You cannot remove the entries contained in the *RunMRU* key by using a REG file.) The following REG file (CLRRNMRU.REG, available in the \chapter4 folder of the downloaded sample files) will reset the *RunMRU* list after you import the file with a double-click.

```
REGEDIT4

[HKEY_CURRENT_USER\Software\Microsoft\Windows\CurrentVersion\Explorer\RunMRU]

"a"=""
"MRUList"=""
```

You could write a similar REG file resetting all 26 entries—*a*, *b*, and so on through *z*—to empty strings, but this isn't required. The REG file above shows you a simple trick: Set only the first entry *a* to an empty string, and clear the *MRUList* value. After the next restart, with the *MRUList* value empty, the shell won't be able to detect an order and thus will show an empty list box in the Run dialog box. (The Run command line will also be empty.)

NOTE: You can create a REG file to reset the Run MRU list, or you can create an INF file to remove the values *b* through *z* from the Registry, reset the *MRUList* value to *" "*, and execute a reboot. INF files are discussed at greater length in later chapters.

Resetting Other MRU Lists

In addition to the Run MRU list is a Find MRU list, which you can access by invoking the Find command. The Find MRU list is maintained in the *HKEY_CURRENT_USER* branch of the Registry in the key *\Software\Microsoft\ Windows\CurrentVersion\Explorer\Doc Find Spec MRU*. This key contains the same entries (*a, b, MRUList*) as *RunMRU*.

The Any Folder function provided in the PowerToys package contains an MRU list maintained in the *HKEY_CURRENT_USER\Software\Microsoft\ Windows\CurrentVersion\Explorer\OtherFolder* key. The structure is identical to the other MRU lists, and you can use a REG file to reset this list.

The Registry key *HKEY_CURRENT_USER\Software\Microsoft\Windows\ CurrentVersion\ Explorer\RecentDocs* contains an MRU list with the entries (15 is the maximum number) shown in the Documents submenu of the Start menu. Setting the *MRUList* entry to *" "* and resetting the shell makes the Documents submenu empty.

If the Have Disk button is enabled on the Windows Setup property page (available through the Add/Remove Programs icon in the Control Panel), the Install From Disk dialog box contains the Copy Manufacturer's Files From list box. Open this list to show the previously used paths during software setups. This MRU list is maintained in the Registry key *HKEY_CURRENT_USER\ InstallLocationsMRU*. This key contains the values *MRUList, a, b, c,* and so on, as described for the other MRU lists.

Modifying Miscellaneous Keys Containing Shell Data

You might be interested to know about other entries in the *\Software\Microsoft\ Windows\CurrentVersion\Explorer* branch of the *HKEY_CURRENT_USER* root key, such as the *Shell Folders* entry, which specifies the paths to the folders used by the shell. The values contained in this key are listed in Table 4-11 on the following page.

Shell Folders Values

Name	Description
Desktop	Defines the path to the desktop folder (*"C:\WINDOWS\Profiles\Born\Desktop"*, for example)
Programs	Defines the path where Windows searches for the Programs subfolder of the Start menu (*"C:\WINDOWS\Profiles\Born\Start Menu\Programs"*, for example)
Fonts	Pointer to the path with the font files (*"C:\WINDOWS\Fonts"*, for example)
Start Menu	Pointer to the Start Menu folder (*"C:\WINDOWS\Profiles\Born\Start Menu"*, for example)
Templates	Pointer to the folder where new templates for the New command in the shell's context menu are stored (*"C:\WINDOWS\ShellNew"*, for example)
Startup	Name of the Startup folder (*"C:\WINDOWS\Profiles\Born\Start Menu\Programs\Startup"*, for example)
Recent	Folder that contains the links to the documents shown in the Start menu's Documents submenu (*"C:\WINDOWS\Profiles\Born\Recent"*, for example)
SendTo	Contains the path and name of the folder where the definitions for the Send To command, shown in the Explorer's context menu, are stored (*"C:\WINDOWS\SendTo"*, for example)
NetHood	Pointer to a path with the Network Neighborhood definitions (*"C:\WINDOWS\Profiles\Born\NetHood"*, for example)

Table 4-11.

These entries are updated by Windows each time a user logs on. (The original data is kept in the *HKEY_USERS* branch.) The key *HKEY_CURRENT_USER\Software\Microsoft\Windows\CurrentVersion\Explorer\User Shell Folders* defines a second set of pointers defining the path to the folders used by the shell. These values are set by default to the same destinations as indicated in Table 4-11. Enabling user profiles allows you to define separate locations for the Desktop, Programs, Start Menu, Startup, NetHood, and Recent folders. The names and locations of these folders are maintained in the *User Shell Folders* key and can be altered with the System Policy Editor (select Local User, then Shell\Custom Folders).

Other entries are located in the key *HKEY_CURRENT_USER\Software\ Microsoft\Windows\CurrentVersion\Policies\Explorer*. If this key contains the value *NoStartMenuSubfolders* set to *0x00000001*, the subfolders of the Start menu will be hidden. This option can be set within the System Policy Editor (in the *Shell\Restrictions* branch).

NOTE: Other options for the Start menu and taskbar (such as the size of the icons) are stored in the *StreamMRU* key, which is contained in the *HKEY_CURRENT_USER\Software\Microsoft\Windows\ CurrentVersion\Explorer* branch. This list is updated dynamically. Some information about the structures used in this key are discussed in the next chapter.

Disabling Save Settings

If the user changes desktop or shell properties and exits Windows, these settings will be saved permanently in the Registry. You can disable this save feature within the System Policy Editor (in the *Shell\Restrictions* branch, by clicking the Don't Save Settings At Exit option). If this option is set, the old settings remain after the system is reset.

The System Policy Editor inserts the *NoSaveSettings* flag into the Registry key *HKEY_CURRENT_USER\Software\Microsoft\Windows\CurrentVersion\Policies\ Explorer*. If the flag is set to *0x00000001*, the settings are not saved upon exiting. A value of *0x00000000* saves the settings.

NOTE: You might enable this option if you want to prevent the user from changing the desktop properties. Disabling the save settings feature has one side effect: If you close a shell window or an Explorer window, the window's properties (size, position, icon size) are stored in the Registry. Windows stores the properties of the most recently opened folders in an MRU list, and if you reopen one of these folders, Windows tries to reuse the settings from the MRU list. If the save settings feature is disabled, the MRU list entries are used only for the current session; after the next restart, the settings you made are gone. Further details about the MRU list are discussed in Chapter 5.

This book brings together all the scattered details about the Registry and provides a comprehensive look at how it works and how you can use it.

Fortunately, the concept of the

The Registry is the central d in Microsoft Windows 95 that s and maintains configuration information and is thus one of th most interesting and important components of Windows 95. Unt now, details about the Registry haven't been readily available. developers, administrators, and end users have all faced the challenge of trying to find information about it.

6810×8850

1080,1170

Customizing the Explorer Menu and Shell Icon Settings

In Chapter 3, we learned how to register new file types in Microsoft Windows 95. Registering file types affects features of the Explorer (such as the context menu). In this chapter, we look at other cool ways to enhance and customize the Explorer and shell functions, and we further examine the internals of the Registry. We'll extend the context menu of the Explorer window, change the icons for the shell, remove the shortcut icons, and extend the templates for the New command of the shell's context menu.

Extending the Explorer's Context Menu

Extending the Explorer's context menu with a new command is fairly simple, as you saw in Chapter 3. When you register a new file type, the context menu for files of that type is extended. You can also register new commands for Explorer elements other than file types, such as folders and drives, and extend the context menu. Inspecting the *HKEY_CLASSES_ROOT* branch reveals keys such as *Folder, Drive,* and so on. If we restrict our view to the way the shell uses command extensions, the shell perceives no differences between a file, a folder, or a drive. So you can add extensions to the context menus of folders and drives in basically the same way you register extensions for files.

Adding the New Explorer Window Command

When you open a folder in the Explorer window, the contents of the selected folder are shown in that window. When you open the My Computer window, you can choose to show the folder contents in the same window or in a second window by setting the Browsing option on the Folder property page, which is available on the Options property sheet. (Select Options from the My Computer View menu.)

Having two open windows on the desktop enables you to copy or move a file using a simple drag-and-drop operation. Wouldn't it be convenient to have this option through the Explorer? Well, you can. You can put a new command on the context menu that enables you to open a second Explorer window with only a right mouse click. Extending the shell with this new command is straightforward—if you know how to use the Registry Editor to register a new file type, you also know how to extend the shell commands applicable to a folder or drive. Here are the steps to set the required entries in the Registry:

1. Open the key *HKEY_CLASSES_ROOT\Folder\shell,* which is where you can add extensions for the folder's context menu. Commands stored in this key are also available from drives and network devices (and from the Start button, because it is a part of the shell).

2. Add a subkey for the verb into the *shell* key. You can use any name for this new key, but the name must be unique in the *\Folder\shell* branch. (For example, you could name it *rootexplore,* as it is named in Microsoft Power Toys, or *newWindow.*)

3. Set the *Default* value of the verb's key to the string you want to see on the context menu—for example, *New Explorer &Window.* The ampersand (&) character defines the accelerator key used on the context menu. (Details about accelerator keys used on context menus can be found on pages 84–87 in Chapter 3.)

4. Add a new *command* subkey to the verb's key (*\Folder\shell\ newWindow\command,* for example), and set the *Default* value of this *command* subkey to the required Explorer command (*Explorer.exe*). Your Registry should look something like Figure 5-1.

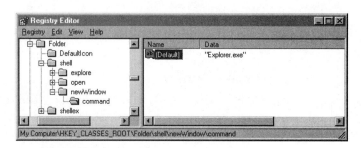

Figure 5-1.
New Registry entries for the New Explorer Window context menu command.

Immediately after you enter these values; the Explorer makes the new command available. Right-click a folder or drive symbol (in the Explorer window, in a shell window, or on the desktop) to show the context menu with the new command.

Defining the Command String

But one question is still open: How useful is it to define the command string that invokes the second copy of the Explorer window by using the method in the preceding steps. We used the command *Explorer.exe* in the *Default* value of the *HKEY_ CLASSES_ROOT\Folder\shell\newWindow\command* key. (A path to the EXE file is not required because EXPLORER.EXE is contained in the Windows folder.) Using this command opens an Explorer window showing the entire desktop hierarchy. We could live with this if we needed only a second Explorer window and were too lazy to launch a second copy of the Explorer using the Start menu. (I created a shortcut icon to the Explorer on the desktop, but this icon is hidden most of the time by application program windows.)

But let's face it—a new Explorer window showing the whole desktop hierarchy is not very convenient, because if you right-click a folder and choose the New Explorer Window command, you have to browse the whole directory structure in the new window to reach your desired folder. (This is too cumbersome for a lazy person like me. When I select a folder, I want to see this folder in the second window.) So why not let the Explorer perform this task? We need the second Explorer window to open with the contents of the desired subfolder displayed. So we will invoke EXPLORER.EXE using the following command syntax:

```
<path>explorer.exe [/e] [,/root,<object>] [[,/select],<sub-objects>]
```

Using this command syntax and options in the Registry *command* key will allow us to control how the Explorer invokes its second copy. Let's look more closely at the command syntax before adding the entry.

All expressions included in square brackets ([]) or angle brackets (<>) are optional and can be omitted. The switches after the name of the EXE file allow you to control some Explorer properties:

■ The */e* switch creates an Explorer-style window with two panes. If you omit this switch and add some other option to the command line, a single window pane with the file list is opened (the shell style).

- The */root,<object>* option defines the root object you want shown in the new Explorer window (such as C:\Text in Figure 5-2).

- With the */select* switch, you can preselect defined sub-objects within an object. This allows you to select a subfolder or a file.

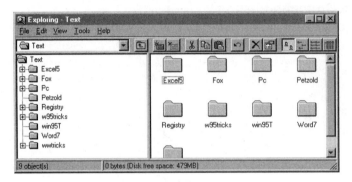

Figure 5-2.
Explorer window using C:\Text as the root.

Example Commands for the Explorer

The Explorer's command syntax appears a little bit complicated, doesn't it? Let's look at a few examples of the command. (You can test them with the Run function, available from the Start menu.) This is an example command for a selected sub-object:

```
Explorer.exe /e ,C:\Text
```

It opens the Explorer window, preselects the C:\Text folder, and shows its contents in the right-hand pane.

Now try to use the following modified command, which was used to create Figure 5-2:

```
Explorer.exe /e ,/root, C:\Text\
```

Carefully place the commas and the backslash that terminates the path. This command opens the Explorer window with the \Text folder shown as the root folder in the left pane and with the folder contents shown in the right pane. You can't switch this construction over to the parent folder of C:\Text because C:\Text is the root.

The next command opens the Explorer window, shows the contents of C:\Text in the right pane, and selects the file AUTHOR.DOC in the C:\Text folder.

```
Explorer.exe /e , C:\Text\ , /select , C:\Text\author.doc
```

176

A command without the /e switch invokes a shell-style window, which shows the contents of C:\Text and the selected file AUTHOR.DOC in the window.

```
Explorer.exe , C:\Text\ , /select , C:\Text\author.doc
```

Adding Placeholders to the Command String

Within the Registry *command* key, you can't define a fixed folder. The Explorer parameters depend on the folder selected by the user. To get around this obstacle, substitute the folder's name with a placeholder. The command line to invoke a copy of the Explorer can contain the following items:

```
Explorer.exe /e , /root, /idlist, %I
```

The placeholder for the folder currently selected with the right mouse-click is *%I*. If you insert this command into the Registry, the New Explorer Window entry on the context menu will invoke a second copy of the Explorer showing the contents of the preselected folder or drive.

Putting It All Together in an INF File

So far, so good. Now, how do you install this new shell extension into the Registry? It is a little difficult to correctly enter all the keys and settings manually, and using a REG file creates a mess if the Windows path is different from the settings in the REG file. My preferred method is to use an INF file.

Following are the statements included in the INF file. All lines starting with a semicolon are comments—I added a lot of comments to clarify what happens. (You can find the EXPLORE1.INF file in the \chapter5 folder of the downloaded sample files.)

```
; File: Explore1.inf  (G. Born)
;
; Install script to extend the Explorer's context menu.
; If the user right-clicks a folder symbol in the
; Explorer's window or in a shell window, the
; New Explorer Window command appears on the context menu.
; Selecting this command opens a new Explorer window.
; This feature can be removed with the Control Panel
; Add/Remove Programs uninstall function.

[version]
signature="$CHICAGO$"
SetupClass=BASE

; During install, add something into the Registry and copy the INF file
; into the \Windows\INF folder. Copy is required because
; we need this file for the uninstall function.
```

(continued)

continued

```
[DefaultInstall]
AddReg = Explore.AddReg
CopyFiles = Explore.CopyFiles.Inf

; This section defines how to uninstall the feature (remove the
; Registry entries and delete the INF file). The
; section name is defined in the [Explore.AddReg]
; section in the UninstallString value.

[DefaultUninstall]

DelReg = Explore.AddReg
DelFiles = Explore.CopyFiles.Inf

; This section adds the keys into the Registry. The feature
; is registered in HKEY_CLASSES_ROOT\Folder\shell.

[Explore.AddReg]

; Add the newWindow verb and the string for the context menu
; contained in %COMMAND_STRING%
HKCR,Folder\shell\newWindow,,,"%COMMAND_STRING%"

; Add the command to activate the Explorer
HKCR,Folder\shell\newWindow\command,,,%COMMAND%

; Required to set up the Uninstall feature

HKLM,SOFTWARE\Microsoft\Windows\CurrentVersion\Uninstall\newWindow,
DisplayName,,"%Explore_REMOVE_DESC%"
HKLM,SOFTWARE\Microsoft\Windows\CurrentVersion\Uninstall\newWindow,
UninstallString,,
"RunDll setupx.dll,InstallHinfSection DefaultUninstall 4 Explore1.Inf"

; Remove the newWindow key in Uninstall by adding this line

HKLM,SOFTWARE\Microsoft\Windows\CurrentVersion\Uninstall\newWindow

; Define the files to be copied. (Source and
; destination directories are defined in the following sections.)

[Explore.CopyFiles.Inf]
Explore1.Inf

; Definition for the source (use the path where the INF file
; is activated; 55 is defined in the SourceDisksFiles section)
```

(continued)

continued

```
[SourceDisksNames]
55="New Explorer Window","",1

[SourceDisksFiles]
Explore1.Inf=55

; Specify the destination. 17 is the logical disk ID for the
; Windows INF subfolder.

[DestinationDirs]
Explore.CopyFiles.Inf = 17

; Define miscellaneous variables with strings.
; These variables are used in the preceding commands. During install, the
; variable will be replaced by its string value.
;
; For this example we define strings for the context menu
; entry and for the name in the uninstall component list

[Strings]
; This section contains two COMMAND declarations, one of which must
; be commented out

; Command to invoke the Explorer window
COMMAND = "Explorer.exe /e,/root,/idlist,%I"
; Command to invoke a shell window
;COMMAND = "Explorer.exe ,/root,/idlist,%I"

; String for the context menu entry
COMMAND_STRING = "New Explorer &Window"

; String for the Uninstall entry
EXPLORE_REMOVE_DESC = "Remove Born's New Explorer Window"

; End ***
```

Right-clicking the file and selecting Install from the context menu modifies the Registry. After installing the extension, right-click a folder or drive to open the context menu showing the New Explorer Window command. (Right-clicking a file won't show this new command.)

NOTE: If you have trouble installing the file, be sure the folders in the path to the source disk do not contain Windows 95 long filenames; only eight-character format names will be found during the install.

If you don't like this context menu extension, you can uninstall it—the most interesting feature of this INF file is the uninstall function.

1. Double-click the Add/Remove Programs icon in the Control Panel, and select the Install/Uninstall property page. This page should show the Remove Born's New Explorer Window entry (Figure 5-3).

2. Click this entry and then click Add/Remove.

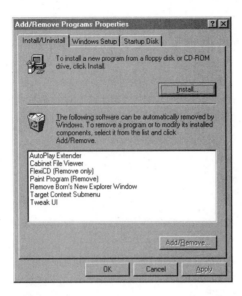

Figure 5-3.
The Install/Uninstall property page, which can be used to uninstall the new extension.

After you perform these steps, the extension will be removed; you can check this using the Registry Editor.

NOTE: You might have noticed in the EXPLORE1.INF program that there are two Explorer command strings. The first string is the command to bring up a new Explorer window. If you comment out this first string and uncomment the second string, the command brings up a shell window. The EXPLORE2.INF program in the \chapter5 folder of the downloaded sample files is the same as the EXPLORE1.INF program, but EXPLORE2.INF has the shell window command active and the Explorer window command commented out.

EXPLORE1.INF file details   If you installed Power Toys, you will find an INF file similar to the file we just examined that installs the Explore From Here function (EXPLORE.INF). Unfortunately, this file contains no comments, some parts are superfluous, and other parts are missing. (But I'm not going to complain—the folks at Microsoft gave us useful tools for free. And I'm sure my own INF files contain a few questionable parts.) The INF file we looked at contains a lot of comments, but I want to explain further.

The file contains different sections (shown in square brackets []) that define actions for the install and uninstall processes. The most important section is [Explore.AddReg], which contains the commands for entering the New Explorer Window function into the *HKEY_CLASSES_ROOT\Folder\shell* key of the Registry. At least two lines are necessary in this section: one to add the *newWindow* key and the other to add the *command* subkey.

The rest of this section prepares the uninstall function. As noted earlier, Windows provides the Install/Uninstall property page so that you can uninstall software and clear the Registry. Windows keeps the entries for this property page in the key *HKEY_LOCAL_MACHINE\SOFTWARE\Microsoft\Windows\ CurrentVersion\Uninstall.* Each application providing an uninstall function can add a subkey to this *Uninstall* key. The [Explore.AddReg] section of the INF file contains lines like the following, which adds the *newWindow* subkey to the *Uninstall* branch:

```
HKLM,SOFTWARE\Microsoft\Windows\CurrentVersion\Uninstall\newWindow...
```

The lines start with the abbreviation for the root key: *HKLM* stands for *HKEY_LOCAL_MACHINE.* Parameters are separated by commas. The second parameter defines the subkey to be altered. If this subkey doesn't exist, a new key is added. The third parameter defines the value's name, and the fourth parameter is left blank. The last parameter can contain the value for the name inserted in the key. The *newWindow* subkey in the *Uninstall* branch contains two entries:

■ The first entry, *DisplayName*, contains the string shown on the Install/Uninstall property page. For our example, I used the text "Remove Born's New Explorer Window." This string is defined in the *%EXPLORE_REMOVE_DESC%* INF variable.

■ The second entry in the *\Uninstall\newWindow* key has the name *UninstallString* and contains a command. This command will be executed when the user selects the entry from the Install/Uninstall property page and clicks Add/Remove.

Some application programs come with their own setup and uninstall programs, and in these cases, the paths and names of the uninstall programs must be set in the *UninstallString* values (*C:\Windows\Unwise.exe\install.log,* for example). My INF file uses the poor man's approach: The command executes the Windows RunDLL program. This is an interface that calls other procedures in DLL routines. All other entries in the command line are parameters for the DLL routine:

- The first parameter defines the name of the DLL file. (I used SETUPX.DLL.)

- Further parameters are DLL-specific (and are documented in the Win32 SDK).

SETUPX.DLL needs several parameters, such as the name of the INF file that will be executed. (In our example, this file is EXPLORE1.INF.) In order to use the INF file for the uninstall, it must be located in the Windows INF folder. (This is why we have to copy the INF file during the install process.) [DefaultUninstall] is the section name in the INF file containing the statements to be executed during the uninstall process. In EXPLORE1.INF, I used a trick: The [DefaultUninstall] section contains a reference to the [Explore.AddReg] section, but DelReg is used instead of the AddReg keyword. This causes SETUPX to remove all Registry entries defined in the [Explore.AddReg] section. (Install and Uninstall use the same commands.)

Is that all? Well, no—I have to mention a pitfall in the Windows uninstall. In theory, you'd have to use only the following two lines to add the *Uninstall*\ *newWindow* key with the two required uninstall entries:

```
HKLM,SOFTWARE\Microsoft\Windows\CurrentVersion\Uninstall\newWindow,DisplayName,...
```

```
HKLM,SOFTWARE\Microsoft\Windows\CurrentVersion\Uninstall\newWindow,UninstallString,...
```

During the install process, the key doesn't exist; it is created automatically. But because the uninstall function (SETUPX.DLL) uses the information found in the INF file and the two lines above specify only the *DisplayName* and *UninstallString* entries, the *newWindow* key remains as an empty key left in the Registry. (This is also the case with the Power Toys Explore From Here INF file.) So I added a third line to the [Explore.AddReg] section:

```
HKLM,SOFTWARE\Microsoft\Windows\CurrentVersion\Uninstall\newWindow
```

This line is superfluous during the install process, but it is required to clean the Registry during uninstall. (Alas—sometimes it's hard to be a programmer.) INF file structures are discussed in Chapter 7.

Activating MS-DOS from the Explorer

Windows provides a great user interface, but sometimes I feel more comfortable running certain commands in the MS-DOS window. Copy, Rename, and Delete, for example, are faster in MS-DOS. Unfortunately, you have to click several commands to reach the MS-DOS window and then you have to use the *CD* (change directory) command to switch to the requested subfolder. Wouldn't it be more efficient to right-click a folder's icon and select an MS-DOS command from the context menu?

All you need to do is hack a little bit in the Registry. At the very least, you have to add a new verb (such as *dos*) with a *command* subkey in the *HKEY_ CLASSES_ROOT\Folder\shell* branch of the Registry. The lines of the following REG file show the commands necessary to register the DOS command processor as a shell extension:

```
REGEDIT4

[HKEY_CLASSES_ROOT\Folder\shell\dos]
@="MS-DOS"

[HKEY_CLASSES_ROOT\Folder\shell\dos\command]
@="command.com"
```

You don't need to indicate a path to invoke the DOS command processor COMMAND.COM, so you can use a REG file to extend the Registry without risk. The only disadvantage of this REG file solution is the missing uninstall feature. If you need this function, use an INF file with the following statements:

```
; File: DOS.inf (G. Born)
;
; Install script to extend the Explorer's context menu with a DOS
; command
;
; If the user right-clicks a folder in the Explorer's
; window or in a shell window, the MS-DOS command
; will appear on the context menu. Selecting this
; command invokes the MS-DOS window and highlights the folder.

[version]
signature="$CHICAGO$"
SetupClass=BASE

; Add the extension into the Registry
```

(continued)

continued

```
[DefaultInstall]
AddReg = DOS.AddReg
CopyFiles = DOS.CopyFiles.Inf

; Uninstall part

[DefaultUninstall]

DelReg = DOS.AddReg
DelFiles = DOS.CopyFiles.Inf

; This part adds the keys to the Registry. The feature
; is registered in HKEY_CLASSES_ROOT\Folder\shell.

[DOS.AddReg]

; Add the dos verb and the string for the context menu
; contained in %COMMAND_STRING%
HKCR,Folder\shell\dos,,,"%COMMAND_STRING%"

; Add the command to activate COMMAND.COM
HKCR,Folder\shell\dos\command,,,%COMMAND%

; *** This stuff is required to set up the Uninstall feature

HKLM,SOFTWARE\Microsoft\Windows\CurrentVersion\Uninstall\dos,DisplayName,
,"%DOS_REMOVE_DESC%"
HKLM,SOFTWARE\Microsoft\Windows\CurrentVersion\Uninstall\dos,
UninstallString,,
"RunDll setupx.dll,InstallHinfSection DefaultUninstall 4 DOS.Inf"

; Don't forget to remove the dos key in Uninstall.
; This is done by adding the following line.

HKLM,SOFTWARE\Microsoft\Windows\CurrentVersion\Uninstall\dos

; Define the files to be copied, and define source and
; destination directories

[DOS.CopyFiles.Inf]
DOS.Inf

; Definition for the source (use the path where
; the INF file is activated; 55 is defined in SourceDisksFiles)
```

(continued)

continued

```
[SourceDisksNames]
55="MS-DOS","",1

[SourceDisksFiles]
DOS.Inf=55

; Now we have to specify the destination. 17 is the
; logical disk ID for the Windows INF subfolder.

[DestinationDirs]
DOS.CopyFiles.Inf = 17

; Define miscellaneous variables

[Strings]
; Command to invoke COMMAND.COM
COMMAND = "command.com"

; String for the context menu entry
COMMAND_STRING = "MS-DOS"

; String for the Uninstall entry
DOS_REMOVE_DESC = "Remove Born's MS-DOS Shell Extension"

; End ***
```

This file sets the Registry entries for the shell extension and uninstall feature. You can remove this extension using the Install/Uninstall property page.

N O T E :   You will find the files DOS.REG and DOS.INF in the \chapter5 folder of the downloaded sample files.

Printing a Directory List from the Explorer Window

Now we have a marvelous Explorer window with cool features such as files, icons, and folders. But if you're like me, you get lost wading through a huge file list. I remember the good old MS-DOS days when I could use the command *DIR *.* >PRN:* to print the directory. I'd use the listing to check which files had to be altered, copied, deleted, and so on. Nothing comparable is available in the Explorer window. (I know this topic is on the wish list of many users.)

What about using the MS-DOS window, which we looked at in the previous section? Couldn't we run the DOS.INF file to register this Explorer extension, right-click a folder or a drive, select MS-DOS from the context menu to get into the MS-DOS window, and then enter the *DIR >PRN:* command?

Well, we *could,* but why perform tasks that Windows will perform for us? Let's evaluate our options. Maybe we should try to use the *DIR *.* > PRN:* command in the Registry. The command makes sense, but I haven't figured out exactly how to get MS-DOS piping to work in a Registry command. So our solution is to store this command in a simple MS-DOS batch file and enter a command to execute this BAT file in the Registry. The BAT file solution is the best one because we also need a form feed at the end of the report to advance the last page. The following lines show the contents of a simple BAT file (PRNDIR.BAT, located in the \chapter5 folder of the dowloaded sample files) that prints a directory:

```
@ECHO OFF
DIR %1 >PRN:
ECHO ^L >PRN:
ECHO ON
```

The form feed is sent by the *ECHO ^L>PRN:* line. The *%1* is the place-holder for the current directory, which is supplied by the Explorer when the BAT file is invoked.

NOTE: By the way, I used the MS-DOS program EDIT.COM to create the BAT file. Notepad won't allow you to enter the ^L character. Just another tip: On PostScript printers, you can use the command *ECHO SHOW >PRN:* to advance one page.

All we have to do is to register the BAT program as a new Explorer command in the Registry. This requires a new verb in *HKEY_CLASSES_ROOT\ Folder\shell* and a *command* subkey defining the string that invokes the BAT file:

```
HKEY_CLASSES_ROOT\Folder\shell\PrnDir = "Print Directory"
HKEY_CLASSES_ROOT\Folder\shell\PrnDir\command ="<Path>PRNDIR.BAT %1"
```

The *<Path>* parameter in the lines above is still undefined, so you can't use these lines in a REG file. The reason is simple. Let me explain where the BAT file is stored and what you need to know to use a BAT file.

Storing and Selecting Properties for the BAT File

The first issue we need to resolve is where we are going to store the BAT file for our planned shell extension. This information will be of interest if you plan to install other shell extensions, too. The simplest solution would be to store it in the \Windows folder because none of the programs in this folder need a path description in a command—but don't do it! Storing software in your Windows folder essentially spoils it with clutter—after I uninstall this kind of software, I have no control over which files are superfluous and can be deleted. (Don't believe that the uninstall function will clear your hard disk—I have hundreds of files on my hard disk and no idea which ones can be wiped out.) Well-designed software uses its own folder to store its files. Here are some locations where you can create such a folder.

- An install program can create a new folder in the root directory of a drive (for example, C:\PRNDIR). If you distribute your application with such a program, the install routine will give the user a chance to select a new name for the destination directory. (We can't use this approach, because I want to use an INF file to install the extension.)

- You can use the \Program Files folder, which is created by Windows, to store common Windows tools (such as WordPad). If you create your own subfolder, you can easily clean it after uninstalling the software.

- You can create a subfolder with its own name in the \Windows directory, indicating that the program belongs to Windows.

I decided to create a Windows subfolder and name it \Born to make it clear who created the mess. (This subfolder will also be used to store other files discussed in this book.)

The second issue we need to resolve is which properties we want to assign to the BAT file. We want this program to always run minimized as an icon on the taskbar, run in the background, and terminate after printing the directory. These options for an MS-DOS window can be controlled with its property sheet: Right-click the BAT file, and select Properties from the context menu. Set the options required for the program to run minimized in the background. When you close the property sheet, a Program Information File (PIF) is created with the settings. You can store this PIF file in the same folder as the BAT file. (See PRNDIR.PIF in the \chapter5 folder of the downloaded sample files.)

You can also set the DOS properties of your BAT program in the APPS.INF file, which is located in the Windows \INF subfolder. APPS.INF is used to register the properties of several MS-DOS applications, but I won't discuss this topic here.

Installing the Print Directory Extension

We need the BAT file, the PIF file, and an INF file to install the Print Directory extension.

NOTE: If you are a programmer, you can write your own Windows application to print a directory list. You can register your file with less overhead—no PIF file is needed—but you should still take a look at the discussion about file locations.

The following INF file contains the commands to register the Print Directory shell extension and copy the required files. (The PRNDIR.INF file can be found in the \chapter5 folder of the downloaded sample files.)

```
; File: PrnDIR.INF  (by G. Born)
;
; Install Print Directory command on Explorer's
; context menu: Copy PRNDIR.BAT and PRNDIR.INF into the
; Windows folder \Born, and add the Registry keys.
; Right-clicking a folder (after installing the
; extension) shows the command.
; The command invokes the PRNDIR.BAT file, which runs
; minimized in the background and prints the directory.
;
; The INF file also provides an uninstall function to
; remove the Registry entries and files copied
; during install. The Windows subfolder \Born will
; not be removed. (It can be used for other extensions.)

[version]
signature="$Chicago$"

; During install: Keep the INF file for uninstall;
; copy BAT and PIF files; and update the Registry

[DefaultInstall]
CopyFiles = Explore.CopyFiles.Inf
CopyFiles = Explore.CopyFiles.Bat
AddReg = Explore.AddReg

; During uninstall: Delete the INF file,
; the BAT and PIF files, and update the Registry

[DefaultUninstall]
DelReg = Explore.AddReg
DelFiles = Explore.CopyFiles.Inf, Explore.CopyFiles.Bat

; Update the Registry keys

[Explore.AddReg]
HKCR,Folder\shell\prnDir,,,"%EXPLORE_DESC%"
HKCR,Folder\shell\prnDir\command,,,"%10%\%MY_FOLDER%\%COMMAND%"
```

(continued)

continued

```
; Add uninstall stuff
HKLM,SOFTWARE\Microsoft\Windows\CurrentVersion\Uninstall\prnDir,DisplayName
,,"%REMOVE_DESC%"
HKLM,SOFTWARE\Microsoft\Windows\CurrentVersion\Uninstall\prnDir,
UninstallString,,
"RunDll setupx.dll,InstallHinfSection DefaultUninstall 4 PrnDir.inf"

; Don't forget this key for the uninstall part
HKLM,SOFTWARE\Microsoft\Windows\CurrentVersion\Uninstall\prnDir,,,

; INF file to be copied in the Windows INF subfolder

[Explore.CopyFiles.Inf]
PrnDir.Inf

; BAT and PIF files needed by the extension, copied
; into the Windows subfolder defined in %MY_FOLDER%

[Explore.CopyFiles.Bat]
PrnDir.bat
PrnDir.pif

[DestinationDirs]
Explore.CopyFiles.bat = 10,%MY_FOLDER%
Explore.CopyFiles.Inf = 17

[SourceDisksNames]
55="Print Directory","",1

[SourceDisksFiles]
PrnDir.inf=55
PrnDir.bat=55
PrnDir.pif=55

; Strings with destination folders, commands, and
; context menu text

[Strings]
MY_FOLDER = "Born"
COMMAND = "PRNDIR.BAT %1"
Explore_DESC = "Print Directory"
REMOVE_DESC = "Remove Born's Print Directory"

; End ***
```

After you run Install on the INF file, you should be able to print the directory contents (right-click the folder and select Print Directory). To remove this shell extension, use the Install/Uninstall property page (available through the Add/Remove Programs icon in the Control Panel).

NOTE: The uninstall process will delete the files copied during the install but will leave the folder \Born in the Windows folder because the Born folder can be used for other files.

Printing a Directory Tree

The Explorer has no option for printing the directory tree, but you can use the concepts in the previous section to easily create a shell extension:

1. Create a BAT file and name it PRNTREE.BAT. Instead of the *DIR* command, use *TREE %1 >PRN:*.

2. Create a PIF file and set the following MS-DOS window properties for this BAT file: icon, background processing, minimized, close after termination.

3. Create an INF file that registers this new extension and copies the required files onto the hard disk.

After these steps, you can install and uninstall the extension as demonstrated in the previous section.

Modifying Miscellaneous Explorer Settings

When you open a folder, the shell opens a window with the folder's contents. By default, the Explorer opens only one window to show the contents of the selected folder. The shell can open one window to show the contents of the most recently opened folder, or it can open a new window for each folder you open. You can change the settings of each folder window that is opened; Windows stores these settings (window size, icon size, and so on) and reuses them the next time the folder is opened. You can also set options to hide or show the file extensions and to exclude system files from the Explorer's view. Let's examine how the Registry supports these and other features.

Hiding and Showing System Files and Extensions

You can hide or show system files (such as DLL, SYS, and VXD files) as well as MS-DOS file extensions in the shell and Explorer windows. Global hide and show options are set on the View property page of the Options property sheet (see Figure 5-4), which is available through the Options entry on the Explorer's View menu. Following is an explanation of these hide and show options:

- The Show All Files and Hide Files Of These Types option boxes control whether you see the system files in the shell windows.

- The Hide MS-DOS File Extensions For File Types That Are Registered option hides (when checked) or shows (when unchecked) the MS-DOS file extensions in the shell windows. The global status of this option can be overruled for certain registered file types through options on the Add New File Type and Edit File Type dialog boxes. Two values, *NeverShowExtension* and *AlwaysShowExtension,* control this option and exist (mutually exclusive) in the key *HKEY_CLASSES_ROOT\file type.* (Further details can be found in Chapter 3.)

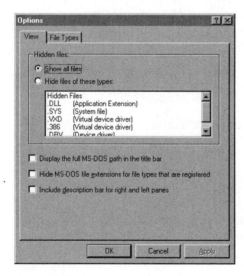

Figure 5-4.
The View property page.

These settings are user-specific. Windows keeps the options in the Registry key *HKEY_CURRENT_USER\Software\Microsoft\Windows\CurrentVersion\Explorer.* This key contains a *ShellState* value, which is defined as four DWORD flags. The second DWORD is a 32-bit flag containing the two options shown in Table 5-1 on the following page.

Hide/Show Settings in the *Explorer* Key

Bit	Value Description
0	*1* = Show all system files
	0 = Hide all system files
1	*1* = Show MS-DOS file extensions for registered file types
	0 = Hide MS-DOS file extensions for registered file types

Table 5-1.
Bits in the second DWORD flag of the ShellState *value.*

Defining the Column Settings of the Explorer Window

When you select the Details mode in the right pane of the Explorer window, the file list is shown with four columns: Name, Size, Type, and Modified. You can change the width of these columns by dragging the columns separator left or right. The information about the most recently used column size is kept in the Registry key *HKEY_CURRENT_USER\Software\Microsoft\Windows\Current-Version\Explorer* in the *DirectoryCols* value. This binary value consists of four WORDs that define the size of each column as shown in Table 5-2.

Column Settings in the *Explorer* Key

WORD	Definition
0	Width of the Explorer's Name column
1	Width of the Explorer's Size column
2	Width of the Explorer's Type column
3	Width of the Explorer's Modified column

Table 5-2.
Coding of the DirectoryCols *value.*

Two other values in this key, *NetDomainCols* and *NetServerCols*, contain four bytes each. Both values are two WORDs that define the Name and Comment columns of the Entire Network folder and the workgroup folders.

NOTE: The shell window (My Computer) uses a similar construction, which is discussed in the following sections.

Removing Shortcut Symbols

When you create a shortcut to an item (a document, folder, drive, and so on), a small arrow is displayed in the lower left corner of the item's icon (Figure 5-5).

PrnDir   PrnDir.inf

Figure 5-5.
You can determine whether an item is a shortcut by the arrow on the icon.

The icons for PIF files are also shown with this small arrow. You can remove this shortcut symbol from the icons in shortcuts and in PIF file types. The information about the shortcut is stored in the *HKEY_CLASSES_ROOT* branch of the Registry:

- Shortcuts are registered in the *lnkfile* key.
- PIF files are registered in the *piffile* key.

If these keys contain the entry *IsShortcut*, the arrow will be shown. The *IsShortcut* value is always set to *""*. Deleting this entry from a key will remove the Shortcut arrow after the screen is refreshed.

> **NOTE:**   The *NeverShowExt* flag in the *lnkfile* and *piffile* keys suppresses the display of file extensions in the Explorer and shell windows. If you remove this flag, the extensions LNK and PIF are shown. The only exception is the LNK extension, which isn't shown on the desktop in an icon title because the extension for the file or application associated with the LNK file is shown instead ("Shortcut to Winword.exe", for example).

You can use the Registry Editor to strip out the *IsShortcut* values, but using the following INF file is more convenient. (You can find the SHORTCUT.INF file in the\chapter5 folder of the downloaded sample files.)

```
; File: Shortcut.INF
;
; Remove the Shortcut arrow shown for shortcuts on the shell.
;
; The INF file also provides an uninstall function to
; recover the factory settings.
```

(continued)

193

continued

```
[version]
signature="$CHICAGO$"
SetupClass=BASE

; During install: Remove IsShortcut entries, set uninstall information

[DefaultInstall]
CopyFiles = Shortcut.CopyFiles.Inf
DelReg = Shortcut.Remove.Reg
AddReg = Shortcut.AddReg

; During uninstall: Delete the INF file,
; the BAT and PIF files, and update the Registry

[DefaultUninstall]
AddReg = Shortcut.Remove.Reg
DelReg = Shortcut.AddReg
DelFiles = Shortcut.CopyFiles.Inf

; Remove the IsShortcut flags

[Shortcut.Remove.Reg]
HKCR,lnkfile,IsShortcut,,""
HKCR,piffile,IsShortcut,,""

; Set uninstall keys

[Shortcut.AddReg]
; Add uninstall stuff
HKLM,SOFTWARE\Microsoft\Windows\CurrentVersion\Uninstall\IsShortcutOn,
DisplayName,,"%REMOVE_DESC%"
HKLM,SOFTWARE\Microsoft\Windows\CurrentVersion\Uninstall\IsShortcutOn,
UninstallString,,
"RunDll setupx.dll,InstallHinfSection DefaultUninstall 4 Shortcut.inf"

; Don't forget to uninstall this key
HKLM,SOFTWARE\Microsoft\Windows\CurrentVersion\Uninstall\IsShortcutOn,,,

; INF file to be copied to the Windows INF subfolder

[Shortcut.CopyFiles.Inf]
Shortcut.Inf
```

(continued)

continued

```
[DestinationDirs]

Shortcut.CopyFiles.Inf = 17

[SourceDisksNames]
55="Shortcut Remove","",1

[SourceDisksFiles]
Shortcut.inf=55

[Strings]

REMOVE_DESC = "Restore Shortcut arrow (Born)"

; End ***
```

Right-clicking the INF file and selecting Install from the context menu removes the Shortcut arrows. You can restore the default settings by clicking the Restore Shortcut arrow (Born) option on the Install/Uninstall property page (select Control Panel, then Add/Remove Programs).

Removing the Shortcut To Prefix from the Icon Title

When you create a shortcut, the "Shortcut to" text is attached to the filename as a prefix, and it's used to build the icon title (for example, "Shortcut to EXPLORER.EXE"). Tweak UI (shipped with Power Toys) provides a function to hide this prefix.

1. Start Tweak UI (available through the Control Panel), and select the Explorer property page.

2. Uncheck the Prefix Shortcut To On New Shortcuts option in the Settings group (see Figure 5-6 on the following page).

3. Apply this setting by clicking OK.

A system reset might be necessary to activate this modification. The "Shortcut to" prefix is controlled by the *link* value, which is available in several Registry keys. One key can be found in the branch *HKEY_USERS\xxxx\ Software\Microsoft\Windows\CurrentVersion\Explorer.* In this key, the *xxxx* stands for the user name (or for *.Default*). If the *Explorer* key contains no *link* value or the value is set to *00 00 00 00,* the prefix is hidden.

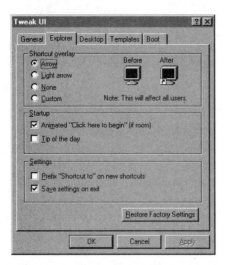

Figure 5-6.
The Tweak UI Explorer property page.

> NOTE: The *link* value in the *HKEY_CURRENT_USER* key is some-
> times used as a counter that is incremented each time a shortcut is
> created. Modifying this value isn't required, because a system restart
> will rebuild the whole branch from *HKEY_USERS* anyway.

Controlling Other Settings in the Explorer Window

You can change options in the Explorer window. For example, you could
decide to show the toolbar, hide the status bar, and switch from Large Icons
to a Details view. The settings for these options are stored in the Registry in
the key *HKEY_CURRENT_USER\Software\Microsoft\Windows\CurrentVersion\
Explorer\ExpView*. This key contains the *Settings* value, which is a byte stream with
several flags controlling Explorer options. Table 5-3 contains a brief overview
of the relevant flags.

Because you can't set individual bytes using REG or INF files, the flags
in Table 5-3 cannot be modified with REG or INF files. But you can access them
with Windows API calls: You can read the original settings, change the flags,
and then rewrite the whole data stream. You might want to do this if you are
developing an Explorer-compatible tool that uses the Explorer settings stored
in the Registry.

Common Explorer Window Settings

Byte Number	Description
44	This byte (at offset 0x2C) controls the view options for the right pane in the Explorer window. The following values can be set by using the Explorer's View menu:
	0 Large Icons
	2 Small Icons
	3 List
	4 Details
48	This byte (at offset 0x30) controls the Auto Arrange Icons option on the Explorer's View menu. The following values can be set:
	01 Auto Arrange Icons (checked in the View menu)
	00 Auto Arrange Icons (unchecked in the View menu)
60	This byte (at offset 0x3C) controls whether the status bar and toolbar are visible:
	Bit 1 If set to *1*, show toolbar
	Bit 2 If set to *1*, show status bar
	Both bits are controlled by the toolbar and status bar entries in the Explorer's View menu.

Table 5-3.
Flags in the Settings *value.*

How the Shell Window Settings Are Saved

You can specify unique characteristics for any folder window opened in the shell mode (such as My Computer)—for example, you might display large icons for one folder and a file list for another. In most cases, when you close the window and reopen it later on, the settings you specified remain.

How does this work? The settings for the folder windows are saved in the Registry in the same way that the settings for the Explorer window are saved, except that Windows uses a behind-the-scenes construction comparable to a "cache" in order to save the settings for more than one window at a time. When you open a folder, Windows checks whether the settings for that folder are still in the cache. If Windows finds the settings in the Registry, those settings are used to open the folder window. If Windows does not find the settings, Windows uses the default settings. When a folder window is closed, one record is written to the cache with the settings. You can store the data for up to 28 different folder windows. If Windows has stored the settings for 28 windows and you close a window that is not stored, the settings for that window overwrite one of the existing records in the cache.

Windows uses a key construction for storing the records in the cache with the shell window settings similar in construction to the MRU lists discussed in Chapter 4. The key *HKEY_CURRENT_USER\Software\Microsoft\Windows\CurrentVersion\Explorer\StreamMRU* contains 28 entries named *a, b, c,* and so on. The value of each entry stores a byte stream containing several flags with status information for the folder. The *MRUList* in this key defines the order of the 28 entries.

The rest of the data for each of the 28 folders is stored in a second subkey, *HKEY_CURRENT_USER\Software\Microsoft\Windows\CurrentVersion\Explorer\Streams.* This *Streams* key contains subkeys with the names *0, 1, 2,* and so on that define the streams for all 28 folders. For each entry in *StreamMRU,* you will find a corresponding subkey in *Streams.* The mapping between the *StreamMRU* values and the subkeys is set to the following: Value *a* corresponds to the subkey *\Streams\0,* value *b* corresponds to the subkey *\Streams\1,* and so on.

A *Streams* subkey can have two entries: *CabView* and *ViewView.* Both entries are byte streams defining options for the folder's window. Table 5-4 shows some available options that are stored in *CabView.* (I interpreted these values as DWORDs starting with the index *0.*)

The *ViewView* value is a buffer describing the folder's contents. The first 28 bytes contain information about the last possible drive (drive Z). The next four WORDs contain the width of the Name, Type, Size, and Modified columns. You should not manipulate these values, because the buffer is updated each time you open a folder.

Settings for the Folder Window

DWORD	Definition
28	At offset 0x1C, defines the X coordinate for the upper left corner of the folder's window.
32	At offset 0x20, defines the Y coordinate for the upper left corner of the folder's window.

Table 5-4. *(continued)*
Coding of the CabView *value for the* Streams *key.*

Table 5-4. *continued*

DWORD	Definition
36	At offset 0x24, defines the X coordinate for the lower right corner of the folder's window.
40	At offset 0x28, defines the Y coordinate of the lower right corner of the folder's window.
44	At offset 0x2C, contains the value for the icon size:
	01 Large Icons
	02 Small Icons
	03 List
	04 Details
48	At offset 0x30, contains the Auto Arrange flag for this folder window. A value of *0x1* enables this option.
60	At offset 0x3C, contains the flags to hide or show the status bar and toolbar. The coding is the same as for the Explorer (see Table 5-3 on page 197).

Modifying Miscellaneous Network Keys

The association of a drive letter to a network service is stored in the key *HKEY_CURRENT_USER\Network\Persistent*. This key contains subkeys with the device name (*G, H, I, LPT1*, and so on) of each drive and printer associated with a persistent network device. The key itself contains several entries defining the network settings:

- *ProviderName* defines the name of the service provider *"Microsoft Network"*, for example).

- *UserName* stores the user name.

- *RemotePath* contains a string with the network path in UNC conventions *"\\C486-1\C486"*, for example).

The key *HKEY_CURRENT_USER\Network\Recent* contains a list of the recent network connections on the computer. Each connection is stored in its own subkey (which is named *././C486-1/C486*, for example). The subkey contains the value with the *ProviderName,* the *UserName,* and the *ConnectionType* (a binary value). These keys are updated each time the user changes a network connection in the shell.

Registering a New Template for the New Command

You can create a new document using the shell's New command (by right-clicking an empty space on the desktop and selecting New from the context menu). The New command contains a submenu with a list of optional document formats (see Figure 5-7). You can modify this list by registering your own document templates.

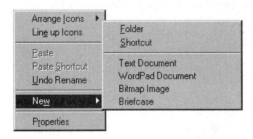

Figure 5-7.
The New command on the shell's context menu.

The Tweak UI property sheet contains a Template property page that lets you register a new template with a simple drag-and-drop operation. However, if you ship a software package, you'll want your install program to register the new template type, and you can't use Tweak UI. So the best way to register a new document template is by following these steps:

1. Use your application program to create a document template in the required format, and store this template file in the Windows subfolder \ShellNew.

2. Search for the file extension key (*.bmp*, for example) in the *HKEY_CLASSES_ROOT* branch, and extend this key with a *ShellNew* subkey.

3. Insert an entry with the name *NullFile* into the *ShellNew* key, and set the value to an empty string. The New command will create an empty file with the file extension used in the Registry (a BMP file, for example). This can also be done for text files.

4. To use your template for the new file, insert an entry with the name *FileName* instead of the name *NullFile* and set the value for this item to the template's filename.

The next time the system is reset, you should find the new file type in the New submenu. The following REG file statements will register a new template for an empty BAT file type. (The BATTEMPL.REG file is in the \chapter5 folder of the downloaded sample files.) The *HKEY_CLASSES_ROOT\.bat* key is already registered in Windows 95, so no path definitions are necessary.

```
REGEDIT4

[HKEY_CLASSES_ROOT\.bat\ShellNew]
"Nullfile"=""
```

After registering this file (by double-clicking it), the New submenu should contain a new MS-DOS Batch File entry. Most of the templates preinstalled by Windows 95 use a *NullFile* entry.

The following INF file copies a template file (BATFILE.BAT) into the *ShellNew* folder and registers the new template in *HKEY_CLASSES_ROOT\.bat\ShellNew*.

```
; File: Batfile.INF
;
; Enter the BAT template to the New command.
;
; The INF file also provides an uninstall function to
; recover the factory settings.

[version]
signature="$CHICAGO$"
SetupClass=BASE

; During install: Copy the template
; batfile.bat into the Windows subfolder ShellNew,
; copy the INF file for uninstall purposes,
; add the ShellNew key to \.bat, and set uninstall feature

[DefaultInstall]

CopyFiles = Bat.CopyFiles.Bat, Inf.CopyFiles.Inf
AddReg = Bat.AddReg

; During uninstall: Delete the INF file and
; the template file, and delete the Registry entries

[DefaultUninstall]
DelReg = Bat.AddReg
DelFiles = Inf.CopyFiles.Inf, Bat.CopyFiles.bat
```

(continued)

continued

```
; Add the ShellNew key into the .bat key
[Bat.AddReg]
HKCR,.bat\ShellNew,,,
HKCR,.bat\ShellNew,FileName,,"Batfile.bat"

; Add uninstall stuff
HKLM,SOFTWARE\Microsoft\Windows\CurrentVersion\Uninstall\battempl,
DisplayName,,"%REMOVE_DESC%"
HKLM,SOFTWARE\Microsoft\Windows\CurrentVersion\Uninstall\battempl,
UninstallString,,
"RunDll setupx.dll,InstallHinfSection DefaultUninstall 4 Batfile.inf"

; Don't forget this key for the uninstall part
HKLM,SOFTWARE\Microsoft\Windows\CurrentVersion\Uninstall\battempl,,,

; INF file to be copied to the Windows INF subfolder

[Inf.CopyFiles.Inf]
Batfile.Inf

; BAT template file to be copied to the Windows ShellNew subfolder
[Bat.CopyFiles.Bat]
Batfile.bat

[DestinationDirs]

Bat.CopyFiles.Bat = 10,ShellNew
Inf.CopyFiles.Inf = 17

[SourceDisksNames]
55="Batfile Template","",1

[SourceDisksFiles]
Batfile.inf=55
Batfile.bat=55

[Strings]
REMOVE_DESC = "Remove BAT template (Born)"

; End ***
```

After installing the INF file (by right-clicking the icon and selecting the Install entry from the context menu), the MS-DOS Batch File item should be available on the New submenu.

N O T E : The files BATFILE.BAT and BATFILE.INF are available in the \chapter5 folder of the downloaded sample files. You can alter this INF file to register other templates. If the settings won't take effect, try restarting the system.

Additional Information About the *ShellNew* Key

I mentioned that *ShellNew* contains the entries *NullFile* and *FileName*, but this is only half the truth. You can use the following entries in this key:

- *Nullfile=""*. Creates an empty file with the extension of the registered file type. Using this option requires that your application opens a file with a zero length.

- *Data=Binary value*. Creates a file with the registered extension and fills it with the specified binary values.

- *FileName="Name"*. Searches for the Name file in the Windows ShellNew subfolder and creates a copy in the destination folder.

- *Command="<Path>application.exe parameters"*. Contains a command to execute an application (such as a wizard) that will create the new file.

Occasionally, more than one application will register a template for a particular file type. This is the case for the DOC file type (see Figure 5-8 on the following page). Windows scans the Registry for *ShellNew* entries and adds all matches into the New subcommand, but because there can be only one *ShellNew* key used for a particular file type, the name of the template that will be used must be set in the parent key of the *ShellNew* subkey. In the *Default* value of the parent key, you will find the key name of the application currently used to open a file of that type. For example, the *Default* value of the *.doc* key shown in Figure 5-8 contains the entry *WordPad.Document.1*, so the template registered in the *\WordPad.Document.1\ShellNew* subkey is used.

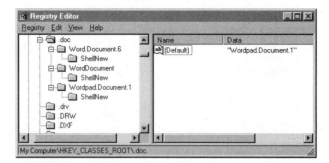

Figure 5-8.
The .doc *key in* HKEY_CLASSES_ROOT.

Changing the Shell Icons

The shell comes with a large set of predefined icons for folders, printers, file types, and so on. The files used for different file types are defined in the Registry in the *HKEY_CLASSES_ROOT* branch in the key that defines the file type properties (for example, the *ascfile* key for the ASC file type). Icons for these file types are all set in the *DefaultIcon* subkey of each file type key, as we've seen in Chapters 3 and 4. But the shell uses a lot more icons for folders, printers, and so on. These icons are registered differently. The following sections discuss how you can customize the shell icons.

How the Shell Icons Are Stored

The icons used by the shell are contained in the file SHELL32.DLL, which is in the Windows\System folder. Icons for shell components are preset and, at first glance, appear unalterable. (Maybe you recognized the *DefaultIcon* key in the branch *HKEY_CLASSES_ROOT\Folder*, but unfortunately, changing this entry has no effect on the icons used for a folder.) You could use one of those special tools available to modify icons contained in a DLL file, but that's a dangerous approach—you could inadvertently change a critical component of a module. Is there any other way?

Well, I've got good news. I've got a solution that was previously undocumented and difficult to find and that I'm happy to let you in on. I came across it while working with Tweak UI (the tool shipped with Power Toys): One optional key in the Registry can be used to redefine the settings for the shell icons. The key belongs to the Registry branch *HKEY_LOCAL_MACHINE* (because these settings are relevant to the whole machine) and is located in the branch *\SOFTWARE\Microsoft\Windows\CurrentVersion\explorer\Shell Icons*.

The *Shell Icons* key is not available by default. You will see it in your Registry only if you have used tools like the Microsoft Plus package or Tweak UI to modify something in the shell icon settings. If you have modified the icon settings, you will see entries like those shown in Figure 5-9 on the following page. (The entry shown in Figure 5-9 was created after I changed the Shortcut arrow icon with Tweak UI's Explorer property page.)

Icons used by the shell can be remapped in the *Shell Icons* key. An entry consists of a name, which is a number starting from *0* through *n*, and its associated value. The numbers are fixed for each shell icon (the number 29 affects the Shortcut arrow icon), and you will find the numbers of the most common entries in Appendix B (on pages 289–292). The value for an entry contains a pointer to the icon source and the icon index. The statement in Figure 5-9 points to SHELL32.DLL and uses the index *29* (which is the 30th icon because the index starts with *0*).

If you inspect the Registry and the *Shell Icons* key is not available, you can create this key. Then insert an entry, set the name to a number, and set the pointer to an icon source as a value. Use your own DLL file as an icon source, or redirect the pointers to other icons in SHELL32.DLL. (If the *Shell Icons* key is already available and contains some entries, you should back up this key before you alter any settings. You can use the Registry Editor export function, as described in Chapter 2, for this purpose.)

The icons shown in Appendix B are used by the shell in different places, and SHELL32.DLL contains more icons than are shown in the table (for example, the Windows flag and additional Recycle Bin icons).

You can reassign most of the icons used by the shell to some of these other icons contained in SHELL32.DLL (or in another DLL file) by adding the number shown in the first column of Appendix B as a name in the *Shell Icons* key. The value for this entry must be set to the icon source. An example of a Registry entry for the shell icon with the index *29* (which is the Shortcut arrow) is shown in Figure 5-9 on the following page.

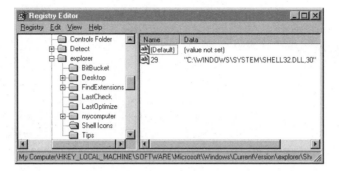

Figure 5-9.
An example of a Registry entry for a shell icon.

Icon Size and Color Depth

You need to pay attention to icon size and colors. In Windows 95, several icon sizes are used (in pixels):

- 16 × 16
- 32 × 32
- 48 × 48

The 32 × 32 pixel icons are shown on the desktop and as large icons in folder windows. The 16 × 16 pixel icons are shown as small icons. A DLL library should contain an icon image for both of these resolutions. You can set other sizes for the desktop icons by using the Appearance property page of the Display Properties property sheet. Because Windows must rescale the 32 × 32 pixel image of the icon to the new size you set, "damaged", or altered, icons are displayed on the desktop.

You can also modify icon colors in Windows 95. Icons can be stored with 16 or 256 colors. You must create six different versions for each icon (one for each color in each of the three sizes listed above) and store them in an icon file. If you create icons, make sure that your icon editor supports this feature. (One such tool is Microangelo, which is offered in various online forums.) For most of your needs, creating a 32 × 32 16-color icon will be sufficient.

Note that icons are stored in ICO files, in EXE files, or in DLL files. Be aware, if you use ICO files as an icon source, that Windows often has problems refreshing icons created from ICO files. Here is a trick that you can use to create an icon: Start a program like Microsoft Paint, create a 32 x 32 pixel image, and save the image as a 16-color or 256-color BMP file. Then use the Explorer to rename the file extension from BMP to ICO. Surprisingly, Windows will display the contents of this file as an icon (although the file is still stored in the BMP format). When using this "pseudo icon," Windows has the same problems refreshing this icon as it does refreshing icons taken from any other ICO file.

Activating Your Icon Changes

You need to know under which circumstances your changes in *Shell Icons* will take effect—simply restarting Windows won't work in every case. You might have noticed that when you use Tweak UI to change the Shortcut arrow icon or when you change the size for desktop icons on the Appearance page of the Display Properties property sheet, icon entries you have redefined in the *Shell Icons* key will also take effect.

Both of these changes cause a reset of the shell (the shell is reloaded), but you need to perform one more step in order for your changes to be visible. The Windows folder contains a file called SHELLICONCACHE. Windows keeps a copy of all icons used by the shell in this cache file. You must delete this file first and then restart the system. During the system restart, the SHELLICONCACHE file is rebuilt with the icons defined in the Registry. After the system restart, the new icons will be used by the shell.

Keeping SHELLICONCACHE to a Manageable Size

Windows keeps several icons used by the shell in the file SHELLICONCACHE. If you change the shell settings frequently, the size of the file will grow. Deleting SHELLICONCACHE from time to time will reduce its size. You can restrict the size of the icon cache by setting an optional entry in the Registry key *HKEY_LOCAL_MACHINE\SOFTWARE\Microsoft\Windows\CurrentVersion\ explorer.* You can insert the value *Max Cached Icons* to set a limit. By default, this value is not in the *explorer* key.

> N O T E :   I have read about cases where icons show up suddenly as black spots on the desktop. This can happen after you change something in the graphics adapter (or tamper too much with the *Shell Icons* key). Most of the time, the spots disappear when you delete the SHELLICONCACHE file and restart the system.

Tips for Customizing Other Shell Icons

We've looked at several techniques for changing the icons used by the shell in this chapter and in Chapter 4, but a few additional tips will help you further customize parts of the shell.

Showing BMP Files as Icons

When you open a folder, each file is shown as an individual icon; many of these are defaults and thus predefined for registered file types. When you open a folder containing icon files (which are files stored in the ICO format), the contents of the ICO files are used to show the icons. Setting the Large Icon option shows you the contents of the icon files as thumbnails. You can also force the shell to show the contents of BMP files as thumbnails by using the Registry key *HKEY_CLASSES_ROOT\Paint.Picture\DefaultIcon*.

The *Default* value is set to something like *"C:\XXXX\MSPAINT.EXE,1"*, where *XXXX* is the path to the MSPAINT.EXE file. This example value defines the second icon stored in MSPAINT.EXE as the icon source. If you set the *Default* value of the *DefaultIcon* key to *%1*, BMP files will be shown in a folder as thumbnails (see Figure 5-10). You can use the files BMPON.REG and BMPOFF.REG in the \chapter5 folder of the downloaded sample files to turn this option on and off.

Figure 5-10.
BMP and ICO files shown as thumbnails.

Maybe you already know this trick, but I bet you don't know why it works with BMP files. Here's the scoop: The Registry contains the entries for registered file types in *HKEY_CLASSES_ROOT*. A file type entry might have a

DefaultIcon key, which defines the icon source for that file type. In Chapter 4, I mentioned that a registered file type can have the placeholder *%1* in the *DefaultIcon* key, which enables the icon handler to set an individual icon for each file instance.

The ActiveX handler for BMP files implements this *%1* placeholder feature. (BMP and ICO are file formats used internally in Windows.) If the *%1* placeholder is found, the handler reads the content of the BMP file, rescales it, and displays it as an icon symbol. (You will get the best results when the BMP file is 32 × 32 pixels in size.) The ICO file handler functions the same way. If other handlers that support the *IExtractIcon* interface are already installed, you can use this feature for other file types.

> N O T E :   You can also register the CLSID of a separate *IconHandler* in the *shellex* branch of a registered file type and add to it the value *DefaultIcon = %1*. The application must provide its own icon handler to implement the *IExtractIcon* interface, which is used by the shell to retrieve icons. Further information about this topic can be found in the *Programmer's Guide to Microsoft Windows 95* and in Nancy Cluts's book *Programming the Windows 95 User Interface*.

Changing the Icon of a Drive

When you open a window containing local or remote drives, the drive symbols are shown. The shell provides default symbols for each drive type, but you can change the icon for a drive type in the *Shell Icons* key. Add the index number as a value into this key, set the string to a new icon source, delete the SHELLICONCACHE file, and reset the computer. All drives of the type you changed will be shown with the new symbol. (See Figure 5-11.)

Figure 5-11.
Folder with the new drive symbols.

Is there a simpler way? Can you assign individual icons to selected drives without hacking in the Registry? Yes, you can. I discovered this trick a few months ago while creating a CD-ROM. If you insert a CD-ROM into a drive, the default icon for the CD-ROM drive will be substituted with another icon. The reason is fairly simple: This CD-ROM contains in its root directory a file with the name AUTORUN.INF, which can be used to start an application when the CD-ROM is inserted into the drive. An AUTORUN.INF file may contain, for example, the following statements:

```
open=Start.exe
icon=BornIcon.dll,10
```

The first line defines the name of an executable application that will be invoked after the CD-ROM is inserted into the drive. The second line defines the name of an icon file used for the drive's symbol. Double-clicking the CD-ROM symbol activates the *open* command defined in the INF file. (The Registry settings will be temporarily overwritten.)

It is possible to store an AUTORUN.INF file containing only this line in the root directory of a hard disk drive:

```
icon=BornIcon.dll,11
```

But you must also store an icon source on this drive. (It can be in the root or in a subfolder like \Icons\BORNICONS.DLL.) The result will be visible the next time that the screen refreshes—the drive gets its own icon. (If you don't want to store an icon file on each drive, assign the same icon index in the icon statement of AUTORUN.INF on the other drives. Windows will cache this icon in SHELLICONCACHE.) If you delete the AUTORUN.INF file, the old drive symbol is shown.

Changing the Shortcut Symbol

You can change the Shortcut arrow icon in two ways. The first way is to define a pointer to a new icon source in the *Shell Icons* key, delete the SHELLICONS-CACHE file, and restart the computer. The more efficient way is to use Tweak UI for this task. If you invoke Tweak UI (an option from the Control Panel) and select the Explorer property page, you will see the Shortcut Overlay section containing options to customize the shortcut icon (see Figure 5-6 on page 196).

Selecting the Custom option button opens a Change Icon window showing all icons in the SHELL32.DLL file. Within this window, you can select a new icon and apply the settings. Tweak UI will handle all the details.

CHAPTER SIX

Miscellaneous Registry Settings

The Registry contains many entries that control internal Windows 95 settings. Some of these entries will influence parts of the shell, others are used only within the Windows kernel. In this chapter, I discuss some of these miscellaneous parts of the Registry.

Sound Events in the Registry

If you have installed a sound card or the SPEAKER.DRV driver, you can assign different sounds to Windows events, such as the Start Windows and Close Program commands. You can also control events for application programs. For example, in Exchange, you can enable or disable a sound event for the receipt of a message. To be able to hear and manipulate sound events, you have to have a sound device installed. In this section, we'll look at how to set up sound events and how Windows handles these values in the Registry.

Where Events Are Registered

Sound events are user-specific, and users can define their own sounds if user profiles are enabled on their systems. Sound events are registered in the *HKEY_CURRENT_USER\AppEvents* key, in the *EventLabels* and *Schemes* subkeys. (See Figure 6-1 on the following page.) Copies of sound event settings are also stored in *HKEY_USERS* under the name of the current user. In most cases, you have to set options in only the *HKEY_CURRENT_USER* key because Windows automatically updates the other branches when you shut down the system. If no user profiles are set, copies of these settings are stored in the key *HKEY_USERS\.Default.*

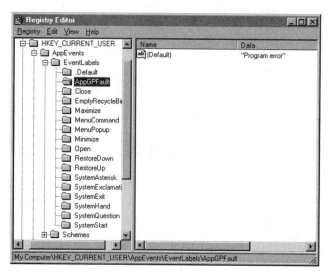

Figure 6-1.
Sound event settings are registered in the \EventLabels *and* \Schemes
subkeys.

The *EventLabels* Key

The subkeys of the branch *HKEY_CURRENT_USER\AppEvents\EventLabels*
(*.Default, AppGPFault, Close, Open*, and so on) define the events available in Windows. The default value of each subkey contains the string (see the Data column in Figure 6-1) that is shown in the Events list of the Sounds property page.
The Sounds property page is shown in Figure 6-2.

Where Can I Edit Sound Events?

You can edit sound events by selecting options on the Sounds property
page (which is available by double-clicking the Sounds icon in the
Control Panel) or by modifying settings in the Registry Editor. The
Sounds property page is the least risky and most convenient tool available for online editing.

If you want to distribute software with sounds associated to specific
events, you should use INF files to register the sound files and events.
(By default, Windows 95 uses the subfolder \Media in the \Windows
folder to store the WAV files used for sound events. Knowing this, you
could use a REG file rather than an INI file, but remember: Folder
names can be changed from the default. In that case, the REG file
won't work.)

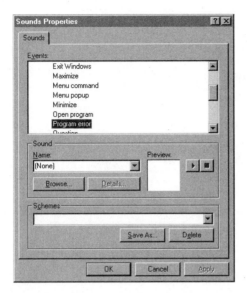

Figure 6-2.
The Sounds property page.

To customize a string shown in the Events list, redefine the value for the *Default* entry of this event. Table 6-1 gives a brief overview of the subkeys in *\EventLabels*.

Keys in *\EventLabels*

Key	Description
.Default	Defines the "Default sound" event
AppGPFault	Activates when a program error occurs
Close	Executes before a program is closed
EmptyRecycleBin	Activates when the Recycle Bin is emptied
Maximize	Activates when a window is maximized
MenuCommand	Indicates that a menu command is clicked
MenuPopup	Activates when a menu pops up
Minimize	Activates when a window is minimized
Open	Executes during opening of a program
RestoreDown	Activates when a window is restored to its default size after being maximized

Table 6-1. *(continued)*
Keys for registering sound events.

Table 6-1. *continued*

Key	Description
RestoreUp	Activates when a window is restored to its previous size after being minimized
SystemAsterisk	Used for the system's Asterisk events, such as when an error message box appears
SystemExclamation	Used in a message box with an exclamation mark icon
SystemExit	Executes before Windows exits
SystemHand	Activates when the system's hand cursor is shown, to imply a critical stop
SystemQuestion	Used in a message box with a question mark icon
SystemStart	Executes during each Windows startup

The *Schemes* Key

Sound schemes are sets of sounds that users define for particular applications to mark events such as the opening of an application or the closing of an application. These schemes can be defined on the Sounds property page or registered in the subkeys of *HKEY_CURRENT_USER\AppEvents\Schemes. Schemes* contains the *ControlIniTimeStamp* entry, which is used internally by Windows. The *Default* value for the *Schemes* key is set to the name of the scheme currently being used (such as *.Current*). The *Schemes* subkey *Apps* contains the applications registered for sound events, and the subkey *Names* contains the names of schemes defined for sound events.

The *Apps* subkey   Applications registered for sound events are listed in the *Apps* subkey, which is shown in Figure 6-3. Note the *.Default* subkey, which contains the keys for Windows events, and the subkeys for additional applications such as the Microsoft Explorer or the Media Player. Each program's EXE file is used as the subkey's name. To register sound files for a particular application, add that application as a key. We'll look at this in more detail later on in the chapter.

Keys for applications such as the Explorer contain subkeys that are named with the verbs of the possible sound events, such as *open* and *MenuCommand*. (These names are defined in the *EventLabels* key we examined earlier.) Take a look at Figure 6-3 and note the *open* subkey of the Explorer branch. It contains three subkeys with the names of available schemes: *.Current*, *.default*, and *born0*. Each of these subkeys contains the path description to a particular sound file. Windows uses the WAV file format by default; these files are stored in the Windows subfolder \Media. Notice in the Data column that I used the RINGOUT.WAV file for the Explorer's open event. Storing this file in the *.Current* subkey of the *open* key means that the sound will be played each time the Explorer is invoked. If I wanted to hear a sound whenever the Explorer terminates, I'd need to add the *close* key and the sound scheme's subkeys to *Explorer* and define a path to the particular sound file. Windows can do a lot of this setting up for you, and we'll look at that a bit later.

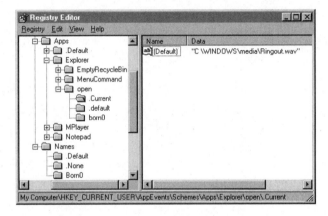

Figure 6-3.
Subkeys of the Apps *subkey.*

The *Names* subkey   The *Names* subkey contains only the names of the schemes defined for sound events and always contains the following two subkeys: *.Default* and *.None*. Any sound modification that the user makes and then stores as a new scheme on the Sounds property page is added to *Names* as a new key. The key name is restricted to seven characters and always terminates with a digit. If a new entry matches an existing key, Windows changes the last digit from *0* to *1*, from *1* to *2*, and so on until there is no match. The name that the user gives this new key is stored in the *Default* value of the key.

215

The *Names* key and its subkeys are used by the Sounds property page. When you save a new scheme, the scheme's name will be inserted as a key into the \Apps\application name\event name subkey for each event of each registered application, and the settings from the .Current key of each branch will be copied into each occurrence of the new key. For example, look again at Figure 6-3 on the preceding page. The scheme Born0 has been defined and added as a subkey to the *Names* key. You can see also that *born0* (case insensitive) has been added as a subkey to the *Apps\Explorer\open* key. The *Default* value of *born0* in the *open* key contains the same information as the *Default* value of the .Current key ("C:\WINDOWS\media\Ringout.wav"). The name of the active scheme is defined in the *Default* value of the *Schemes* key. (This is different from the way Windows stores the color schemes, for example, and it may be a little difficult to use the Registry Editor to maintain the Registry entries for a scheme. Therefore I advise you to use the Sounds property page to fine-tune the settings, and leave it to Windows to ensure that the right settings will be used.)

NOTE: Sound events can be very helpful to people with disabilities, enabling them to use their computers more efficiently. Sound events are also a great gimmick, but having too many of them slows down the system considerably because an action will not occur until the associated sound is played. So it's a good idea to limit sound events to critical actions.

Registering a Sound Event for an Application

The way you set up a sound event for an application depends on whether that application is registered. If the application is registered, you can associate sounds with particular application events on the Sounds property page. Double-click the Sounds icon in the Control Panel, and follow these steps:

1. Search for the entry with the application name.

2. Click the entry for the event (open or close, for example), and associate one of the available sound files. Repeat this step for all sound events available for this application.

3. If you want to keep the original settings and your new settings, click Save As to save the settings into a new scheme, and close the property page. (See Figure 6-4.)

The last step generates all necessary subkeys to define the sound events in the *Apps* subkey. If Windows detects some missing subkeys (in the *open* and *close* branches, for example), these keys are added automatically.

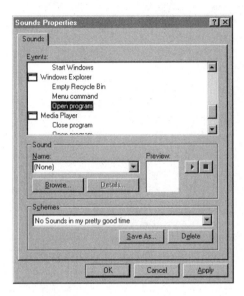

Figure 6-4.
Entries for an application's sound events.

If the application isn't yet registered, you won't be able to find the application name in the Events list of the Sounds property page, and you'll need to add the filename of the application to the following key:

HKEY_CURRENT_USER\AppEvents\Schemes\Apps

Suppose, for example, we want to extend the Registry with and assign sounds to the open and close events for the Notepad text editor. To register the events, follow these steps:

1. Extend the *HKEY_CURRENT_USER\AppEvents\Schemes\Apps* key with a *Notepad* subkey. Notepad is the name of the EXE file, so the Windows Session Manager should recognize the application when it loads it into memory.

2. Add the *open* and *close* subkeys to *HKEY_CURRENT_USER\AppEvents\ Schemes\Apps\Notepad*. Both subkey names are already registered in the *HKEY_CURRENT_USER\AppEvents\EventLabels* key as global system events. The new subkeys enable you to supersede the global settings with individual parameters for this application.

217

Steps 1 and 2 prepare the system for the new sound event by registering the application and the events. You could also register the application and events using a REG file. At this point we can use a REG file because we don't need paths for the Registry settings and we don't have to ensure, yet, that sound files are available. Here's the SOUND.REG file (located in the \chapter6 folder of the downloaded sample files):

```
REGEDIT4

[HKEY_CURRENT_USER\AppEvents\Schemes\Apps\Notepad]
@="Windows Notepad"

[HKEY_CURRENT_USER\AppEvents\Schemes\Apps\Notepad\open]

[HKEY_CURRENT_USER\AppEvents\Schemes\Apps\Notepad\close]
```

So now the System is aware of the new open and close events, but no sounds are associated with them. (This is the default for most events.) You've got to tell Windows which sounds you want to hear when the events occur. You could do this by messing around in the Registry, but it would be a little bit difficult for several reasons. First, you'd have to be sure that the WAV files were in the correct folder (preferably, in the Windows\Media subfolder). Sound files are optional components in the Windows 95 setup, so if you didn't intend to create your own sound files, you would have to be sure the Windows 95 sound files have been installed. Second, you'd have to know the status of schemes already defined in the *Apps* subkeys. You would need to define a subkey with an associated sound file for each existing scheme.

You could handle only about half of this job with a simple INF file by adding a fixed subkey name to the scheme (for example, \open\.default). The entries would be updated when the user saved a new scheme using the Sounds property page. As a result, you'd want to be careful using the .Current scheme to store your new settings, because these settings could get lost if the user didn't save the new scheme after changing the entries on the Sounds property page.

So as you can see, hacking in the Registry is probably not the best way to associate sounds with events. Your best bet, once you've registered the application, is to define the sound events on the Sounds property page.

Establishing a Sound Event for an Empty Recycle Bin

If you inspect the *HKEY_CURRENT_USER\AppEvents\Schemes\Apps* branch, you'll find the *Explorer* key containing an *EmptyRecycleBin* subkey. (See Figure 6-3 on page 215.) The EmptyRecycleBin event occurs when the user empties the Recycle Bin, and you can associate a sound file to this event.

1. If the *EmptyRecycleBin* subkey is not available, use a REG file (such as BINSOUND.REG, located in the \chapter6 folder of the downloaded sample files) or the Registry Editor to add this entry into the *HKEY_CURRENT_USER\AppEvents\Schemes\Apps\Explorer* branch.

2. Invoke the Sounds property page (by opening the Control Panel and selecting Sounds). Select the Empty Recycle Bin entry in the Windows Explorer branch and associate a sound file.

After you close the property sheet by clicking OK, the new sound event is registered. If you right-click the Recycle Bin icon and select the Empty Recycle Bin command from the context menu, a sound notification is sent to your sound device.

Setting Up Application Paths in the Registry

A path defines where program files (EXE) and DLL libraries are located. In Windows 95, you can define a path in two ways. One way is to define a global path in the MS-DOS PATH environment variable, which is set in the AUTOEXEC.BAT file during system startup. This solution isn't state of the art, however, because AUTOEXEC.BAT is used only for compatibility purposes with old application programs. The path environment variable set in AUTOEXEC.BAT defines a global path used for all applications, so if you use many applications that have their own folders, the path command gets too long to fit into the environment variable. The more efficient option, then, is to define paths in the Registry. The Registry contains a key where application programs can register their own paths.

Entries in the *App Paths* Key

An application that conforms to the standards set in the *Windows Interface Guidelines for Software Design* stores files in different folders: The EXE file of an application is located in a subfolder with the application's name (for example, the BornTool application is stored in the ...\BornTool subfolder); the DLL and HLP files are located in a system folder (for example, ...\BornTool\System). This file structure is contained in the following Registry key:

*HKEY_LOCAL_MACHINE\SOFTWARE\Microsoft\Windows\CurrentVersion\
App Paths*

A setup program for this application adds a new subkey into this branch. The key's name is defined by the EXE file. For example, if the application is executed with the BORNTOOL.EXE file, the following key is added into the Registry:

HKEY_LOCAL_MACHINE\Microsoft\Windows\CurrentVersion\App Paths\ BornTool.Exe

This new key can contain two values with path strings:

- *The* Default *value.* The *Default* value of the key must be set to the path and name of the EXE program. Windows uses this string to load the application into the memory. If the application program BORNTOOL.EXE is stored in the folder C:\Born\, the *Default* value of the key is set to *C:\Born\BornTool.exe*. This value may also contain additional parameters to control the application.

- *The* Path *value.* If the application uses DLL files, an optional *Path* value can be inserted into the key. This *Path* value contains the paths to the folders required by the application. This value can contain several path definitions separated by semicolons (*"C:\Born; C:\Born\System;"*, for example).

The following lines show the *App Paths* entry for the Microsoft Network Signup program SIGNUP.EXE:

```
REGEDIT4

[HKEY_LOCAL_MACHINE\SOFTWARE\Microsoft\Windows\CurrentVersion\
AppPaths\SIGNUP.EXE]
@="C:\\Progra~1\\TheMic~1\\SIGNUP.EXE"
"Path"="C:\\Progra~1\\TheMic~1;"
```

The *Default* value points to the \Program Files\The Microsoft Network folder, which contains the file SIGNUP.EXE. The *Path* value uses the same path to direct Windows 95 to the folder where the DLL and data files will be found. In this example, the old eight-character file conventions are used in the folder names, but you can also use the long filenames allowed by Windows 95 within the folders.

NOTE: If you start an application by typing the name of the EXE file—without a path—in the Run dialog box accessible from the Windows Start menu, Windows will look for the file in the current directory. If the file is not in the current directory, Windows will look at the *Default* value in the appropriate *EXE* subkey of the *App Paths* key.

Entries in the *SharedDLLs* Key

When an application shares DLL files with other programs, the install program creates a new entry in the following key:

HKEY_LOCAL_MACHINE\SOFTWARE\ Microsoft\Windows\ CurrentVersion\SharedDLLs

The value name is set to the name and path of the shared DLL file. The value itself is a binary counter. Each install program will increment this value if the installed application uses this shared DLL file. If the application is removed, the uninstaller should decrement this value by 1. If the counter reaches the value *0*, the user can remove the Registry value and the DLL. Figure 6-5 shows example entries in the *SharedDLLs* key. These DLL routines are currently used by only one application each.

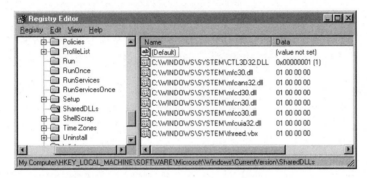

Figure 6-5.
Keys for shared DLL routines.

> NOTE: An uninstall routine removes all application files, including the DLL files. When files are shared, the uninstall routine does not remove the files because they might be used by other applications. So it's a good idea to use the values in *SharedDLLs* to determine whether a shared DLL file can be removed. If the key value is decremented to *0*, you can safely remove the DLL file.
>
> The only problem I foresee is with install and uninstall programs that misbehave. A good install program detects when a user tries to install the same application several times and does not increment the value for the shared DLL. (If this were not the case, you would never be able to remove the DLL files after uninstalling all other applications.) Likewise, a good uninstall program detects when a user tries to uninstall a program more than once and so decrements

the counter only once. (If the uninstall feature did not detect this, the counter would be decremented to zero and the file would be removed, disabling the other applications relying on that DLL.)

Entries in the *Shared Tools* Key

Some Microsoft application programs share software tools that enable them to perform certain functions. For example, Microsoft Word, Microsoft Excel, and Microsoft Access share graphics filters that allow them to import a variety of file formats. Information about shared software components that are already installed is stored in the following Registry key:

> *HKEY_LOCAL_MACHINE\SOFTWARE\Microsoft\Shared Tools*

These filter modules are installed from application setup programs and stored in folders. For example, when Windows 95 is installed, the MSPAINT.EXE program is installed in the \Program Files\Accessories folder. This folder also contains a PCX graphics filter required by MSPaint. When you install Microsoft Office components, other graphics components will be copied onto the hard disk as well and stored in folders.

This key can contain subkeys that define the location of shared tools provided by Microsoft applications. Graphics filters are located in the subkey *Graphics Filters\Import*, with each graphical file type having a subkey such as *BMP* or *PCX*. Each subkey has three values:

- *Extensions,* which contains the file extensions for the file types that use the graphical filter interface
- *Name,* which contains the name of the filter
- *Path,* which contains the path to the filter file

Other applications can access this information from the Registry to use existing filter interfaces.

Other subkeys of *Shared Tools* (such as *AutoCorrect, Equation,* and *JPEG*) contain information about other shared components available in Windows 95. A related key, *HKEY_LOCAL_MACHINE\SOFTWARE\Microsoft\Shared Tools Location,* is used by Microsoft Office products to find the path to the folder that contains additional shared modules specific to Office.

Miscellaneous Application Settings

The Registry contains several keys that store system and application settings. These keys are described in the following sections.

HKEY_LOCAL_MACHINE\SOFTWARE

Application programs insert subkeys that define machine-specific settings in this key. Microsoft uses a key with the name *\Microsoft* to store such settings for all Microsoft products. If you have installed different software packages, you'll notice other subkeys in *HKEY_LOCAL_MACHINE\SOFTWARE* (such as the *SCC* key and the *ODBC* key for ODBC driver settings). The names and contents of these subkeys are vendor-specific.

Windows System programs store information in the subkeys of the *\Microsoft\Windows\CurrentVersion* key of this branch. For example, Backup stores backup configurations and the flag denoting whether a tape drive is detected in the *\Applets\Backup* key. ScanDisk stores information about the error-checking status in the *\Applets\Check Drive* key. (This information can be viewed on the Tools property page of a drive. Right-click the drive symbol and select Properties.) Other keys, such as *\explorer\LastOptimize* and *\explorer\ LastCheck*, are used by ScanDisk and Defrag to store information about the time the user ran the last optimize and check procedures.

HKEY_CURRENT_USER\Software

An application's user-specific settings are stored here. Windows keeps the settings for all registered users in the *HKEY_USERS* branch upon system exit (unless the No Save Settings On Exit option is enabled).

HKEY_USERS\xxxx\Software\Microsoft\Windows\CurrentVersion\ Applets

This key contains subkeys that are inserted by application programs in order to store settings for the specific user *xxxx*. For example, MSPaint and WordPad store their *Recent File List* and other application-specific parameters under this key, and user-specific data for ScanDisk can be found in the *Check Drive* subkey. (None of the values used by ScanDisk should be altered by the user; the tool maintains the data during each check and optimize process.)

Launching Programs During the Windows Startup

During Windows startup, you can have Windows automatically start applications for you by putting a shortcut to the application in the Windows\Start Menu\Programs\Startup folder. This works well for users, but when a developer creates an application that needs to run at Windows startup, the most reliable method is for the application's setup program to store the startup information in the Registry. This is where the *Run* keys come in.

Registry Keys for Launching Applications and Services

The four Registry keys that launch applications and services are located in the branch *HKEY_LOCAL_MACHINE\SOFTWARE\Microsoft\Windows\CurrentVersion*. These *Run* keys are shown in Figure 6-6 and described in the following sections.

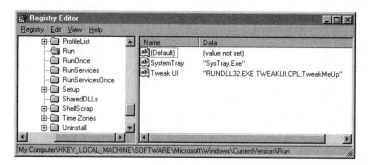

Figure 6-6.
The Run *keys launch applications during a system startup.*

Run

Applications registered in the *Run* key are executed during each Windows 95 startup. Each entry in this key consists of the application's name and a string value. This string value contains the path and the name of the application to launch. Figure 6-6 shows two entries, *SystemTray* and *Tweak UI*, in the *Run* key.

RunOnce

This key contains values with the names and paths of applications that will be executed only once during a Windows startup; Windows removes the entries in this key after the system successfully starts. If an install program must execute a reset, it can enter its own name and the required options into this key and force a Windows restart. After a successful restart of Windows, the install program is executed and can continue the install process.

RunServices

This key is used to launch network or system services during a Windows startup. The entries are structured in this key as they are in the *Run* key: a value with the name of the service and a string pointing to the name of the program to execute.

RunServicesOnce

This key can be used by the setup programs of network components in order to execute a network service only once during the next Windows startup. After a successful restart, the entries in this key are removed.

Modifying the *Run* Keys

You can modify these four Registry keys using the Registry Editor, a setup program, an INF file, or the System Policy Editor, which contains a few modification options in the System branch. (See Figure 6-7.) To modify the keys using the System Policy Editor, follow these steps:

1. Start the System Policy Editor, and open the Registry by selecting Open Registry from the File menu.

2. Double-click the Local Computer icon.

3. Select one of the Run key checkboxes (Run, Run Once, or Run Services) from the System branch, and then click Show.

4. Edit the list of applications in the Show Contents window.

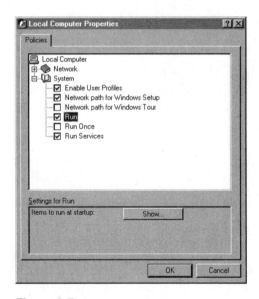

Figure 6-7.
Entries in the System Policy Editor to set the Run, RunOnce, *and* RunServices *keys.*

> NOTE: Not only is it easy for a setup program to modify these keys during a software installation, but you can also use these keys in an INF file. The *Run* keys also enable you to launch an application without the user knowing about it. If you use the Startup folder, there is a risk that the user will accidentally delete these entries.

Settings for the File System

The Windows 95 file system features long filenames, a tool for remapping long filenames to standard DOS 8.3 names, and other options such as caches. This section examines Registry entries that relate to file system settings.

Disabling Long Filenames

If your network environment is not fully compatible with the long filenames of Windows 95, you can disable this long filenames feature, thus enabling a Windows 95 client to generate only filenames in the 8.3 format. The settings for the file system are kept in the following Registry branch:

HKEY_LOCAL_MACHINE\System\CurrentControlSet\control\FileSystem

NOTE: This key contains several subkeys and values containing the file system settings used on hard disks and floppy disks. (See the *Windows 95 Resource Kit* for information about the architecture of the Windows modules used by the file system.)

The information about long filenames is kept in a value with the name *WIN31FileSystem*. This value is set to *00* by default. If you switch the value to *01* and restart the computer, the old DOS and Windows 3.1 file system with 8.3 filenames will be used.

You can use the Registry Editor to change this flag, but a better way is offered by the System Policy Editor. (Click the Local Computer icon, then select Microsoft Client For Netware Networks under the Network branch, and check the Support Long File Names option.)

Modifying the Mapping of Alias Names

For reasons of compatibility with older applications, Windows 95 provides a function to generate 8.3 aliases from long filenames. The alias name is created from the beginning characters of the long filename (typically, the first six), a tilde (~), and a numerical tail (as in BORNJA~1.DOC). If two alias names match in a folder, Windows distinguishes one from the other by modifying one of the numerical tails, which generates a new alias. In the best case, the result is a six-character name. Abbreviated alias names are more difficult to read, and you can force Windows 95 to use eight characters for the alias name by entering the value

NameNumericTail = 0

to the following key:

HKEY_LOCAL_MACHINE\System\CurrentControlSet\control\FileSystem

This can be done with the Registry Editor or with the following REG file:

```
REGEDIT4

[HKEY_LOCAL_MACHINE\System\CurrentControlSet\control\FileSystem]
"NameNumericTail"=hex:00
```

After you reboot the system, the feature that maps the long filenames to the alias names will use eight characters whenever using these eight characters doesn't create duplicate filenames. The ALIASOFF.REG file is located in the \chapter6 folder of the downloaded sample files.

Setting Miscellaneous Options in the *FileSystem* Key

The *FileSystem* key contains additional entries for configuring the file system. All of these entries can be set through the Hard Disk, CD-ROM, and Troubleshooting property pages of the File System Properties property sheet. This property sheet is available by clicking the System icon in the Control Panel and then clicking File System on the Performance property page. If values for these entries are not in the *FileSystem* key, Windows uses the default setting.

AsyncFileCommit

This value is set to *00* by default, which enables a synchronous commit of buffers to disk. Setting this value to *01* enables an asynchronous file commit. The flag is affected by the setting of the Disable Synchronous Buffer Commits option, which is available from the Troubleshooting property page (see Figure 6-8).

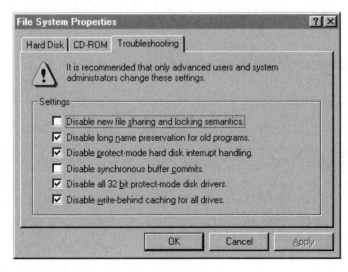

Figure 6-8.
The Troubleshooting property page.

LastBootPMDrvs

This flag is set to the number of the last boot driver.

ReadAheadThreshold

This value defines a threshold for the read-ahead buffer. When an application requests data, Windows automatically reads ahead, in increments, up to the threshold value. *ReadAheadThreshold* is set with the Read-Ahead Optimization slider, available on the Hard Disk property page. This property page is available through the File System Properties property sheet.

DriveWriteBehind

This value enables and disables the write-behind caching for all drives, ensuring that data is continually flushed from caches to the hard disk. This value can be set using the Disable Write-Behind Caching For All Drives checkbox on the Troubleshooting property page. Selecting this option sets the value to *00 00 00 00*; deselecting this option sets the value to *FF FF FF FF*. By default, the flag is deselected and *DriveWriteBehind* is not displayed in the Registry.

PreserveLongNames

This value enables and disables the Windows 95 feature that preserves long filenames even after a file has been opened and saved by an application that does not support long filenames. The value can be set using the Disable Long Name Preservation For Old Programs option on the Troubleshooting property page. Selecting this option sets *PreserveLongNames* to *FF FF FF FF*; deselecting it sets the value to *00 00 00 00*. By default, the option is deselected and *PreserveLongNames* is not displayed in the Registry.

ForceRMIO

If this flag is set to *01*, the Real Mode disk IO is forced (in other words, 32-bit access is disabled). This flag is controlled using the Disable All 32 Bit Protect-Mode Disk Drivers option, available on the Troubleshooting property page. By default, this flag is set to *00*.

VirtualHDIRQ

Enabling this option prevents Windows 95 from terminating interrupts from the hard disk controller and is controlled using the Disable Protect-Mode Hard Disk Interrupt Handling checkbox, available on the Troubleshooting property page. A value of *0* enables this feature; a value of *1* (the default) disables this feature.

SoftCompatMode

This value enables and disables the rules for file sharing and locking and can be set using the Disable New File Sharing And Locking Semantics option on the Troubleshooting property page. Selecting this option sets the value to *00*; deselecting it sets the value to *01* (the default).

CDFS Subkey

The *CDFS* subkey contains the entries *CacheSize, PrefetchTail,* and *Prefetch,* which control the CD-ROM cache settings. You can set or view these entries on the CD-ROM property page of the File System Properties property sheet.

The *CacheSize* value defines the size of one cache buffer block. The *PrefetchTail* value defines the number of cache buffer blocks. Multiplying these two values will tell you the size of the physical memory used by Windows to read CD-ROM data. This combined value is shown on the CD-ROM property page. (See Figure 6-9.) The *Prefetch* value, which is set in the Optimize Access Pattern For list box, specifies the speed of the CD-ROM drive.

> **N O T E :** Other settings for the CD-ROM driver, including *Required Pause Tolerance* and *Desired Lru1 Percentage,* are located in the following key:
>
> *HKEY_LOCAL_MACHINE\SOFTWARE\Microsoft\Windows\CurrentVersion\ CD-ROM*

The subkey *\FileSystem\NoVolTrack* contains values for devices that don't have a volume track (such as ROM disks).

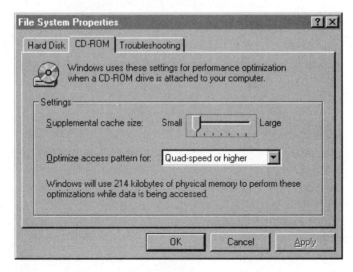

Figure 6-9.
Set the values for the CD-ROM cache.

NameCache and *PathCache*

On the Hard Disk property page, which is shown in Figure 6-10, you can define the role of the machine you are using: Desktop Computer, Mobile Or Docking System, or Network Server. Your role selection here determines the size of the *NameCache* and *PathCache* values.

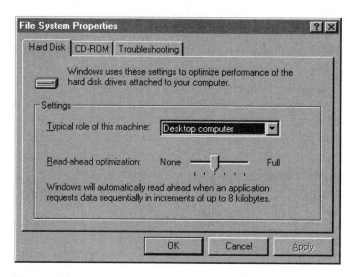

Figure 6-10.
On the Hard Disk property page, you determine the role of the computer you are using.

How does this feature work? Windows 95 stores and retrieves the names and paths of the last files read in caches. The *NameCache* entry defines the size of the cache used to buffer filenames. The *PathCache* entry defines the size (number of entries in) of the path cache. Both caches are implemented in the Windows 95 system heap. Table 6-2 shows the sizes of the values for each machine "role":

NameCache and *PathCache* Values

Machine Role	Cache	Value
Desktop Computer	*NameCache*	*32*
	PathCache	*677*
Mobile Computing	*NameCache*	*16*
	PathCache	*377*
Network Server	*NameCache*	*64*
	PathCache	*2729*

Table 6-2.
The entries define the size of the values for each machine role.

These cache settings are stored in the *Desktop, Mobile,* and *Server* subkeys of the following Registry key:

HKEY_LOCAL_MACHINE\SOFTWARE\Microsoft\Windows\CurrentVersion
FS Templates

The *Default* value of the *FS Templates* key contains the name of the selected file system template (for example, *Desktop*). The *Default* value of each subkey contains the name shown in the list box on the Hard Disk property page. If the *PathCache* and *NameCache* values are not shown in the *Desktop* key settings, the default values will be used.

You can define your own profile and fine-tune the cache size. To do this, insert a new subkey into the *FS Template* key, insert a text string into the default value of the added key, and then define the values for *NameCache* and *PathCache.* (In Figure 6-11, I defined the new profile *Born* with my own settings.) After you define a new key and its values, this subkey will be shown as an entry in the Settings group list box on the Hard Disk property page.

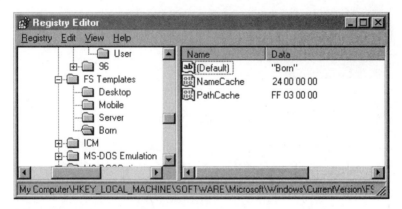

Figure 6-11.
Entries defining the file system templates.

System Properties in the Registry

The Registry contains the settings for the system properties. Most of these settings are defined during Windows Setup and during the installing and uninstalling of hardware components. Some of these properties can be altered on the System Properties property sheet. (Open the Control Panel, then select System.) In this section, we'll look at how the information for hardware profiles and device manager data is stored.

Hardware Profiles

Windows detects the hardware components currently available for dockable computers. You can create profiles for the current configuration on the Hardware Profiles property page (Figure 6-12).

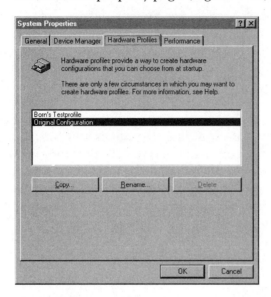

Figure 6-12.
Create profiles on the Hardware Profiles property page.

If you have a mobile computer with different docking stations, you might want to create a hardware profile for each configuration and set a unique name for each profile. You can do this by clicking Copy, which saves the current settings in a separate hardware profile. During the next system startup, you will see a menu asking which hardware profile should be used, and you can select the appropriate configuration.

Windows uses two keys in the Registry to store information about the hardware profiles:

- *HKEY_LOCAL_MACHINE\System\CurrentControlSet\control\ IDConfigDB* stores global information about the profiles. The *CurrentConfig* value defines the name of the profile currently used. The value is set to a string, such as *"0001"*, which is just a pointer to a subkey of this name that is contained in the *HKEY_LOCAL_MACHINE\Config* branch. So an entry such as *friendlyName0001* would contain the profile names shown in Figure 6-12.

■ *HKEY_LOCAL_MACHINE\Config* stores the hardware profile itself. This key has an additional subkey for each defined hardware profile. These profile subkeys are named *0001, 0002*, and so on. The current profile is indicated by the *CurrentConfig* value mentioned in the preceding bullet. A profile subkey contains the subkeys *Display* and *System*.

The *Display* subkey contains the subkeys *Fonts*, with the font properties used by the system, and *Settings*, with the screen settings. The *Settings* key contains data about the screen resolution, metrics, and so on. Changing the Hardware Acceleration slider on the Advanced Graphics Settings dialog box affects some of the entries in the *Settings* key. (The Advanced Graphics Settings dialog box is available by clicking Graphics on the Performance property page.) By default, the Hardware Acceleration slider is set to Full. Moving the slider to the left adds values to the *Settings* key. For example, moving the slider one notch to the left adds a value named *SwCursor*, set to *1*, which indicates that the hardware cursor support in the display driver is disabled. Setting the slider to None sets the entries *Advanced=0* and *SwCursor=1*.

The *System* subkey contains the *CurrentControlSet* subkey with additional subkeys that define the names of the printer drivers.

Storing and Manipulating Hardware Component and Plug & Play Information

The *HKEY_LOCAL_MACHINE\Enum* key and the device manager allow you to view the status of and customize your system components. Specifically, *\Enum* stores information about the hardware and Plug & Play (PnP) components of your system, and the device manager enables you to manipulate the device configuration. The device manager uses the information stored in *\Enum*.

Values in the *\Enum* Key

The *\Enum* key contains subkeys for the specific hardware components used by the computer. Windows uses this information to allocate resources, such as IO addresses, interrupts, and so on, for the devices. All values in the *\Enum* branch are vendor- and device-specific, so specific information about parameters is not available. The following list briefly describes entries contained in the *\Enum* key. Figure 6-13 on page 235 shows the *\Enum* key.

■ *BIOS*. This subkey contains entries for PnP components of the *BIOS* (which includes timers, controllers, and DMA chips). Each *BIOS* subkey starts with the string **PNP* and is followed by a four-digit number that represents classes by which the components are grouped: *PNP0000*. (Table 6-3 below lists some of the PnP component codes.) Each *PNPxxxx* key contains subkeys (*00, 01*) that contain the data (such as class name, device description string, driver name, and hardware ID) for the device configuration.

- *ESDI*. This subkey contains the configuration data of the ESDI controller used for hard disk drives and other devices.

- *FLOP*. This subkey contains the configuration data of the floppy disk controllers used in the system.

- *HTREE*. This subkey is reserved for future use by Windows.

- *ISAPNP*. This subkey contains entries for PnP equipment used on an ISA bus system.

- *MF*. This subkey defines manufacturer-specific information about hardware components.

- *Monitor*. This subkey contains information about the monitor used in the system. If the setup can't detect the monitor type, the selection is set by the user.

- *Network*. This subkey contains information about the network (redirectors, services, NetBEUI, and so on). The network adapter is specified in the *Root\Net* subkey.

- *PCI*. This subkey contains entries for PnP equipment used on a PCI bus system.

- *Root*. This subkey contains *PNPxxxx* entries for old, non–Plug & Play hardware (such as the CPU, BIOS, network adapters, and printer drivers).

- *SCSI*. This subkey contains the configuration data of the SCSI controllers used in the system.

Values for PnP Components

Value	Description
PNP0000-PNP0004	Interrupt controllers
PNP0100-PNP0102	System timers
PNP0200-PNP0202	DMA controllers

Table 6-3.   (*continued*)
PnP codes are contained in the \Enum\BIOS *key.*

Table 6-3. *continued*

Value	Description
PNP0300-PNP0313	Keyboard controllers
PNP0400-PNP0401	Printer ports
PNP0500-PNP0501	Communication ports
PNP0600-PNP0602	Hard disk controllers
PNP0700	Standard floppy disk controller
PNP0800	System speaker
PNP0900-PNP0915, PNP0930-PNP0931, PNP0940-PNP0941	Display adapters
PNP0A00-PNP0A04	Expansion buses
PNP0B00	CMOS real-time clock
PNP0C01	System board extension for PnP BIOS
PNP0C02	Reserved
PNP0C04	Numeric data processor
PNP0E00-PNP0E02	PCMCIA controllers
PNP0F01	Serial Microsoft mouse
PNP0F00-PNP0F13	Mouse ports
PNP8xxx	Network adapters
PNPA030	Mitsumi CD-ROM controller
PNPB0xx	Miscellaneous adapters

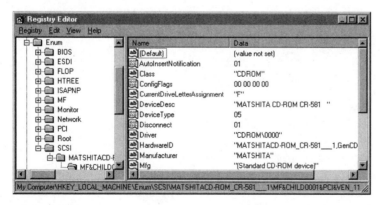

Figure 6-13.
The \Enum *key.*

PnP codes are grouped in classes according to their four-digit code. Further information about the Plug & Play standard can be found in different specifications, which are located on the Microsoft FTP site ftp.microsoft.com in the /developr/drg/Plug-and-Play/Pnpspecs/README.TXT file and related subdirectories.

Modifying the Device Configuration

You can view and manipulate the device configuration used on your computer through options on the Device Manager property page (Figure 6-14), which is available by clicking the System icon in the Control Panel. This property page lists all devices recognized by Windows (and registered in the Registry) as well as any hardware conflicts. Device conflicts and the current status of each device in the configuration are stored in the Registry key *HKEY_DYN_ DATA\ Config Manager\Enum*.

Figure 6-14.
Modify the device configuration using the Device Manager property page.

To inspect or change device properties, you need to access the Properties property sheet. (Click the desired entry on the device list, and then click the Properties button. A property sheet opens with a General tab and other tabs appropriate for the specific device.) You can use these property pages to modify the device settings (such as drive letter, I/O range, and Interrupts). All settings are device-specific.

Changing CD-ROM Drive Letters

The drive letters for hard disks and CD-ROMs are defined by Windows 95. Some application programs rely on CD-ROM drives having a specific drive letter. This can cause trouble if the hard disk is partitioned (using FDISK) and drive letters are reassigned. Each partition gets its own drive letter (two partitions will use the drive letters C: and D:), and the CD-ROM is assigned a new drive letter (E:, for example). Some device drivers allow you to reassign the drive letter used by the devices.

Select the drive (CDROM or Disk Drives, for example) from the device list in the Device Manager and click Properties. A property sheet opens with a property page that shows the drive letters available for this device. For a CD-ROM drive, you can alter the range of possible drive letters (for example, E: through H:).

The drive letters used by a particular controller are stored in the drive controller's subkey of the *HKEY_LOCAL_MACHINE\Enum* branch. These subkeys contain the *CurrentDriveLetterAssignment* value with the names of the assigned drives. (See Figure 6-13 on page 235 for a list of *Enum* subkeys and controller values.) The assignment of a drive letter to a specific piece of hardware is vendor-specific information, so you need detailed advice from the vendor about how to change a drive letter.

The *AutoInsertNotification* value controls Windows notification regarding whether a CD-ROM is inserted into a drive. A value of *01* enables notification.

Local System Properties: *HKEY_LOCAL_MACHINE\System*

The *HKEY_LOCAL_MACHINE\System* key contains only one subkey that defines the system properties of the local machine: *CurrentControlSet. CurrentControlSet* has two subkeys: *control* and *Services*.

The *control* Subkey

The *control* subkey contains all settings necessary for the current Windows configuration. There you will find a list of keys for installed system files, file system settings, information about the password and service provider, and so on. The *control* key contains one value with the name *Current User*, which contains the name used during logon. Here is a short overview of the subkeys of *control*:

■ *ComputerName.* This key contains subkeys that also have the name *ComputerName.* The last key in this hierarchy contains the value *ComputerName* that defines the computer name of the local machine used for identification in a workgroup. You can alter this name on the Identification property page of the Network property sheet (available by selecting Network in the Control Panel).

■ *FileSystem.* This key contains settings for the file system. (See pages 227–229 for a description of this key.)

■ *InstalledFiles.* This key contains a list of the system files (VXD, SPD, DLL) already installed in Windows. This is one of the lists that uninstallers use to detect unused files that can be removed from the \System subfolder.

■ *keyboard layouts.* This key identifies subkeys named for the country code used for international settings in Windows. Subkeys are named like this: *00000409.* Each subkey contains two values: *layout file* (such as *"kbdus.kbd"*) and *layout text* (which contains a readable text string such as *"United States"*).

■ *MediaProperties.* This key contains subkeys with the properties for Joysticks and MIDI schemes.

■ *MediaResources.* The resources for multimedia devices are defined in this key. This key contains subkeys with the data for audio-compression (*acm* subkey), image compression (*icm* subkey), the media mapper, a filter list, and so on. The data of the *Media-Resources* key is controlled by the Multimedia Properties property sheet (select Control Panel, then Multimedia). The Advanced property page of this sheet contains a list of the multimedia devices; from this list you can select an entry to modify. Selecting a device and clicking Properties enables you to view and change the device's settings.

■ *NetworkProvider.* This key contains the name and the order of the network providers used on the local machine.

■ *Nls.* The *Nls* key contains the definition for national language settings (names of the code pages and the mapping between the country codes and the country names).

■ *PerfStats.* This key contains configuration information for the System Monitor (available from the System Tools submenu of the Accessories menu) and is used to show performance values of memory usage, system components such as the kernel, and so on. The information contained in the *PerfStats* key is static. Use the key entries to customize the options shown in the Add Item dialog box of the System Monitor. The entries in the Category list are defined by the *Name* value of keys such as *KERNEL, VFAT,* etc. The *Name* entries in the subkeys define the strings shown in the Item list of the System Monitor. The *Description* value contains the string that will be shown in a message box if you select an item and click the Explain button on the Add Item dialog box. Dynamic data for the system monitor is collected in the *HKEY_DYN_DATA\PerfStats* key.

- *Print.* The print key contains several subkeys (*Environments, Monitors, Printers, Providers*) that define the data for the installed printers.

- *PwdProvider.* All services needing an access password (screen saver, networks, and so on) store the options for the password provider here.

- *ServiceProvider.* This key contains information about service providers used in Windows 95.

- *SessionManager.* Windows uses a session manager to control all applications and routines loaded into memory. Microsoft keeps in the *SessionManager* key information that controls applications. The data in these *Session Manager* subkeys should be modified only by Microsoft, in cooperation with affected software vendors, and distributed with Windows and software upgrades:

  - *AppPatches.* This key contains the names of applications and the patch data that forces these applications to run under Windows 95.

  - *CheckBadApps.* This key contains the names and versions of application programs (each filename is also a key name) that cause trouble in Windows 95. If the user tries to load such an application in Windows, a message box with a warning occurs.

  - *CheckVerDLLs.* This key contains a list of DLL routines whose versions are checked during loading.

  - *HackIniFiles.* This key contains information for modifying the INI files of applications so that they run properly in Windows 95.

  - *Known16DLLs.* This key contains the name of all 16-bit DLL routines installed in Windows 95. (If you add a driver in SYSTEM.INI, for instance, it will be shown in the list.)

  - *KnownDLLs.* This key contains a list of 32-bit DLL routines.

  - *WarnVerDlls.* Loading a DLL included in *WarnVerDLLs* results in a warning during loading.

- *Shutdown.* This key contains data relevant to a shutdown process. By default, this key is empty.

- *TimeZoneInformation.* This key contains the settings for the current time zone. Some of its entries are used on the Date/Time Properties property sheet (available by double-clicking the current time display on the Windows taskbar).

- *Update.* This key, which contains the values *NetworkPath* and *UpdateMode*, specifies how Windows is updated: *UpdateMode = 0* (no update), *UpdateMode = 1* (automatic update, use network path), *UpdateMode = 2* (manual update, requests a path). The values *UpdateMode, NetworkPath,* and the optional flags *LoadBalance* and *Verbose* can be altered with the System Policy Editor (select Local Computer, then the path *\Network\Update*).

- *VMM32Files.* This key contains a list of all VXD files installed in Windows 95.

The *Services* Subkey

HKEY_LOCAL_MACHINE\System\CurrentControlSet\Services contains a list of services used under Windows 95. The content of this list depends on the software installed under Windows 95.

- *Arbitrators.* This key contains other subkeys with specific data for the bus arbitrators (address, DMA, IO, IRQ).

- *Class.* This key contains device data organized by class (adapter, CDROM, disk drivers, display, keyboard, and so on).

- *VxD.* This key contains the names of all VxD drivers loaded during the Windows startup.

- *RemoteAccess, MSNP32, NcpServer, Winsock.* These keys contain information specific to optional services. These keys contain valid data only if the service is already installed. *RemoteAccess* is used to allow remote access to the local Registry through the System Policy Editor. *Winsock* is necessary if you use the TCP/IP protocol to establish, for example, an Internet connection with the Microsoft Internet Explorer.

Settings for System Software

Information about installed fonts, settings for starting an MS-DOS window, and so on is controlled in keys in the Registry.

Installed Fonts

By default, fonts are stored in TTF files in the \Windows\Fonts folder, but they can also be stored in other folders on the local system. Information about the fonts available in Windows 95 is stored in the following key:

HKEY_LOCAL_MACHINE\SOFTWARE\Microsoft\Windows\CurrentVersion\Fonts

Names of the values for this key are the same as the font names, and the value data are text strings containing the names of the TTF files.

To take a look at the currently installed fonts, open the Fonts folder (open the Control Panel, and then click Fonts). If you want to add any fonts to this list, you can do so through the Add Fonts dialog box (open the File menu and select Install New Font). Windows 95 allows you to install approximately 1,000 fonts; this limit exists because Windows 95 can read keys with a maximum size of 64 KB. (In Microsoft Windows NT, the size of a key is limited to 1 MB.) Here are some tips for installing fonts efficiently.

- If you can, install all fonts in the \Windows\Fonts folder. Font files take up space on the hard disk and can slow the system down, so you don't want duplicate fonts on your system.

- If an application requires its fonts to be stored in a separate folder, you can still ensure that there are no duplicates by creating a shortcut (a LNK file) from the \Fonts subfolder to the folder the font file is actually stored in. You do this by deselecting the Copy Fonts To Fonts Folder option in the Add Fonts dialog box when you add the font. Fonts are stored in a font cache (TTFCACHE) and are loaded during the system startup.

Besides the TrueType fonts kept in the *Fonts* key, there are also settings for raster fonts. These settings are stored in the key *HKEY_LOCAL_MACHINE\ Config\000x\Display\Fonts*. Definitions for the small and large fonts are stored in the *HKEY_LOCAL_MACHINE\SOFTWARE\Windows\CurrentVersion\fontsize* key. The *120* subkey defines large fonts, and the *96* subkey defines small fonts.

User-Supplied Install Information

During the Windows install process, setup asks you to enter the owner name, the organization, the CD key, and so on in a series of dialog boxes. These settings are then used in several other dialog boxes and message boxes. What if some of this information has changed? Do you need to reinstall Windows 95? No—by using the Registry Editor, you can modify these types of settings, which are all stored in the following single key:

HKEY_LOCAL_MACHINE\SOFTWARE\Microsoft\Windows\CurrentVersion

In this key, you will find interesting information about the install parameters and other miscellaneous settings, some of which are described here:

- *ConfigPath.* This is the path to the \config subfolder, which contains the file GENERAL.IDF, which is used for MIDI instruments.

- *DevicePath.* This value points to the \INF subfolder containing the INF files for the uninstall feature.

- *MediaPath.* This value defines the path where the media files (WAV, AVI, MDI) are stored.

- *ProductId.* This value contains the CD-ROM key code that you must enter during the install process.

- *RegisteredOrganization.* The name of the organization for whom the installed Windows 95 copy is registered.

- *RegisteredOwner.* This is the registered owner for the installed Windows 95 copy.

Besides these values, you will find other entries containing the installation date, the Windows version number, the path of the old Windows folder, and so on.

If you must change the name of the owner/organization, you can use the following statements in a REG file:

```
REGEDIT4

[HKEY_LOCAL_MACHINE\SOFTWARE\Microsoft\Windows\CurrentVersion]
"RegisteredOwner"="xxxxx"
"RegisteredOrganization"="yyyyy"
```

These lines are in the OWNER.REG file in the \chapter6 folder of the downloaded sample files. You must insert the required names in place of *xxxxx* and *yyyyy* and then save the lines in a REG file. After double-clicking the REG file, the information is added to the Registry. You can check whether the values have taken effect by double-clicking the System icon in the Control Panel. The General property page of the System Properties property sheet should show the new entries.

Setup Data

The following key contains several entries that control the Windows 95 Setup process and that are used to install and remove optional components:

HKEY_LOCAL_MACHINE\SOFTWARE\Microsoft\Windows\CurrentVersion\Setup

All values in these entries are set by Windows, so you shouldn't modify them. The entries are as follows:

- *BaseWinOptions.* This key can contain the names of INF files that are used to configure the basic Windows options. An entry like *msmail.inf* can be set to *0x00000001* to indicate that Windows should use the INF file for the settings.

- *EBD.* This key contains subkeys that control the keyboard settings and locale settings in AUTOEXEC.BAT and CONFIG.SYS.

- *OptionalComponents.* This key contains a value for each optional component; this value identifies the name of that component (such as the value name *CharMap*, which identifies the Character Map program). The value associated with this value name is set to the component's name (such as *"CharMap"*). For each value in *OptionalComponents*, you will find, also under *OptionalComponents*, a subkey with the component's name. For example, if the value *CharMap* is set to *"CharMap"*, then you will find also the subkey *\OptionalComponents\CharMap*. The entries in the *CharMap* subkey define whether the optional component is installed.

  - ❑ The value *INF* defines the name of the INF file used to install or remove the optional component (such *as "appletpp.inf"*).

  - ❑ The *Installed* entry indicates whether an optional value is installed. A value of *"1"* in *Installed* indicates that the optional component is already installed. A value of *"0"* indicates that the component isn't installed yet.

  - ❑ The *Section* entry defines the section in the INF file that is used to install the optional component.

- *WinbootDir.* This key contains the entry *devdir*. The value is set to the Windows subfolder (for example, *"C:\Windows"*).

Setting Keyboard Speed and Delay

When you press down on a single keyboard key for an extended period of time, the keyboard eventually generates the character repeatedly. You can control the keyboard delay (the time it takes the system to begin generating the letter) and the keyboard speed (how quickly the character repeats) on the Speed property page of the Keyboard Properties property sheet (available by selecting the Control Panel and then clicking the Keyboard icon). Values are set using the Repeat Delay and Repeat Rate slider settings. When you set these values and then click Apply, a new *Keyboard* subkey is generated in the *HKEY_USERS\xxxx\Control Panel* key, and the values *KeyboardDelay* and *KeyboardSpeed* are added. (The characters *xxxx* stand for the user's name or for *.Default.* The *Keyboard* key is not available by default.)

> NOTE: The value for the cursor blink rate is stored in the *CursorBlinkRate* entry, which can be found in the *HKEY_CURRENT_ USER\Control Panel\Desktop* key.

Settings for the MS-DOS Mode

Windows offers an MS-DOS window that allows you to run old DOS application programs. The following key contains the subkeys *MS-DOS Emulation* and *MS-DOSOptions*:

HKEY_LOCAL_MACHINE\SOFTWARE\Microsoft\Windows\CurrentVersion

MS-DOS Emulation contains a *DisplayParams* value that defines the display properties of the MS-DOS window. It also contains several predefined subkeys with settings for certain MS-DOS applications. (Users cannot alter these subkeys.)

You can also run each MS-DOS application in single MS-DOS mode. You can configure the options for this mode with the following steps:

1. Right-click the MS-DOS file, and select Properties to open the file's Properties property sheet.

2. Click the Program tab, and then click Advanced. This invokes the Advanced Program Settings dialog box. (See Figure 6-15.)

3. Check the MS-DOS mode option, and then select Specify A New MS-DOS Configuration.

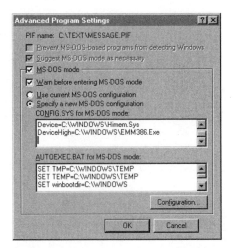

Figure 6-15.
Advanced Program Settings dialog box.

4. Click the Configuration button to invoke the Select MS-DOS Configuration Options dialog box. (See Figure 6-16.) You can set different options for the MS-DOS mode in this dialog box.

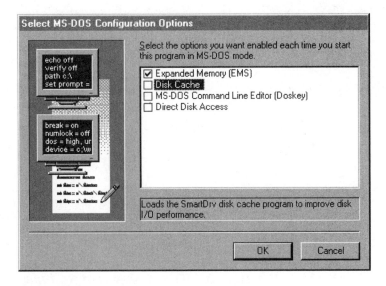

Figure 6-16.
The MS-DOS configuration options.

When you check one of the options in the Select MS-DOS Configuration Options dialog box and click OK, Windows generates the statements for CONFIG.SYS and AUTOEXEC.BAT to support the selected feature (Disk Cache, EMS, and so on).

The options for the single MS-DOS mode are stored in the following key:

HKEY_LOCAL_MACHINE\SOFTWARE\Microsoft\Windows\CurrentVersion\ MS-DOSOptions

If you open this key in the Registry Editor, you will see several subkeys containing the settings for the various options. (See Figure 6-17.)

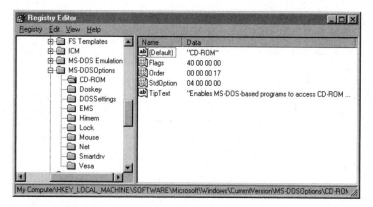

Figure 6-17.
The MS-DOSOptions *branch.*

Each key can contain several values that set the options for the feature defined by the key. Table 6-4 contains a brief description of these values.

Values for the Subkeys of the *MS-DOSOptions* Key

Value	Description
Default	The *Default* value of each key contains the string shown in the Select MS-DOS Configuration Options window (Figure 6-16). You can change the string to customize the option.
Autoexec.Bat	This value contains a string with the statement inserted in AUTOEXEC.BAT (*"LoadHigh %WINDIR%\Command\ DOSKey"*, for example). The placeholder *%WINDIR%* defines the Windows folder.

Table 6-4.   *(continued)*

246

Table 6-4. *continued*

Value	Description
Config.Sys	This value contains a string value with the command line that must be inserted into CONFIG.SYS.
Flags	This is a binary value that can be set to the following values: *00* Disable the key *02* Show this option; uncheck the box *07* Hide this option; select option by default *1B* Show this option; check the box The values *01* and *40* disable the option. The *Flags* value is stored sometimes as a binary and sometimes as a DWORD.
Order	The statements in AUTOEXEC.BAT and CONFIG.SYS must be ordered. Windows uses this DWORD to order the lines in *Autoexec.Bat* or *Config.Sys*. If several entries use identical *Order* values, Windows arranges these lines as it reads them from the Registry. If one entry should precede another entry, set the *Order* value of the preceding entry to a lower number.
StdOption	This value is used internally by Windows 95.
TipText	The string found in this value is shown in the Configuration window in the footer "tip" box when you click the entry (Figure 6-16 on page 245). This string may be treated as online-help text to show the user additional information about the selected option.

You can change the settings in the *MS-DOSOptions* subkeys. Use the strings in the *Autoexec.Bat* and *Config.Sys* values to customize the commands for your computer. (You can overwrite settings of your old MS-DOS configuration files, such as the commands to include the CD-ROM driver and MSCDEX.EXE, which are commented out by the Windows setup program. The same occurs with network and mouse statements.)

When you click OK, Windows takes the *Autoexec.bat* and *Config.sys* values in the *MS-DOSOptions* subkey and inserts the strings in the Advanced Program Settings window. If you miss a command necessary to run the MS-DOS application in *Autoexec.bat* or *Config.sys*, you can add the line manually into the Advanced Program Settings window. However, this requires that you know which command is needed, its order in the configuration file, and all parameters or options requested for this command.

Wouldn't it be nice to extend the options available in the configuration window? This would allow you to check an option to make Windows use the Registry to change the command. (You need to set the option for the *MS-DOSOptions* subkey only once.) To extend the *MS-DOSOptions* key, you must add a subkey and set the values defined in Table 6-4. This can be done with a simple REG file:

```
REGEDIT4

[HKEY_LOCAL_MACHINE\SOFTWARE\Microsoft\Windows\CurrentVersion\
MS-DOSOptions\Born]
@="NumLock off (Born)"
"TipText"="Switch off the Numlock key."
"Flags"=hex:02,00,00,00
"Order"=hex:00,00,00,13
"Config.sys"="NUMLOCK=OFF"
```

After you double-click the REG file, you will find the new *Born* subkey in the Registry (Figure 6-18). You will find the MSDOS.REG file in the \chapter6 folder of the downloaded sample files.

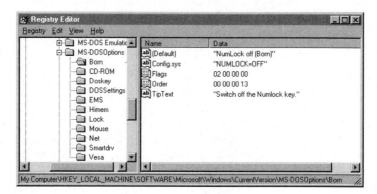

Figure 6-18.
The new Born *subkey for* MS-DOSOptions.

The entries shown in Figure 6-18 create a new option, NumLock Off (Born), in the configuration window (Figure 6-19). If this option is checked, Windows inserts the NUMLOCK=OFF command into CONFIG.SYS, which switches off the NumLock key after a system startup.

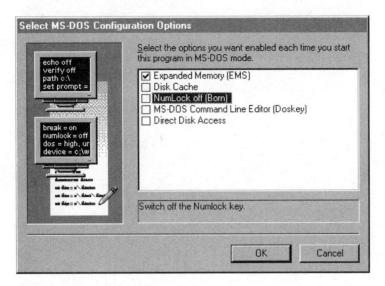

Figure 6-19.
A new option in the configuration window.

NOTE: If you want to offer a remove option for these options,
you must create an INF file that adds the uninstall commands to remove the new subkeys. Examples of similar INF files are given in
other chapters.

6810×8850

1080.1170

This book brings
together all the
scattered details
about the Registry
and provides a
comprehensive look
at how it works and
how you can use it.

Fortunately, the
concept of the

The Registry is the central
in Microsoft Windows 95 that s
and maintains configuration
information and is thus o
most interesting and important
components of Windows 95. Un
now, details about the Registry
haven't been readily available.
developers, administrators, and
end users have all faced the
challenge of trying to find
information about it.

CHAPTER SEVEN

Programming Issues

Throughout the book, we've looked at how software components can be registered using different techniques. If you are writing software that will be distributed to end users, using the Registry Editor to register components is appropriate only for test purposes—you can't distribute modifications to end users. REG files, setup programs, and INF files offer more convenient and safer methods for customizing the Registry, and they offer more practical methods for distributing those modifications.

If you write your own software, this chapter will be especially relevant to you. We address in more detail how and where you register software components, how you update the Registry using a program, and how you can use INF files to a greater extent.

Registering Version and Status Information

Some of the information about software is inserted into the Registry by the software's setup program; other information is stored later by the application. An application stores this information in the \Software key of these two root keys:

- *HKEY_LOCAL_MACHINE.* Settings that pertain to the software, such as a version number, are stored here.

- *HKEY_CURRENT_USER.* Settings that are user-dependent, such as the most recent file list, are stored here.

If you are writing software, your application must enter its settings in the appropriate keys. Let's look at an example to determine where certain kinds of information would be stored. Suppose your software had multiple versions (one for the typical end user and one for the experienced professional user).

This information is pertinent to your machine and would therefore be stored in *HKEY_LOCAL_MACHINE*. Your setup program would add the following entries (generic names are used in this example) in the Registry:

HKEY_ LOCAL_MACHINE\SOFTWARE\company\product\settings

For the first two subkeys under the *\SOFTWARE* key, use your actual company and product names. For example, Microsoft inserts the key *\SOFTWARE\ Microsoft*, which contains entries for Microsoft products, such as Windows, Word, and Excel, as well as entries for system extensions such as SCC viewers. After the *\product* key, you can use your own structure. You might, for example, want to insert all settings relevant to all users as values in the *\product* subkey. Note that Windows uses the *\CurrentVersion* subkey of the *\Windows* product key to separate miscellaneous entries. Take a look at the key structure of other software programs to learn how to build your own.

You've also got to build a structure for user-dependent settings. As we've seen, they're stored in the *HKEY_CURRENT_USER\Software* branch. This branch also has a key structure that includes the vendor and product names: *\company\product\settings*. What you've got to decide now is which entries should be keys and which entries should be values. Let's assume you want to store a recent file list for the current user. I don't recommend you use subkeys like *File, File1, File2*, and so on. Rather, you should create a subkey such as *Recent Files* and then add values with names such as *File, File1*, and *File2*.

Remember that a key's name cannot be changed without using the Registry Editor. If you want to change the name of a key, you'll have to delete the key and add the entries under a new key name.

> **NOTE:** The distinction between the *HKEY_CURRENT_USER* branch and the *HKEY_USERS* branch is important. The branch *HKEY_ CURRENT_USER* is built during each Windows startup (after the user logs on to the system). This branch contains all data relevant for the current user.
>
> Windows collects the settings for all registered users in the *HKEY_USERS* branch. Therefore you'll find subkeys such as *HKEY_USERS\.default* and *HKEY_USERS\Born*. If you change a setting in *HKEY_CURRENT_USER*, the change is immediately reflected in *HKEY_USERS* in the user's subkey.
>
> You should update all values in the *HKEY_CURRENT_USER* branch, not in the *HKEY_USERS* branch. If you want to apply the settings to all users, you can do so in *HKEY_LOCAL_MACHINE*.

Application-Specific Registry Entries

If you are a developer writing software that will be installed under Microsoft Windows 95, you'll want your setup program to set specific Registry entries. These entries have been discussed in previous chapters, so we'll just outline them here.

- *New file types.* If you want your application to start automatically when a file of a given file type is double-clicked, you need to register the file type and associate it with your application. You'll probably also want to register a unique icon for this file type. See Chapter 3 for details on where in the Registry this information belongs.

- *Handlers.* Handlers that are provided by your application, such as an icon handler or a context menu handler, must be registered under the *shellex* subkey of the associated file type. See Chapter 3 for more details.

- *Path information.* If your application relies on data in specific paths, you need to register these paths. See Chapter 6 for details on Registry locations.

- *Uninstall.* Every application designed for Windows 95 should have an uninstall feature. You must add your application to the Registry to make this feature available through the Add/Remove Programs Properties property sheet (which is available from the Control Panel). See Chapter 5 for more information on using the Registry with the uninstall feature.

NOTE: Further information about application-specific entries can be found in *The Programmers Guide to Microsoft Windows 95*.

Accessing the Registry Using a Program

If you use Microsoft Visual Basic, Visual C++, and so on, you can write your own setup routine to perform the install process. This setup routine copies the required files and updates the Registry entries. Microsoft programming language packages are shipped with setup wizards and install programs (such as InstallSHIELD) that provide you with the functions to install and uninstall software packages you create. Further information about these tools can be found in the online reference shipped with the compilers.

In some cases, you must access the Registry from a program in order to read settings or store specific settings for the next session. Windows 95 provides a set of API functions for accessing the Registry. Table 7-1 contains an overview of the API functions provided by Windows 95 (or, more precisely, by Win32). Both Win16 and Win32 API functions are supported by Windows 95.

API Functions Supported by Windows 95

Function	Description
RegCloseKey	A Win16 API function that closes the defined key.
RegCreateKey	A Win16 API call that creates the specified key. New Win32 applications should use the Win32 *RegCreateKeyEx* function.
RegCreateKeyEx	A Win32 API call that creates the specified key. If the key already exists in the registry, this function opens it.
RegDeleteKey	A Win16 function that deletes a defined key by removing the key and all its values. It cannot delete a key that contains subkeys.
RegDeleteValue	A Win32 function that deletes a named value from a specified key.
RegEnumKey	A Win16 API function that enumerates subkeys of the given open Registry key. The function retrieves the name of one subkey each time it is called. Win32 applications should use *RegEnumKeyEx*.
RegEnumKeyEx	A Win32 API call that enumerates the subkeys of a given open key.
RegEnumValue	A Win32 API call that enumerates all values of a given open key.
RegFlushKey	Writing information to the Registry can take several seconds before the cache is flushed onto the hard disk. An application can use the Win32 *RegFlushKey* function to force Windows to write the buffers to the hard disk, but this function uses many system resources and should be called only when necessary.
RegOpenKey	A Win16 function that opens a key. *RegOpenKey* does not create the specified key if that key does not exist in the Registry. *RegOpenKey* is provided for compatibility with Microsoft Windows 3.1. New Win32 applications should use the *RegOpenKeyEx* function.

Table 7-1.   *(continued)*

These API calls are supported by Windows 95 and can be used to read and change the settings in the Registry.

Table 7-1. *continued*

Function	Description
RegOpenKeyEx	A Win32 API function that opens a specified key.
RegQueryInfoKey	A Win32 API function that delivers information about a key.
RegQueryValue	A Win16 API function that retrieves the value associated with the unnamed value for a specified open key in the Registry. New Win32 applications should use the *RegQueryValueEx* function.
RegQueryValueEx	A Win32 API function that returns the value of an entry associated with a given open key.
RegSetValue	A Win16 API function that sets a value of a given key. New Win32 applications should use the *RegSetValueEx* function, which allows an application to set any number of named values of any data type.
RegSetValueEx	A Win32 API function that sets the value in the specified key.

NOTE: The Win32 API functions are defined for Windows 95 and for Microsoft Windows NT. Windows NT contains additional attributes (security attributes) for Registry keys. A detailed description of the API calls can be found in the Win32 SDK.

The application must open the Registry key by using *RegOpenKey* or *RegOpenKeyEx* before a value is read or stored. Both API functions deliver a handle to the key; that handle will be used in other API calls. *RegCreateKey* and *RegCreateKeyEx* create a new subkey for an already open key. *RegCloseKey* closes an open key and writes the data to the Registry. The data is cached, and you can use *RegFlushKey* to flush the cache to the hard disk.

The CD-ROM shipped with Nancy Cluts's book *Programming the Windows 95 User Interface* contains a source code example that uses some of the commands shown in Table 7-1 from within a C program.

The commands needed to read/write information to the Registry depend on the language platform you use. Visual Basic 4.0, for example, provides built-in functions such as *SaveSettings*, *GetAllSettings*, and *GetSettings* to read/write Registry entries, and you don't need any commands at all to open or close the Registry. (The Registry is opened and closed in the run-time library.) The following is a simple Visual Basic for Applications procedure that accesses application settings in the Registry. You can find this procedure in the REGISTRY.BAS file in the \chapter7 folder of the downloaded sample files.

This procedure can be used with Visual Basic 4.0 or later, and with Microsoft Office 97 VBA.

```
Sub Registry()
'
' Visual Basic Code (by G. Born)
'
' Sample program to show how to access application
' settings in the Registry with Visual Basic

Dim Settings As Variant

' Create a new key "G_Born\Init" in:
' HKEY_CURRENT_USER\Software\VB and VBA Program Settings
'
' Command: SaveSetting appname, section, key, setting
'
' All four parameters are required, and they are string expressions:
' appname   containing the application or project name
' section   containing the section name
' key       containing the name of the key
' setting   containing the value

' An error occurs if the key setting can't be saved
'

Response = MsgBox("Add keys?", vbYesNo + vbQuestion _
          + vbDefaultButton2, "Registry access")
If Response = vbYes Then       ' User chose Yes
' Add the new keys with fixed values
    SaveSetting appname:="G_Born", Section:="Init", _
              Key:="Version", setting:=1.3

    SaveSetting "G_Born", "Init", "LRUFile", "C:\Text\Born.doc"

    SaveSetting "G_Born", "Init", "Author", "G. Born"
End If

' Try to read the Version number back

Version = GetSetting(appname:="G_Born", Section:="Init", _
                  Key:="Version", Default:="Key not found")

' Show the result in a message box
Response = MsgBox("Key: Version = " + Version, _
          vbOKOnly + vbInformation, "Key value")
```

(continued)

continued

```
' Test to see if the key exists--"Version" is set to "Key not found"
If Version <> "Key not found" Then
    crlf = Chr(10) + Chr(13)
    test = ""                       ' Clear string

    ' Now try to list all subkeys in Init

    Settings = GetAllSettings(appname:="G_Born", Section:="Init")
    For Count = LBound(Settings, 1) To UBound(Settings, 1)
        test = test + Settings(Count, 0) + ": " _
                + Settings(Count, 1) _
                + crlf
    Next Count

    Response = MsgBox(test, vbOKOnly + vbInformation, "Key values")

    ' Ask before deleting the key
    Response = MsgBox("Delete key?", vbYesNo + vbQuestion _
                + vbDefaultButton2, "Registry access")
    If Response = vbYes Then         ' User chose Yes
        ' Remove the section "Init" and all its settings from Registry.
        ' The key "G_Born" can't be removed!
        DeleteSetting "G_Born", "Init"
    End If
End If

End Sub
```

This code creates a *G_Born* subkey and adds to that the *Init* subkey with the values *Version, LRUFile,* and *Author.* Different message boxes control the program flow to access, show, and delete the *G_Born* key's Registry settings.

When you access the Registry through Visual Basic 4.0 or later, you must use the 32-bit version—16-bit code will create INI files instead. Also, the functions used in the above procedure support access only to this key:

HKEY_CURRENT_USER\Software\VB and VBA Program Settings

N O T E : If you use Microsoft Word for Windows 95, WordBasic provides the GetPrivateProfileString and SetPrivateProfileString commands to alter the Registry. (You will find an example for accessing the Registry in the RegOptions macro shipped with the MSOffice\WinWord\Macros\MACROS7.DOT file.)

More About INF Files

We've looked briefly at INF files and used them throughout this book to perform such tasks as registering file types, customizing the Recycle Bin icon, and adding commands to the Microsoft Explorer window. In this section, we look in more detail at INF files to help you write your own. We'll use them to create a Components list for the Have Disk dialog box.

Advantages and Disadvantages of Using INF Files

Windows 95 offers the INF file format to run an automatic install script that allows you to copy, rename, and delete files; update INI files; and control the entries in the Registry. You can use placeholders for path descriptions and specify what will happen to a new value if a duplicate entry exists.

But it is complicated to write such an INF file. You must know the INF file format, and you must create the complete install script. Windows 95 provides no debug tool for testing an INF file step-by-step. When there is a problem, Windows doesn't automatically tell you what's wrong with the file. (Later on, we look at how to squeeze some debug information out of the setup process.)

Another disadvantage is that INF files do not provide commands to detect special conditions. If you use shared libraries, for instance, you must increment the counter programmatically. (This counter indicates how many installed applications rely on this module.) You cannot increment the counter by using an INF file.

Although you can't use INF files for all purposes, an INF file is a good choice in many cases if the setup is not too complicated and you don't want to ship a separate install program.

Details About the INF File Structure

INF files provide information that is used by Windows 95 to install software and hardware devices. (The primary purpose of the INF file is to support hardware devices.) The INF file format is based on the Windows 3.x INI file format:

- The file is divided into sections.

- Each section name must be unique within the INF file. A section name is enclosed in brackets (as in [Version]). The INF file contains predefined section names ([Version]) and user-defined section names ([Born]).

■ Each section contains one or more keywords. These keywords do not have to be unique, but their order within a section is significant.

Defining an INF Header in the [Version] Section

The [Version] section is simply a header of the INF file. It identifies whether the INF file is valid and defines whether the INF file is used for Plug & Play components or for some other purpose. The following lines define entries for the [Version] section:

```
[Version]
Signature="$Chicago$"          ; Identify the INF file
SetupClass=Base
```

For a Windows 95 program, the *Signature* keyword of your INF file must be set to the value *"$Chicago$"*, as shown above. (The signature value *"$Windows 95$"* is also valid, but I've found the file doesn't always process correctly.) The *Class* keyword is optional. *Class* indicates that the file is used for Plug & Play. *SetupClass*, as shown in our example, indicates that the INF file will be loaded by the setup program. If both the *Class* and *SetupClass* keywords are missing, the file will not be loaded by the setup program. If you install software that has nothing to do with a hardware device, you can set the *SetupClass* value to *BASE*.

Another optional keyword is *LayoutFile=filename*. This keyword defines the name of a second file that contains information about the layout of the distribution media. If you omit this keyword, you must insert the sections [SourceDisksNames] and [SourceDisksFiles] in the INF file in order to define where the files come from.

Other optional keywords include *ClassGUID* (the device GUID stored in the Registry for a device installed by the INF file) and *Provider* (the name of the INF file creator, usually a company name).

Creating a Components List for the Have Disk Dialog Box

For some of your software purposes, you'll find it helpful to offer a list of optional components that users can install. Take a look at the Components list on the Windows Setup property page shown in Figure 7-1 on the following page. (You can access this page by double-clicking the Add/Remove Programs icon in the Control Panel and then selecting the Windows Setup property page.) Any hardware-related components offered by Microsoft are automatically contained in this list.

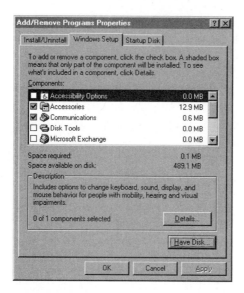

Figure 7-1.
Optional Windows 95 components.

To ensure that you don't modify this list, Microsoft makes third-party vendors supply the INF file for each hardware component installed in a computer running Windows 95. (This INF file is typically supplied on a disk. For example, if you have a new graphics card, you receive a driver's disk from the manufacturer.) You must install these components to make them appear in the Components list. First you click Have Disk to invoke the Install From Disk dialog box, which contains a text box for the path to the INF file (see Figure 7-2). You then enter the path manually or click the Browse button to select the appropriate path. If you have a disk or a directory containing an INF file, you can specify the path to this location. After clicking OK, the INF file is read. (If the directory or disk contains several INF files, the first entry in the file list is used. You will see the filename when you click Browse and select the directory in the Open dialog box.) If the hardware vendor supports several hardware components, all options will appear in the Components list.

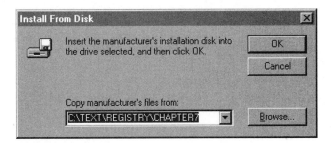

Figure 7-2.
Enter the path to an INF file.

Wouldn't it be a perk to provide an identical feature for installing software components? Figure 7-3 shows a simple example of a Components list containing four entries. These four entries add or remove keys in the Registry. (This is just an example to show the technique.) All you need to do to add the first two entries to *HKEY_CURRENT_USER\Software* is click the checkboxes next to the entries and then click the Install button. Selecting the last two entries and clicking Install removes the keys.

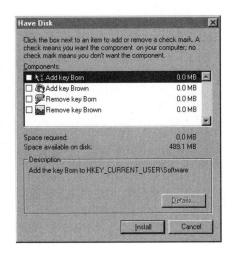

Figure 7-3.
New options added to the Components list.

The INF file that created the Components list shown in Figure 7-3 contains the following lines:

```
; File: Options.inf  G. Born
;
; Demonstrates how to create a Components list with
; optional entries in the Have Disk dialog box.
; Checked components will be included in the install
; process.

[version]
signature="$CHICAGO$"
Provider=%author%
SetupClass=Base

[DestinationDirs]
; This section is left empty in this example


;*******************************************************
; Here we define all components for the Components list
;*******************************************************

[Optional Components]
Born                    ; Optional components sections
Brown
BornUninst
BrownUninst

[Born]
; For the Born option, you can add keywords
; like DelReg, CopyFiles, and DelFiles.
; In this example, I will add an option into the Registry.

AddReg = Born.AddReg

; Here is the optional information shown in the
; Have Disk dialog box

OptionDesc   = %Option1_DESC%    ; Define the entry
Tip          = %Option1_TIP%     ; Define the tip text
InstallType  = 0                 ; Allow manual only
IconIndex    = 45                ; Windows Logo mini icon for dialogs

[BornUninst]
; BornUninst removes the key added in [Born]

DelReg = Born.AddReg
```

(continued)

continued

```
; Here is the optional information shown in the
; Have Disk dialog box

OptionDesc  = %Option3_DESC%     ; Define the entry
Tip         = %Option3_TIP%      ; Define the tip text
InstallType = 0                  ; Allow manual only
IconIndex   = 46                 ; Windows Logo mini icon for dialogs

[Brown]
AddReg = Brown.AddReg

OptionDesc  = %Option2_DESC%     ; Define the entry
Tip         = %Option2_TIP%      ; Define the tip text
InstallType = 0                  ; Allow manual only
IconIndex   = 47                 ; Icon

[BrownUninst]
DelReg = Brown.AddReg

OptionDesc  = %Option4_DESC%     ; Define the entry
Tip         = %Option4_TIP%      ; Define the tip text
InstallType = 0                  ; Allow manual only
IconIndex   = 48                 ; Icon

; Information about Registry keys (used in AddReg, DelReg)

[Born.AddReg]
HKCU,Software\Born,,Test,"Hello there"

[Brown.AddReg]
HKCU,Software\Brown,,Test,"Hello there"

[Strings]
; Localizable strings
author = "Born"
Option1_DESC = "Add key Born"
Option1_TIP = "Add the key Born to HKEY_CURRENT_USER\Software"

Option2_DESC = "Add key Brown"
Option2_TIP = "Add the key Brown to HKEY_CURRENT_USER\Software"

Option3_DESC = "Remove key Born"
Option3_TIP = "Remove the key Born from HKEY_CURRENT_USER\Software"

Option4_DESC = "Remove key Brown"
Option4_TIP = "Remove the key Brown from HKEY_CURRENT_USER\Software"

; *** End
```

The important part of this code, which creates the Components list, is the [Optional Components] section. In this section you can insert the names of other sections, which are scanned by the install routine. In my example, I inserted the section names [Born], [Brown], [BornUninst], and [BrownUninst]. These sections contain other INF commands. (You can copy files, add keys to the Registry, etc. I discuss the required commands later on.) In a section like [Born], for example, you can set some additional information for the Have Disk dialog box:

- *OptionDesc.* This keyword specifies the string displayed for this option in the Components list.

- *Tip.* This keyword defines the string shown in the Description section of the Have Disk dialog box.

- *InstallType.* This keyword specifies the type of installation for Windows 95 setup. Valid values are *0* (compact), *1* (typical), *2* (portable), and *3* (custom). The default value is *1*.

- *IconIndex.* This keyword defines the mini icons shown in the Components list. (See Figure 7-4.)

You can also add other keywords that define the install options, such as the required disk space.

NOTE: Further information about keywords can be found in the *Windows 95 Resource Kit* and in the *Windows 95 Software Development Kit.* The file OPTIONS.INF containing the commands listed in our example code can be found in the \chapter7\Options folder of the downloaded sample files.

TIP: To examine the icon index, use the file ICONS.INF contained in the \chapter7\Icons folder of the downloaded sample files. Opening this folder from the Install From Disk dialog box reveals a list of the first 30 icons (see Figure 7-4). Because indexing starts with 0, the *IconIndex* value used in the INF file is always one less than the number shown in the Have Disk dialog box Components list. You can extend the ICONS.INF file to show the other mini icons provided by the Windows setup routines.

Figure 7-4.
Mini icons for the Have Disk dialog box.

Installing and Uninstalling Files

During a software installation, you need to copy files from the install disk to the destination directories of the computer. Some files go into the Windows directories; others must be copied into new folders. Some files must be deleted from the hard disk after they perform their functions. For example, temporary files must be deleted after installation, and an uninstall feature must remove all files for an application from the hard disk. All these jobs can be accomplished with a simple INF file. The next sample file copies two files: the sample file itself, FILECOPY.INF, and TSTFILE.TXT. The file FILECOPY.INF is copied into the Windows\INF subfolder. This file is needed later on for the uninstall feature. The file TSTFILE.TXT is copied into the Windows\Born subfolder. (If this subfolder doesn't exist, it will be created by the INF file. If you don't want this subfolder to be created, you can designate an existing subfolder.)

The sample file also provides an uninstall feature. After you run this file, you'll find the option Remove Testfile (Born) on the Install/Uninstall property page. (Access this property page by invoking Add/Remove Programs, which is available from the Control Panel.) This entry allows you to remove the INF and TXT files—which were copied during the install process—from the hard disk.

```
; File: Filecopy.INF
;
; Demonstrate how to copy and delete files
;
; This INF file provides an uninstall function to
; remove the files

[version]
signature="$CHICAGO$"
SetupClass=BASE

; This is the install part. Here we copy the files,
; but you can add other commands as well.

[DefaultInstall]

CopyFiles = Tst.CopyFiles, Inf.CopyFiles
AddReg=Tst.AddReg              ; Add uninstall entries

; This is the uninstall section. We use the DelFiles keyword
; to remove the files. The destination section is the same as
; for the CopyFiles section, so Windows will do the job.

[DefaultUninstall]

DelReg=Tst.AddReg             ; Remove uninstall entries
DelFiles = Inf.CopyFiles, Tst.CopyFiles

; Add the uninstall stuff to the Registry

[Tst.AddReg]

HKLM,SOFTWARE\Microsoft\Windows\CurrentVersion\Uninstall\tst,DisplayName
,,"%REMOVE_DESC%"
HKLM,SOFTWARE\Microsoft\Windows\CurrentVersion\Uninstall\tst,
UninstallString,,
"RunDll setupx.dll,InstallHinfSection DefaultUninstall 4 Filecopy.inf"

; Don't forget this key for the uninstall part
HKLM,SOFTWARE\Microsoft\Windows\CurrentVersion\Uninstall\tst,,,

; INF file to be copied in the Windows\INF subfolder

[Inf.CopyFiles]
Filecopy.Inf
```

(continued)

continued

```
; Test file to be copied in the Windows\Born subfolder
[Tst.CopyFiles]
Tstfile.txt

[DestinationDirs]

Tst.CopyFiles = 10,Born        ; Create new subfolder
Inf.CopyFiles = 17             ; INF subfolder

[SourceDisksNames]
55="Testfile Disk","",1

[SourceDisksFiles]
Filecopy.inf=55
Tstfile.txt=55

[Strings]
REMOVE_DESC = "Remove Testfile (Born)"

; End ***
```

I kept the contents of this INF file simple to illustrate my points. The first section [Version] contains the signature for an install file. The [DefaultInstall] and [DefaultUninstall] sections, which come next, contain commands to copy and delete files:

- To copy one or more files, you must insert the *CopyFiles* keyword in a section. After the equal sign, list the names of the sections that identify which files will be altered.

- To delete a file, insert the *DelFiles* keyword into the section. The equal sign is followed by a list of sections that describe the files to manipulate.

In our example, the [DefaultInstall] section contains the *CopyFiles* keyword designating the [Tst.CopyFiles] and [Inf.CopyFiles] sections, which contain information about the files to be copied. You can define the names of these sections—the only requirement is that each section name be unique within the INF file.

The next issue in our example concerns the files that will be copied. This information is contained in the sections referenced in the *CopyFiles* line. Note in our sample that the [Tst.CopyFiles] section contains only one entry, *Tstfile.txt*, which is copied from the source to the destination. We will take a closer look at source and destination in a moment.

Details About the Uninstall Feature

The file FILECOPY.INF contains a section called [DefaultUninstall]. This section seems as if it might have something to do with an uninstall feature provided by the Install/Uninstall property page (available by selecting Control Panel, then Add/Remove Programs), but this is only partially true—[DefaultUninstall] is just a section name. You could name this section [Born] and you would get the same results. The uninstall feature offered by Windows 95 requires that you add a key to the following branch:

HKEY_LOCAL_MACHINE\SOFTWARE\Microsoft\Windows\CurrentVersion\Uninstall\xxxx

You can use the program's EXE name instead of the subkey *xxxx* to create a unique subkey. This subkey must contain two values: *DisplayName* and *UninstallString*. *DisplayName* defines the string shown on the Install/Uninstall property page. *UninstallString* contains the command to remove all settings provided during the install process. (I have discussed these topics in the examples shown in Chapters 4 and 5.) The *UninstallString* value can contain, for example, the following command to activate RUNDLL.EXE:

```
"RunDll setupx.dll, InstallHinfSection DefaultUninstall 4 Filecopy.inf"
```

As mentioned in previous chapters, RUNDLL.EXE is a stub program that calls other DLL routines. The line above activates the Windows SETUPX.DLL routine, which reads the INF file. (Therefore, the INF file must be located in the Windows\INF subfolder). SETUPX.DLL uses this syntax:

```
Setupx.dll, InstallHinfSection <section> <reboot-mode> <inf-name>
```

The following list describes the SETUPX.DLL parameters:

- The first parameter is always set to the string *InstallHinfSection*.

- The next parameter defines the name of the INF file section that will be executed. (In my examples, I've named this section [DefaultUninstall]. If you prefer a different section name, you must also alter the entry in the *UninstallString* value.)

- The third parameter defines the reboot mode. This value is a little bit mysterious because in some INF files you will find it set to *4* and in other INF files you'll find it set to *132*.

- The last parameter is always set to the name of the INF file used to uninstall the settings. In most cases, the INF file used for the install is also used for the uninstall. (In these cases, you could use the same structures in *CopyFiles* and *DeleteFiles*, *AddReg* and *DelReg*, and so on.)

The possible values for the reboot mode are defined in Table 7-2.

Reboot Mode Values

Value	Description
0	*NeverReboot.* The PC will not be rebooted. It is up to the client program to determine whether or not the PC should reboot. The setup program must add entries to the WININIT.INI file or create a new WININIT.INI file and copy it to the \Windows folder to ensure that settings will be initialized at the next reboot.
1	*AlwaysSilentReboot.* The PC will always reboot without prompting the user.
2	*AlwaysPromptReboot.* The user will always be asked to respond to a Reboot The Machine, Yes/No dialog box. Setup does not attempt to determine whether or not a reboot is necessary.
3	*SilentReboot.* If setup determines a need for a reboot, the PC is rebooted without prompting the user.
4	*PromptReboot.* If setup determines that the PC needs to reboot, setup prompts the user with a Reboot The Machine, Yes/No dialog box.

Table 7-2.
The reboot mode is the third parameter of SETUPX.DLL.

If the parameter <inf-name> specifies your INF file instead of a Windows 95 INF file, you must add the value *128* to the values shown in Table 7-2. If you install optional components, you should add *128* to the value *4*, resulting in a reboot value of *132*. (I used the value *4* successfully.) It is recommended that you use *4* or *132* as the reboot value. If you add *128* to the reboot mode value, all the files that your installation program is installing must be in the same directory on the installation disk as the INF file.

> N O T E :   Many other commands can be included in INF files, but giving you a complete overview of all INF file options is beyond the scope of this book. The *Windows 95 Resource Kit* contains an appendix with a description of the INF file format.

Defining the Source and Destination
How do we define the source and the destination? This is a little bit tricky in an INF file.

Defining the source   The source must be either the source disk or a folder that contains the files. This information is provided in the [SourceDisks Names] section. Each entry in this section specifies a disk containing the files to be copied:

```
55="TestfileDisk","",1
```

The number *55* is a disk ordinal used in the [SourceDisksFiles] section. This number is associated with a specific filename or with several filenames. The string after the equal sign is the name of the source disk. This text is displayed in a message box if the file cannot be found. The second parameter after the equal sign defines the disk label, and the last parameter is used for the serial number of a disk.

Defining the destination   The destination directories are defined in the [DestinationDirs] section of the INF file. The syntax of a line contained in the [DestinationDirs] section is as follows:

```
section name=destination directory
```

The section name, which identifies the section that contains the files that will be copied, must be defined in the INF file. In our example, we use the two section names [Tst.CopyFiles] and [Inf.CopyFiles]. Each of these entries defines a separate destination directory.

Now let's have a look at the destination directory. INF files are designed to install a device driver into the Windows folders, so Microsoft has defined Logical Disk IDs (LDIDs) that allow you to specify a destination directory. Table 7-3 lists the LDID values for the most often used predefined directories.

LDID Values for INF Files

LDID	Destination Directory
10	Windows
11	System
12	IOSubsys
13	Command
14	Control Panel

Table 7-3.   *(continued)*
Use the LDID codes to specify predefined destination directories for INF files. These codes are defined by Microsoft.

Table 7-3. *continued*

LDID	Destination Directory
15	Printers
16	Workgroup
17	INF
18	Help
20	Fonts
30	Root directory of the boot drive
31	Root directory of the host drive (of a virtual boot drive)
32	Old Windows
33	Old MS-DOS

If you wanted to copy the files defined in the [Tst.CopyFiles] section into the Windows folder, you would use the following line:

```
Tst.CopyFiles = 10
```

I want to copy the files in [Tst.CopyFiles] to the subfolder \Born, so I've added the \Born subpath after the LDID. You could add other subfolder names after the LDID number. Adding 30\MyProgram, for example, creates the folder \MyProgram on the boot drive.

The *DelFiles* keyword is handled in the same way as the *CopyFiles* keyword. You have to use the defined sections to specify the names of the files to be deleted and the destination directory. In our sample, I used a simple trick. The sections [Inf.CopyFiles] and [Tst.CopyFiles] already contain the information about the files copied during the install process, so I added only this line to the [DefaultUninstall] section:

```
DelFiles = Inf.CopyFiles, Tst.CopyFiles
```

Windows recognizes the *DelFiles* keyword and uses the information in [Inf.CopyFiles] and [Tst.CopyFiles] to remove the files. Only the subfolder \Born, which was created during the install process, can't be removed.

NOTE: You can find the files TSTFILE.TXT and FILECOPY.INF in the \chapter7\ Filecopy folder of the downloaded sample files. Right-clicking the INF file and selecting Install copies both files included in the folder onto the hard disk. If you use the Install/ Uninstall property page, you can remove the files with the Remove Testfile (Born) option.

Adding and Deleting Registry Entries

An INF file can contain the *AddReg* keyword to add a new key or value into the Registry and the *DelReg* keyword to delete a key or value. The FILECOPY.INF file we've been looking at (pages 266–267) contains both keywords. This line defines the [Tst.AddReg] section in the INF file:

```
AddReg=Tst.AddReg
```

This [Tst.AddReg] section contains all information necessary to add an entry into the Registry. If you use the following line, the information in the [Tst.AddReg] section will be used to remove entries:

```
DelReg=Tst.AddReg
```

Don't be confused by the [Tst.AddReg] name. This is just a name of a section—the term AddReg in this name has nothing to do with the *AddReg* keyword mentioned above. I used this as the section name to indicate that information is added to the Registry. You are free to use the same section to remove these settings.

We looked briefly in Chapter 3 at the syntax for a line that enters a key into the Registry, but let's review it again here:

```
root-key, [subkey], [value name], [flag], [value]
```

You must first enter the root key in this line—the root key is inserted as an abbreviation (see Table 7-4). Parameters included in brackets are optional and can be left blank, and they must be separated by commas.

Abbreviations for Root Keys

String	Meaning
HKCC	*HKEY_CURRENT_CONFIG*
HKCR	*HKEY_CLASSES_ROOT*
HKCU	*HKEY_CURRENT_USER*
HKLM	*HKEY_LOCAL_MACHINE*
HKU	*HKEY_USERS*

Table 7-4.
When you enter a key into the Registry, you must enter the appropriate root key abbreviations in the line first.

The root key name is followed by a string specifying the subkey (*Software\ Microsoft*, for example). The third parameter defines the name of the value entry in the subkey. If this parameter is empty, Windows sets the *Default* value. The fourth parameter contains an optional flag defining the insertion mode for data. This flag is defined in Table 7-5. (The sample files in this book do not set this flag, so the default value *0* is set.)

Flag Codes

Value	Meaning
0	Default. Use an ANSI string for the value, and replace the key's value if it exists.
1	Use a HEX record, and replace the key's value if it exists.
2	Use an ANSI string. Don't replace an existing key's value.
3	Use a HEX record. Don't replace an existing key's value.

Table 7-5.
Optional flags for the fourth parameter.

The last parameter in the line is also optional and defines the value to be set. This value can be an ANSI string or a hexadecimal representation of a binary record in Intel format (least significant byte first). Binary value entries can be extended beyond the 128-byte line limit with a backslash (\) appended on each line. Look at the following statement:

```
HKLM,SOFTWARE\Born, MyEntry,,"Hello I was there"
```

It creates the key *HKEY_LOCAL_MACHINE\SOFTWARE\Born*, adds the value *MyEntry* into the key, and inserts the string *"Hello I was there"* into this value. The parameter with the value can also contain commands including path settings like this:

```
"C:\WINDOWS\Notepad.exe %1"
```

If the pathname is changed by the user (for example, the user might rename the Windows folder during setup), you can use the LDID numbers shown in Table 7-3 (on pages 270–271) as placeholders. The previous command, then, could also be written like this:

```
"%10%\Notepad.exe %1"
```

Windows will substitute the *%10%* placeholder with the current Windows folder name.

The INF section pointed to by the *DelReg* keyword also contains a similar command:

```
root-key, subkey, [value name]
```

The root key here is also an abbreviation as shown in Table 7-4 on page 272. The subkey is required for a *DelReg* statement, but the value name is optional. If you omit the value name, the key and all its values will be removed. The first parameters to add or delete a Registry entry are the same, so you can use the same lines for *DelReg* and *AddReg*. (I've used this trick in several INF files in this book.)

Putting It All Together in an INF File

Let's put all these details about INF files to work in an INF file that copies a new icon library to the hard disk and sets the icons for the Recycle Bin. (This situation should sound familiar—we dealt with the Registry key for setting the Recycle Bin icon and looked at RECYCLE0.INF and RECYCLE1.INF in Chapter 4.) Our INF file will also support the uninstall feature in order to recover the default system settings. The following code handles these requirements:

```
; File: Recycle.INF
;
; Redefine the icons used by the Recycle Bin
;
; This INF file provides an uninstall function to
; remove the files and recover the factory settings

[version]
signature="$CHICAGO$"
SetupClass=BASE

; This is the install part. Here we will copy the files.

[DefaultInstall]

CopyFiles = DLL.CopyFiles, Inf.CopyFiles
AddReg=Bin.AddReg              ; Add uninstall entries

; This is the uninstall section. We use the DelFiles keyword
; to remove the INF file.
```

(continued)

continued

```
[DefaultUninstall]
DelReg=Bin.AddReg          ; Remove uninstall entries
AddReg=BinOld.AddReg       ; Reset factory values
DelFiles = Inf.CopyFiles   ; Delete INF file; let DLL file
                           ; set new icons and add the
                           ; uninstall stuff to the Registry


[Bin.AddReg]
; Use HKEY_CLASSES_ROOT\CLSID.
; Set "Full" to icon no 5 in BornIcon.dll.
HKCR,CLSID\{645FF040-5081-101B-9F08-00AA002F954E}\DefaultIcon,Empty
,,"%10%\Born\BornIcon.dll,0"
HKCR,CLSID\{645FF040-5081-101B-9F08-00AA002F954E}\DefaultIcon,Full
,,"%10%\Born\BornIcon.dll,5"

HKLM,SOFTWARE\Microsoft\Windows\CurrentVersion\Uninstall\bin,DisplayName
,,"%REMOVE_DESC%"
HKLM,SOFTWARE\Microsoft\Windows\CurrentVersion\Uninstall\bin,
UninstallString,,
"RunDll setupx.dll,InstallHinfSection DefaultUninstall 4 Recycle.inf"

; Don't forget this key for the uninstall part
HKLM,SOFTWARE\Microsoft\Windows\CurrentVersion\Uninstall\bin,,,

; INF file to be copied to the Windows\INF subfolder

[BinOld.AddReg]
; Reset factory settings in HKEY_CLASSES_ROOT\CLSID
HKCR,CLSID\{645FF040-5081-101B-9F08-00AA002F954E}\DefaultIcon,Empty
,,"%11%\\shell32.dll,31"
HKCR,CLSID\{645FF040-5081-101B-9F08-00AA002F954E}\DefaultIcon,Full
,,"%11%\\shell32.dll,32"

[Inf.CopyFiles]
Recycle.Inf


; Test file to be copied to the Windows\Born subfolder
[Dll.CopyFiles]
BornIcon.dll

[DestinationDirs]

Dll.CopyFiles = 10,Born    ; Create new subfolder
Inf.CopyFiles = 17         ; INF subfolder
```

(continued)

continued

```
[SourceDisksNames]
; Set folder names to the correct path
55="Set folder to: \RegBook\chapter7\recycle","",1
56="Set folder to: \RegBook\chapter4","",1

[SourceDisksFiles]
Recycle.inf=55
BornIcon.dll=56                    ; Icon source in ...\chapter4

[Strings]
REMOVE_DESC = "Reset Recycle Bin icons (Born)"

; End ***
```

These lines copy the BORNICON.DLL file from the \chapter4 subfolder into the Windows subfolder named \Born. The Registry is also updated with the new icon settings for the Recycle Bin and for the uninstall feature. The INF file is copied into the \INF subfolder to support the uninstall feature.

NOTE: The file RECYCLE.INF is in the \chapter7\Recycle folder of the downloaded sample files. Right-click the INF file, and select the Install option from the context menu. During installation you will be prompted to change the disks. Set the new path to \chapter4 to continue the file copy operation. After installing the file, you must open and close the Recycle Bin window before the new icons will be visible. Recovering the factory settings requires the Install/ Uninstall property page (select Control Panel, then click Add/ Remove Programs). Select the Reset Recycle Bin icons (Born) option, and click Add/Remove. The old icons return after the next change occurs in Recycle Bin (such as the deletion of a file).

Executing and Testing an INF File

We've seen that you can execute an INF file and force Windows to process the commands it contains in two ways:

- By right-clicking the filename and selecting Install from the context menu

- By using the Windows Setup property page, which enables you to select the path to the INF file on the Install From Disk dialog box

The advantage of the first option is that you can select any INF file and let Windows process it; the disadvantage of this feature is that it does not show a dialog box with a Components list. The second option is preferable if the INF file supports options shown in the Have Disk Components list; the disadvantage is that only the first INF file of a source is processed.

The progress of the INF file's copy operation is shown in a progress bar in the Copying Files window (see Figure 7-5). This window is visible only if you have defined several files to be copied.

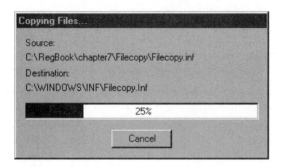

Figure 7-5.
Progress bar shown during the copy operation.

If a file defined in the FileCopy section of the INF file cannot be found on the source disk or in the source folder, setup invokes the dialog box shown in Figure 7-6. You must either change the path shown in the Copy Files From text box or click Skip File to omit the file.

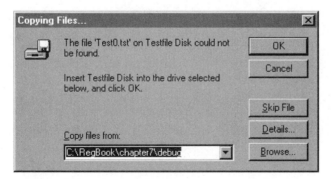

Figure 7-6.
Asking for a new source path.

Debugging an INF File

One big source of mistakes in INF files is typing errors, especially in section names, and these can be hard to detect. Unfortunately, Windows does not offer a method for debugging your INF files during processing, so if an INF file contains the wrong instructions, you won't receive an error message stating that the section with the error was not processed. What do you do? Let's take a look at lines that contain an error and then figure out how to track it down.

```
[DefaultInstall]
CopyFiles = Tst.CopyFiles, Inf.CopyFiles

[CopyFiles.Inf]
Filecopy.Inf
```

The CopyFiles line in the [DefaultInstall] section contains a reference to the [Inf.CopyFiles] section. This section, however, doesn't exist because there is a typing error in the name of the section [CopyFiles.Inf]. Thus it's never processed, and the FILECOPY.INF file isn't copied into the destination folder. You won't be able to detect this until you try to uninstall the feature—uninstalling reveals that FILECOPY.INF is missing in the \INF subfolder. Windows removes the uninstall entry in the Install/Uninstall property page, but all other keys and files remain. (I was caught in this trap while creating the FILECOPY.INF example.)

How did I detect such a problem? I inspected the Registry entries and folders and also tested the features, but to no avail. So I came to the conclusion that something must be wrong in the INF file itself. I printed it and had a look (a very long look) at the listing—not a very efficient way to test huge INF files.

What we need is a kind of breakpoint that we insert in several places to check whether this point is reached or not. Unfortunately, there is no breakpoint command in the INF file syntax that allows us to do this. If you haven't got a tool to create and check INF files, you can use a simple (and dirty) trick to debug the INF files:

1. Insert the name of a nonexistent file into the section that is used to copy files. If you insert several file names into the INF file (TEST0.TST, TEST1.TST, and so on), you can inspect several sections in an INF file. When Windows detects the missing file, a dialog box showing the filename is invoked (see Figure 7-6 on the preceding page). Now you know that Windows has reached the section containing this so-called breakpoint.

2. Click Details to invoke the message box shown in Figure 7-7, which has information about the source and destination paths. Click Skip File to skip the breakpoint and continue the setup process.

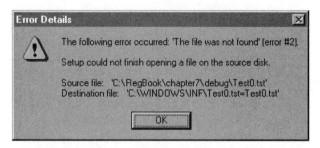

Figure 7-7.
The Error Details message box contains information about the missing file.

Following are lines I prepared for test purposes:

```
[Inf.CopyFiles]
Filecopy.Inf
Test0.tst                  ; *** Breakpoint 0

; Test file to be copied in the Windows\Born subfolder
[Tst.CopyFiles]
Tstfile.txt
Test1.tst                  ; *** Breakpoint 1
```

NOTE: You will find the tweaked file FILECOPY.INF in the \chapter7\Debug folder of the downloaded sample files. If you try to execute the file (by right-clicking it and selecting Install from the context menu), you will see the messages mentioned.

Conclusion

I have discussed most of the Registry entries relevant to Windows 95 settings and a lot of topics relevant to dealing with the Registry. There are still many things to say about INF files and other Registry topics, but it was never my goal to address all these topics—just some of the more critical issues. Use the references listed in the Further Readings section to find more information.

6810 × 8850

1080,1170

This book brings together all the scattered details about the Registry and provides a comprehensive look at how it works and how you can use it. Fortunately, the concept of the

The Registry is the central in Microsoft Windows 95 that s information and is thus one of most interesting and important and maintains configuration components of Windows 95. Un now, details about the Registry haven't been readily available developers, administrators, and end users have all faced the challenge of trying to find information about it.

The MCA Bus

Icons Contained in SHELL32.DLL

This appendix contains two tables. The first table describes the standard icons used by Windows 95. The second table lists other, less frequently used icons that you can use as you want.

Common Icons Used by Windows 95

Icon Index	Icon	Description
0		Default used for unregistered file types and for files for which no icon is available.
1		Default used for files with the extension DOC. As discussed in Chapters 3 and 4, you can redefine this icon using the *DefaultIcon* subkey in the *docfile* key of the Registry.
2		Used for executable programs that have no icon, such as MS-DOS, EXE, and COM files. (This icon can be overwritten by PIF file settings.) To change the icon, click Change Icon on the Program property page of the file's Properties property sheet.
3		Used by the shell (comprising the Microsoft Explorer, desktop, Start menu, and shell windows) to indicate a closed folder. This icon must be redefined in the *Shell Icons* key.
4		Used by the shell to indicate an open folder. This icon must be redefined in the *Shell Icons* key.
5		Used by the shell for a 5¼" floppy disk drive. This icon must be redefined in the *Shell Icons* key.

(continued)

Common Icons Used by Windows 95 *continued*

Icon Index	Icon	Description
6		Used by the shell for a 3½" floppy disk drive. This icon must be redefined in the *Shell Icons* key.
7		Used by the shell for a removable drive. This icon must be redefined in the *Shell Icons* key.
8		Used by the shell for a hard disk drive. You can redefine this icon in the *Shell Icons* key, or you can use the AUTORUN.INF file trick described on page 210.
9		Used by the shell for the drives associated with a network device (folder or drive). You can redefine this icon in the *Shell Icons* key.
10		Used by the shell if the connection to an associated network device is broken. You can redefine this icon in the *Shell Icons* key.
11		Used by the shell for a CD-ROM drive. You can redefine this icon in the *Shell Icons* key, but this icon is always temporarily overwritten when a CD-ROM contains an AUTORUN.INF with an icon definition. (See Chapter 5.)
12		Can be used for RAM drives or for hardware settings. (I see no need to redefine the icon.)
13		Used in the Network Neighborhood window to show the Entire Network. (I see no need to redefine this icon in *Shell Icons*.)
14		Another icon for a network connection. (I haven't found the place where this icon is used by the shell.)
15		Used in the Network Neighborhood window to show workgroup computers. (The icon is defined in the *HKEY_CLASSES_ROOT\CLSID* key of the network ActiveX server.) This icon belongs to one of the shell's namespace objects. (See Chapter 4.)
16		Used for local printer drivers in the Printers folder, and used in links that you create in folders or on the desktop. (This icon can't be redefined.)

(continued)

Common Icons Used by Windows 95 *continued*

Icon Index	Icon	Description
17		Used by the shell for the Network Neighborhood. This icon belongs to the shell's namespace objects. (See Chapter 4 to learn how to change this icon.)
18		Used in the Entire Network window to show a workgroup entry. (The icon can't be redefined in *Shell Icons*.)
19		Used for the Programs entry on the Start menu and for the entries of the program groups in the submenus. The icon also represents program groups entries in the window of the Start Menu folder and subfolders (such as Accessories, Startup, etc.).
20		Used for the Documents entry on the Start menu.
21		Used for the Settings entry on the Start menu.
22		Used for the Find entry on the Start menu and other places.
23		Used for the Help entry on the Start menu. (The symbol shown for help files is defined in *HKEY_CLASSES_ROOT\hlpfile* and is contained in WINHLP32.EXE.)
24		Used for the Run entry on the Start menu.
25		Used for the Suspend mode if the computer supports a power saving feature.
26		Used for computers with a docking station.
27		Used for the Shut Down entry on the Start menu. The icon can be changed in the *Shell Icons* key.
28		Used in combination with other icons (of drives, folders, and printers) to represent sharing within a workgroup. Any icon you substitute for this one must have a transparent background.

(continued)

Common Icons Used by Windows 95 *continued*

Icon Index	Icon	Description
29		Superimposed over other icons (of drives, folders, printers, and files) to indicate a shortcut (or a PIF file). You can suppress this icon by removing the *IsShortcut* entry in the *lnkfile* and *piffile* keys. (This topic is discussed in Chapter 5.) If you want to use a substitute for this arrow, use an icon with a transparent background. Tweak UI offers a feature to suppress the Shortcut arrow or to set another icon (such as the big arrow icon).
30		Can be superimposed over other icons to indicate shortcuts (or PIF files). The icon has a transparent background. Tweak UI provides an option to use this icon as a Shortcut symbol.
31		The standard icon used to represent Recycle Bin Empty. This icon is set in the *DefaultIcon* key of the ActiveX server in the *HKEY_CLASSES_ROOT\CLSID* branch. (See Chapter 4 for further information.)
32		The standard icon used to represent Recycle Bin Full. This icon is set in the *DefaultIcon* key of the ActiveX server, in *HKEY_CLASSES_ROOT\ CLSID*. (See Chapter 4 for further information.) Other icons that can be used to represent a filled Recycle Bin are located in the SHELL32.DLL file.
33		Used by the Dial-Up networking function. (You have the option to install this in Microsoft Windows 95.) This icon is set in the *CLSID* key of the ActiveX server.
34		Used in the shell for the Desktop entry (Explorer window).
35		Used for the Control Panel panel folder. This icon can be shown or hidden on the desktop. (See Chapter 4.)
36		Used to represent the large icons for the program group folders on the Start menu.
37		Used for the Printers folder. This icon can be shown or hidden on the desktop. (See Chapter 4.)

(continued)

Common Icons Used by Windows 95 *continued*

Icon Index	Icon	Description
38		Shown for the Fonts folder in the Control Panel.
39		The Microsoft Windows symbol used as an icon on the Start button.
40		Icon used for the CD Player utility that comes with Windows 95.

Other Icons Available for General Use

Icon Index	Icon	Description
41		Tree symbol.
42		Multiple documents symbol.
43		Find files and folders symbol.
44		Find computers symbol.
45		Shut down symbol.
46		Control panel folder symbol.
47		Printer folder symbol.
48		Add new printer symbol.
49		Network printer symbol.

(continued)

Other Icons Available for General Use *continued*

Icon Index	Icon	Description
50		Print to file symbol.
51		Recycle Bin symbol.
52		Recycle Bin symbol.
53		Recycle Bin symbol.
54		Document symbol.
55		Document copy symbol.
56		Rename folder symbol.
57		Copy symbol.
58		Document symbol.
59		Document symbol.
60		Executable program symbol.
61		Document symbol.
62		Font symbol.
63		TrueType font symbol.

(continued)

Other Icons Available for General Use *continued*

Icon Index	Icon	Description
64		Run application symbol.
65		Send file symbol.
66		Backup symbol.
67		ScanDisk symbol.
68		Defragment symbol.
69		Printer symbol.
70		Network printer symbol.
71		Print to disk symbol.

Values for the *International* Key

Listed in this table are the possible values contained in the following Registry key: *HKEY_ CURRENT_USER\Control Panel\International*. These values can be set by clicking Regional Settings in the Control Panel and then selecting the appropriate property page. If the default for a given value is selected, the value will not be shown in the *International* key.

Value Name	Description
Number Settings	
sDecimal	Decimal symbol for numbers.
iDigits	Number of digits after the decimal. The value can be *0* through *9*.
sThousand	Digit grouping symbol. An example of the format is 1,000.
sGrouping	Number of digits in a group. The value is *x;0*.
sNegativeSign	Negative sign symbol.
iNegNumber	Negative number. The following list shows the value and the format, respectively: *0* (1.1) *1* −1.1 *2* − 1.1 *3* 1.1− *4* 1.1 −
iLZero	Display leading zeroes. The following list shows the value and the format, respectively: *0* .7 *1* 0.7

(continued)

continued

Value Name	Description
Number Settings *(continued)*	
iMeasure	Measurement system. The following list shows the value and the format, respectively: *0* Metric *1* U.S.
sList	List separator.
Currency Settings	
sCurrency	Currency symbol.
sMonDecimalSep	Decimal symbol.
iCurrDigits	Number of digits after decimal. The value can be *0* through *9*.
sMonThousandSep	Digit grouping symbol.
sMonGrouping	Number of digits in group. The value is *x;0*.
iCurrency	Position of currency symbol. The following list shows the value and the format, respectively: *0* $1.1 *1* 1.1$ *2* $ 1.1 *3* 1.1 $
iNegCurr	Negative number format. The following list shows the value and the format, respectively: *0* ($1.1) *1* -$1.1 *2* $-1.1 *3* $1.1- *4* (1.1$) *5* -1.1$ *6* 1.1-$ *7* 1.1$- *8* -1.1 $ *9* -$ 1.1 *10* 1.1 $- *11* $ 1.1- *12* $ -1.1 *13* 1.1- $ *14* ($ 1.1) *15* (1.1 $)

(continued)

continued

Value Name	Description

Time Settings

iTime	Time format. The following list shows the value and the format, respectively:

0	12 hours as 1:30
1	24 hours as 13:30

iTLZero	Display leading zeros in time. The following list shows the value and the format, respectively:

0	9:15
1	09:15

sTimeFormat — Time style (*h* represents 1 through 12, *H* represents 0 through 23). The following list shows the value in the left-hand column and the AM and PM formats in the middle and right-hand columns, respectively:

h:mm:ss tt	1:15:00 AM	1:15:00 PM
hh:mm:ss tt	01:15:00 AM	01:15:00 PM
H:mm:ss	1:15:00	13:15:00
HH:mm:ss	01:15:00	13:15:00

sTime	Time separator.
s1159	AM symbol.
s2359	PM symbol.

Date Settings

sLongDate — Long date style with date and weekday(*M* is month, *d* is day). *M:* month as 1–12. *MM:* month as 01–12. *MMM:* month as Jan–Dec. *MMMM:* month as January–December. *d:* day as 1–31. *dd:* day as 01–31. *ddd:* day as Mon–Sun. *dddd:* day as Monday–Sunday. The following list shows the value and the format, respectively:

dddd, MMMM dd, yyyy	Wednesday, January 01, 1997
MMMM dd, yyyy	January 01, 1997
dddd, dd MMMM, yyyy	Wednesday, 01 January, 1997
dd MMMM, yyyy	01 January, 1997

sShortDate — Short date style (only day, month, and year).

M/d/y	1/1/97
M/d/yyyy	1/1/1997
MM/dd/yy	01/01/97
MM/dd/yyyy	01/01/1997
yy/MM/dd	97/01/01
dd-MMM-yy	01-Jan-97

(continued)

continued

Value Name	Description
Date Settings *(continued)*	
sDate	Date separator.
iDate	Date style. The following list shows the value and the format, respectively: *0* USA *1* Europe *2* Japan
sLanguage	Language code for sorting and ordering.
Locale	Windows 95 country code (USA is 409).

The Registry in Windows NT 4.0 Workstation

Microsoft Windows NT 4.0 Workstation and the server version both have the Microsoft Windows 95 shell and a Registry, so you're correct to assume that they are compatible in some ways. A brief look at the NT Registry shows that several topics we address for the Windows 95 Registry are also likely to apply to the Windows NT Registry.

But there is a limit to the similarities—Windows NT 4.0 Workstation *is* a different operating system, and in many ways its Registry is remarkably different from the Windows 95 Registry. I can't address all the NT-specific topics in detail in this book, but I can provide you with some important insights that will help you with your work. (An examination of the Windows NT Registry really requires its own book. Perhaps I'll write it!)

NOTE: You can find further information about the Windows NT 4.0 Registry in the file REGENTRY.HLP, which is provided on the CD shipped with the *Windows NT 4.0 Workstation Resource Kit*. The *Resource Kit* also contains printed information about several Registry keys.

The Role of INI Files

As discussed in Chapter 1, Windows 95 still supports the old INI files for compatibility reasons. In Windows NT, however, the Registry is used in place of most of the INI files—Windows NT doesn't use the INI files. So when you install Windows NT 4.0 Workstation over Windows 3.*x*, all entries in the INI files will be moved into the Registry and those entries will be deleted from the INI files. After the install is complete, a few INI files will remain in the Windows NT folder, including WIN.INI and SYSTEM.INI. These files contain a small number of entries that aren't compatible with the Windows NT Registry and are maintained only for compatibility with 16-bit Windows software (and will be used by only those programs).

NOTE: For additional information about the mapping of the Windows 3.*x* INI file entries into the Windows NT 4.0 Registry, take a look at the *Windows NT 4.0 Workstation Resource Kit.* (See the *Further Reading* section for details about this title.)

The NT Registry Architecture

Like the Windows 95 Registry, the Windows NT 4.0 Registry is structured as a hierarchical database. The information stored in this database is organized in keys; each key contains a value or other subkeys. (See Chapter 1 for details about this type of structure.) The difference between Windows 95 and Windows NT 4.0 Workstation is in the root keys.

The Five Root Keys in the NT Registry Structure

The Windows NT 4.0 Registry consists of only five root keys that reflect different parts of the configuration data—user data and machine-dependent settings. (The sixth key, *HKEY_DYN_DATA*, is not available, as explained in the Note on page 295.) Related information about a particular aspect of the system (about the user, the hardware, the application, and so on) is grouped together in a key, or branch. Each root key, named *HKEY_xxxx*, is followed by several subkeys. The root keys are displayed when you start the Registry Editor. (See Figure C-1.)

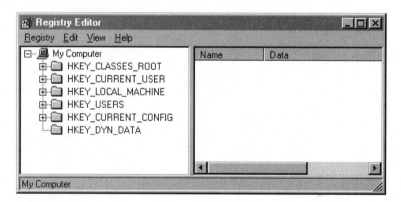

Figure C-1.
The Windows NT Registry Editor.

The following sections describe the contents of the five branches within the Registry. These branches are discussed in more detail later in this appendix in the section "Windows NT 4.0 Workstation Registry Entries" on pages 314–321.

HKEY_CLASSES_ROOT

This branch contains all data used in Windows NT for OLE and drag-and-drop operations, including the names of all registered file types and their properties. All entries of this branch can also be found in the key *HKEY_LOCAL_MACHINE\SOFTWARE\Classes*. You can use the Explorer's File Types property sheet (invoked by selecting View and then Options) to change the file type associations. The entries and steps explaining how to change these entries are discussed in Chapters 3 and 4.

HKEY_USERS

In Windows NT, more than one user can log on to a single computer, and each of those users can have unique settings for the desktop, application software, and so on. Information about each of these users, as well as settings for the desktop, Start menu, application defaults, and so on, is located in the *HKEY_USERS* key. Default values for new users logging on to the system are stored in the *.DEFAULT* subkey of *HKEY_USERS*. The information in the *.DEFAULT* subkey is also used when no user is logged on to the system. Unlike Windows 95, which uses a user's name as a subkey, Windows NT uses the user's Security ID string as the subkey.

HKEY_CURRENT_USER

Settings for the current user are stored in this key. This information is built from *HKEY_USERS* during the logon process.

HKEY_LOCAL_MACHINE

Configuration data for the local computer that is not user-dependent is stored in this key. This information is used by applications, drivers, and the NT system. Some parts of this key are built during each system startup. (We examine this more closely later in this chapter.)

HKEY_CURRENT_CONFIGURATION

This branch is new to Windows NT 4.0 and contains the configuration data for the hardware profile currently used in the computer. This branch was added for compatibility with Windows 95 (which means that the application can use this branch to run under Windows 95 and Windows NT 4.0).

> N O T E : A close look at Figure C-1 reveals a sixth key, *HKEY_DYN_DATA*. This key is actually not available—you will see it in only the REGEDIT.EXE program. If you try to open this key, the Registry Editor displays an error message.

What Are Hives?

In Windows 95, the Registry is stored in only two files: USER.DAT and SYSTEM.DAT. In Windows NT 4.0, Registry entries are saved into a more atomized structure. (This is related to the security concept used in Windows NT.) One component of this atomized structure is a "hive."

As we know, some Registry keys are rebuilt dynamically during each system startup, and other keys are essential for Windows NT 4.0 and must be available during each system startup. A hive is one of those essential keys. It is a permanent Registry key. The values for hives are stored in separate files in the Windows NT folder. Table C-1 contains a brief overview of these hives and files. You can find the names and directory locations of hives on a computer in the Registry in this key:

HKEY_LOCAL_MACHINE\SYSTEM\CurrentControlSet\Control\hivelist

Hive	Description
HKEY_LOCAL_MACHINE\SAM	Stores information for the security access manager in the System32\Config subfolder in the files SAM, SAM.LOG, and SAM.SAV. This key can't be inspected by the user.
HKEY_LOCAL_MACHINE\SECURITY	Stores security information in the System32\Config subfolder in the files SECURITY, SECURITY.LOG, and SECURITY.SAV. This key can't be inspected by the user.
HKEY_LOCAL_MACHINE\SOFTWARE	Stores information in the System32\ Config subfolder in the files SOFTWARE, SOFTWARE.LOG, and SOFTWARE.SAV.
HKEY_LOCAL_MACHINE\SYSTEM	Stores information about the hardware profiles of this subkey in the System32\ Config subfolder in the files SYSTEM, SYSTEM.LOG, and SYSTEM.SAV.
HKEY_CURRENT_CONFIG	Stores information about the *System* subkey of this hive in the System32\ Config subfolder in the files SYSTEM, SYSTEM.LOG, SYSTEM.SAV, and SYSTEM.ALT.

Table C-1. *(continued)*
Hives, keys, and their associated files.

Table C-1 *continued*

Hive	Description
HKEY_USERS\.DEFAULT	Stores information for a new user who is logged on to the system. The information for this hive is stored in the System32\Config subfolder in the files DEFAULT, DEFAULT.LOG, and DEFAULT.SAV.
HKEY_CURRENT_USER	Stores information for the current user under the \Profiles subfolder in the files NTUSER.DAT and NTUSER.DAT.LOG.

The Registry Database

The Windows NT 4.0 Registry is spread over several files, which you can inspect using the Explorer. (See Table C-1 for a detailed description of these hives and files.)

Files in the \Profiles Subfolder

The files that support the entries in *HKEY_CURRENT_USER* are stored in the \Profiles subfolder of the Windows NT folder. Selecting this subfolder in the Explorer shows the All Users and Default User subfolders as well as a subfolder for each user with an account under Windows NT. All subfolders except All Users contain the files NTUSER.DAT and (sometimes) NTUSER.DAT.LOG. The file NTUSER.DAT contains the user profile for the current machine (desktop settings, applications, and so on). The file NTUSER.DAT in the Default User subfolder contains the hive for each new user. If a new user logs on to the system for the first time, the data in the NTUSER.DAT file in the Default User subfolder is copied to a file in the user's subfolder.

Files in the \System32\Config Subfolder

The other supporting files for the hives are stored in the Windows NT subfolder \System32\Config. Some of these files, such as SAM, DEFAULT, and SOFTWARE, do not contain an extension and do contain a copy of the hive content. All files with the extension SAV, such as DEFAULT.SAV and SOFTWARE.SAV, contain a copy of the hive file. This copy is made at the end of the text-mode Setup. All changes made to a key in a hive are recorded in a file with the extension LOG (such as SAM.LOG). The file SYSTEM.ALT contains a copy of the critical hive *HKEY_LOCAL_MACHINE\SYSTEM*.

NOTE: The USERDIFF file in the NT subfolder\System32\Config does not contain a hive. It is used only for compatibility reasons with older NT versions. If a user logs on to the system for the first time, the settings from the old user profile will be read from USERDIFF and incorporated into the Registry.

Recovery in the NT Registry

Windows NT 4.0 uses a different strategy from Windows 95 to record all changes in the Registry and allow a recovery. After you modify a Registry entry, the changed data is written by the system to the hive's LOG file and the value is stored on the hard disk when the next flush operation occurs. This flush operation can occur within a few seconds automatically, or it can occur when an application forces it to.

During this flush, the first sector of the LOG file is marked to indicate that a Registry transfer is under construction. After the flush, the changed data is also written to the actual hive file. If this transfer operation is successful, the hive file and the LOG file are marked as complete. If the system crashes during the transfer, the system detects the incomplete transaction (the mark in the LOG file is still available) and recovers the hive from the previous value recorded in the LOG file.

The *SYSTEM* hive is processed a little bit differently. After Windows stores the changed data in the hive and LOG files, the SYSTEM.ALT file is updated in the same manner. If Windows restarts with a *SYSTEM* hive still under construction, the contents of SYSTEM.ALT will be used.

NOTE: Backing up, recovering, and restoring the NT Registry is discussed on pages 310–314.

Data Types Used in the NT Registry

In earlier chapters, we examined the data types available for the Windows 95 Registry: string, DWORD, and binary. If you use the Registry Editor REGEDIT.EXE to modify entries, you can use these three data types. In Windows NT 4.0, you can also use the Registry Editor REGEDT32.EXE (see "Tools for Accessing the NT Registry" on page 300) to use additional data types to define a key's value. Table C-2 contains an overview of these data types.

Data Type	Description
REG_BINARY	This type describes raw binary data as a byte stream. The data type is named BINARY in REGEDIT.EXE.
REG_DWORD	An entry of this data type represents a 4-byte (or 32-bit) number. This data type is also available as DWORD in REGEDIT.EXE.
REG_SZ	Values for this data type can contain a sequence of characters (a string) that are easily understood by a user. (We've seen many of these strings in the previous chapters.) This data type is also supported as the string data type by REGEDIT.EXE.
REG_EXPAND_SZ	Windows NT recognizes expandable data strings, which are not supported in Windows 95. Such a string contains a variable that can be expanded when an application is called. You can insert, for example, the variable *%SystemRoot%* into an expandable data string, and the variable will be replaced by the name of the Windows NT directory (for example, *%SystemRoot%\ NOTEPAD.EXE*). This data type can be created by a program or by REGEDT32.EXE.
REG_MULTI_SZ	This value describes a multiple string that contains several user-readable entries separated by NULL characters. This data type is also supported only by a program or by REGEDT32.EXE.

Table C-2.
Data types available for Windows NT Registry values.

As Table C-2 points out, keys containing some data types can be created only by a program or by using the REGEDT32.EXE Registry Editor. An NT Registry key entry can be as long as 1 MB—that's a lot longer than a Windows 95 Registry key, which is restricted to a length of 64 KB. However, a Registry full of long values will result in very large Registry hive files, and a lot of memory is required to load such large files. So Microsoft recommends storing entries longer than 2048 bytes in separate files and storing the paths and filenames of these files in the Registry key. A key name can be up to 16000 Unicode characters long. One important fact in Windows NT is that, unlike in Windows 95, the key names are case-sensitive.

NOTE: Other data types might be added by various programs, but this data can't be edited by the Registry Editor.

Tools for Accessing the NT Registry

Because the Windows NT 4.0 Registry file structure is different from the Windows 95 Registry file structure, you need special tools to access and modify it. These tools include the two Registry Editors, REGEDIT.EXE and REGEDT32.EXE, as well as a diagnostics tool, the Explorer, the Control Panel, and REG and INF files.

REGEDIT.EXE

After you install Windows NT 4.0 Workstation, you will find in the Windows NT folder the REGEDIT.EXE file. REGEDIT.EXE is the new style of Registry Editor provided by NT. The NT Registry Editor has the same functionality and structure as the Windows 95 Registry Editor, so you can use it in the same way. (See details for using the Registry Editor in Chapter 2 of this book.) The disadvantage of this Registry Editor is that it doesn't support the extended data types defined for Windows NT. (These data types are listed in Table C-2 on the preceding page.)

REGEDT32.EXE

Windows NT 4.0 Workstation is shipped with a second Registry Editor, REGEDT32.EXE, that is available in the Windows NT\System32 subfolder after you install Windows NT. This second Registry Editor was based on older NT versions, so its user interface is different from the REGEDIT.EXE interface. Context menus are not available, and the Registry keys are displayed in separate windows (as shown in Figure C-2 on the facing page). The menu bar in the Registry Editor's window contains commands for viewing, editing, and storing Registry data.

Registry Menu Commands

Registry menu commands available to you with REGEDT32.EXE include the Save Subtree As command, which allows you to save a selected subkey to a text file, commands for printing a subkey (or "subtree"), and commands for loading and unloading a hive.

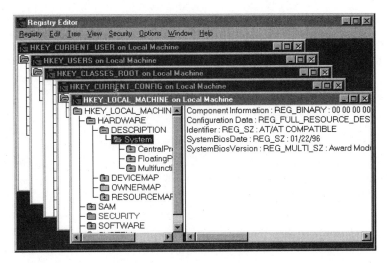

Figure C-2.
The Registry structure shown in REGEDT32.EXE.

Loading and unloading a hive   The Load Hive and Unload Hive options
are available from the Registry menu only if you select a subkey that is actually a hive. These options enable you to load a copy of another computer's hive
files into the Registry Editor and modify them. The hive files of the current
machine are loaded automatically when you start REGEDT32.EXE. To load
another computer's hives, select the *HKEY_LOCAL_MACHINE* key or the
HKEY_USERS key and then click the Load Hive command on the Registry
menu. The Load Hive dialog box opens, which allows you to select another
computer's hive from a file copied to a floppy disk. After you select the hive
file, you can modify it, save it back to the original computer, and restart Windows NT.

> NOTE: To export a key into a hive file, select the key and use the
> Save Subtree As command. To import the hive file, click the key and
> select the Restore command from the Registry menu of the Regis-
> try Editor. After these steps, you can select the name of the hive file.
> (As you can see, this export and import process is different from the
> export and import process used for REG files that are provided by
> REGEDIT.EXE.)

View and Options Menu Commands

The View menu contains a Find Key command that allows you to search for a key. (REGEDIT.EXE also allows you to search for a key, as well as for a key's value.) Luckily, the Options menu offers the Read Only Mode command. This is a cool function because it allows you to inspect the Registry without the risk of inadvertently modifying it.

The Security Menu's Permissions Command

Each key in the Windows NT Registry contains an access permission attribute. The system administrator can use REGEDT32.EXE to limit a user's access to any key in order to prevent that user from modifying the key. The Permissions command on the Security menu of the Registry Editor allows you to set the access permission to Read, Full Control, and Special Access. The Special Access command allows users to modify specific values of a key.

> WARNING: Be careful when you restrict access permission to system keys because you might inadvertently restrict people like the system administrator from modifying them. Always back up the Registry before changing any access privilege, and let the system administrator "own" all keys. Further information about this topic can be found in the *Windows NT 4.0 Workstation Resource Kit.*

Windows NT Diagnostics

You can use the Windows NT Diagnostics tool WINMSD.EXE to inspect important system settings. This file is available in the Windows NT subfolder \System32. After you invoke WINMSD.EXE (by clicking the Start menu and then selecting Programs, Administrative Tools, and Windows NT Diagnostics), you will see a property sheet with several property pages, as shown in Figure C-3.

Through these property pages, you can view various system components (each component corresponds to a property page). This diagnostic tool allows only a Read access, which prevents you from accidentally changing something in the Registry.

Figure C-3.
The Windows NT diagnostics program.

Explorer

You can use the Explorer to change file type associations by invoking the Explorer and then selecting the Options command from the View menu. The File Types property page contains the settings for all registered file types. You can change these settings as explained in Chapter 3 of this book.

Control Panel

When you want to change the system settings in the Registry, *always go through the Control Panel first.* To open the Control Panel window, click the Start menu, and then select Settings, then Control Panel. Double-click the desired icon to open its property sheet. On the property sheet, you can safely inspect and modify the settings. We examined how to do this for Windows 95 in earlier chapters, and you can use the same steps for Windows NT 4.0.

Windows NT includes the functions of the Windows 95 Plus! Pack, which simplify some tasks, such as how to change desktop icons for My Computer, Recycle Bin, and Network Neighborhood. Under Windows NT 4.0 Workstation, you don't have to use all those tricks we examined in earlier chapters. All you have to do is invoke the Display Properties property sheet, which you can do from the Control Panel, and select the Plus! property page, which contains options for changing the desktop icons. (See Figure C-4.) Clicking a desktop icon on this property page and then clicking Change Icon allows you to select a new icon source.

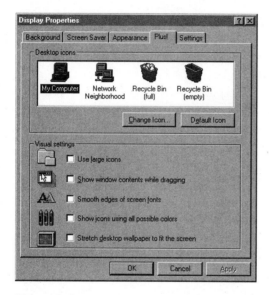

Figure C-4.
Changing the desktop icons on the Plus! property page.

> N O T E : The Policy Editor for Windows 95 isn't available in Windows
> NT 4.0 Workstation. POLEDIT.EXE is shipped only with Windows NT
> 4.0 Server and the Windows 4.0 WorkStation Resource Kit.

REG Files

You can use a valid REG file to import a key into the Windows NT 4.0 Registry by double-clicking the filename. The REG file must be stored in the same format as a REGEDIT.EXE export file. (We looked at this format in Chapter 2.) Importing with a REG file has its risks and disadvantages—the same ones we noted for Windows 95. If you use REG files created under Windows 95, you must carefully check the paths and keys before you import those files into Windows NT 4.0. Although Windows NT 4.0 uses different paths to store the files and the Registry structure is somewhat different from Windows 95, you can try to customize the Windows NT 4.0 shell by using some of the REG files described in the previous chapters.

INF Files

A better solution for accessing the Registry is provided by INF files, which allow you to add placeholders for the path description. In Chapter 7, we examined how to manipulate the Windows 95 Registry by writing and using INF files. Using similar INF files, you can modify the Windows NT 4.0 Registry, but you must understand how the Registries and their file structures differ (described further in the next section). Also keep in mind that Windows NT flushes the internal write buffers to the hard disk only occasionally. If you change a setting in the Registry (using a Registry Editor, a REG file, or an INF file), several seconds might pass before the new data is stored to all locations on the hard disk. (See page 310 for an explanation of how Windows NT saves information to the hive files.)

What Should I Know About
Using INF Files Under Windows NT 4.0?

Before you use INF files, you need to be aware of several differences between Windows 95 and Windows NT 4.0. As long as you accommodate these differences (as described in the following sections), you can use INF files in Windows NT 4.0 in the same way we have used them throughout the book.

> NOTE: Are you using the INF files provided for Windows 95? For your convenience, I've ported several INF files from Windows 95 to Windows NT 4.0 Workstation. These are located in the\NTApendx subfolder of the downloaded sample files.

Placeholders First of all, your INF file should start with these lines:

```
[version]
signature="$Windows NT$"
```

Next you should be aware of the different ways that Windows 95 and Windows NT use placeholders in an INF file. In Chapter 7, we examined how to use the placeholders *%10%* and *%11%* in a statement. These placeholders are also used in Windows NT. As in Windows 95, these placeholders stand for the Windows folder and the system subfolder and are replaced when the INF file is processed. If you inspect a Registry entry you've set using these placeholders, you will find the name of the current drive and folder containing the Windows NT system files. If you omit these placeholders, you should keep in mind that the Windows 95 system subfolder is named System whereas the Windows NT system subfolder is named System32.

Another placeholder that can be used in a Windows NT Registry command is *%SystemRoot%*. This placeholder is not converted to a path when the INF file is installed; it is inserted as a string value directly into the Registry. Windows NT 4.0 recognizes the *REG_EXPAND_SZ* data type, which allows you to insert variables into a command. During the execution of a command, Windows NT will replace *%SystemRoot%* with the name of the current Windows folder.

Keys for identical tasks differ   Windows 95 and Windows NT 4.0 use the same shell, but only some Registry structures are similar in both operating versions—unfortunately, you can be easily misled by these similarities. For example, let's take a closer look at our trick for changing the desktop icons (discussed in Chapter 4). Can we use the INF file RECYCLE1.INF to change the Recycle Bin icon? The INF file itself can be used, but the keys you need to modify are different. Under Windows 95, the entries for the Recycle Bin icons are stored in this key:

> *HKEY_CLASSES_ROOT\CLSID\{645FF040-5081-101B-9F08-00AA002F954E}\DefaultIcon*

This key is also available in Windows NT 4.0, but it's not the key you want to modify to affect the Recycle Bin icons on the desktop. In Windows NT 4.0, the Recycle Bin icons are defined in a different key:

> *HKEY_CURRENT_USER\Software\Classes\CLSID\{645FF040-5081-101B-9F08-00AA002F954E}\DefaultIcon*

If you modify the entries in the INF file, you can change the desktop icon for the Recycle Bin as you would in Windows 95. Following are the statements contained in an INF file that sets a new icon for the Recycle Bin under Windows NT 4.0:

```
; File: Recycle1.INF (Windows NT 4.0)
; by Guenter Born
;
; Set the Recycle Bin Full icon to a new symbol
[version]
signature="$Windows NT$"

[DefaultInstall]
AddReg = Recycle.AddReg
```

(continued)

continued

```
[Recycle.AddReg]
; Use HKEY_CURRENT_USER\Software\Classes\CLSID
; Set "Full" to icon no 54 in shell32.dll
HKCU,Software\Classes\CLSID\{645FF040-5081-101B-9F08-00AA002F954E}
\DefaultIcon,Empty,,"%11%\\shell32.dll,31"
HKCU,Software\Classes\CLSID\{645FF040-5081-101B-9F08-00AA002F954E}
\DefaultIcon,Full,,"%SystemRoot%\\system32\\shell32.dll,53"
; End ***
```

The file that resets these icons must have a similar structure. Other desktop icon entries (such as My Computer and Network Neighborhood) are also stored in this branch.

32-bit versions of programs and libraries must be used
Another difference is that you must always use the 32-bit version of programs and libraries, so you can't take advantage of the uninstall commands described in Chapter 7. Although the *Uninstall* subkey is still available in the NT 4.0 Registry, you can't use RUNDLL.EXE to invoke other libraries. Instead, Windows NT provides the RUNDLL32.EXE program to call other DLL libraries. The library SETUPX.DLL isn't available under Windows NT 4.0, so you must insert the library SETUPAPI.DLL, which has the same calling interface as SETUPX.DLL. Following are INF file statements that install the DOS Window as a shell extension. This INF file also provides an uninstall feature that can be invoked in the Install/Uninstall property sheet. (You can access this property sheet by selecting Settings from the Start menu, then Control Panel, and then Add/Remove Programs.)

```
; File: DOS.inf (c) G. Born ** Windows NT 4.0 Version
;
; Install script to extend the Explorer's context menu
; with a DOS command under Windows NT 4.0
;
; If the user right-clicks a folder symbol in the
; Explorer's window or in a shell's window, the command
; "MS-DOS" will appear on the context menu. Selecting this
; command invokes the MS-DOS window and selects the folder.

[version]
signature="$Windows NT$"
SetupClass=BASE

; Add the extension into the Registry
```

(continued)

continued

```
[DefaultInstall]
AddReg = DOS.AddReg
CopyFiles = DOS.CopyFiles.Inf

; Uninstall part

[DefaultUninstall]

DelReg = DOS.AddReg,
DelFiles = DOS.CopyFiles.Inf

; This part adds the keys to the Registry. The feature
; is registered in HKEY_CLASSES_ROOT\Folder\shell.

[DOS.AddReg]

; Add the DOS verb and the string for the context menu
; %COMMAND_STRING%
HKCR,Folder\shell\dos,,,"%COMMAND_STRING%"
; Add the command to activate command.com
HKCR,Folder\shell\dos\command,,,%COMMAND%
; *** This stuff is required to set up the uninstall feature.
; *** Attention: The UninstallString is different from Windows 95!!!
HKLM,SOFTWARE\Microsoft\Windows\CurrentVersion\Uninstall\dos,
DisplayName,,"%DOS_REMOVE_DESC%"
HKLM,SOFTWARE\Microsoft\Windows\CurrentVersion\Uninstall\dos,
UninstallString,,
"RunDll32 setupapi.dll,InstallHinfSection DefaultUninstall 4 DOS.Inf"
; Don't forget to remove the newShellWindow key in Uninstall
; by adding the following line:
HKLM,SOFTWARE\Microsoft\Windows\CurrentVersion\Uninstall\dos
; Here we define the files to be copied. Source and
; destination directories are defined in the following sections.

[DOS.CopyFiles.Inf]
DOS.Inf

; This is the definition for the source. (Use the path where
; the INF file is activated; 55 is defined in SourceDisksFiles.)
[SourceDisksNames]
55="MS-DOS","",1
[SourceDisksFiles]
DOS.Inf=55

; Now we have to specify the destination. The
; logical disk ID for the Windows subfolder INF is 17.
```

(continued)

continued

```
[DestinationDirs]
DOS.CopyFiles.Inf = 17

; Define miscellaneous variables

[Strings]
; Command to invoke command.com
COMMAND = "command.com"

; String for the context menu entry
COMMAND_STRING = "MS-DOS"

; String for the Uninstall entry
DOS_REMOVE_DESC = "Remove Born's Win NT 4.0 MS-DOS Shell Extension"
; End ***
```

Modifying the Registry Size

The Registry data is kept in an area of physical memory that is used for system data. This data area is flushed from time to time to the hard disk. The Registry size is limited by default to 25 percent of the paged memory pool. You can set this limit within the *RegistrySizeLimit* value in this Registry key:

> *HKEY_LOCAL_MACHINE\SYSTEM\CurrentControlSet\Control*

The *RegistrySizeLimit* value is defined as a DWORD. The size for the paged memory pool is kept in the *PagedPoolSize* DWORD value in the following key:

> *HKEY_LOCAL_MACHINE\SYSTEM\CurrentControlSet\Control\
> Session Manager\Memory Management*

If the Registry grows, you must either increase the memory limits or remove unused hives.

Removing Unused Registry Parts

As mentioned in the other chapters of this book, you should keep the Registry up-to-date. After using Windows NT 4.0 for a while, you will find unused Registry entries. Eventually, the Registry will become too large to back up, so you should clean it up from time to time.

You can use the Registry Editor to delete unused keys in the Registry. Although this keeps the Registry clean, it won't reduce its size significantly.

Cleaning up user profiles, however, can have an impact on the size of the Registry. Each user who has an account on a workstation gets his or her own Registry profile, which is stored in the *HKEY_USERS* branch. Viewing the *HKEY_USERS* branch of the Registry with a Registry Editor shows the

.DEFAULT key and a key with the name of each user's Security ID string. During a system startup, Windows NT loads into memory the entries in the *HKEY_USERS\.DEFAULT* key. Pressing the Ctrl-Alt-Del key combination invokes the logon dialog box. If the user enters a name and password, Windows NT uses the user's Security ID string to load the associated branch from *HKEY_USERS*. This means that Windows NT keeps only the data for the current user in the memory pool.

Nevertheless, for each user having an account under Windows NT, the operating system keeps a profile in the file NTUSER.DAT. If many unused user accounts exist, it is always a good idea to remove the corresponding profiles from the computer. This can be done in the Windows NT Setup by clicking the Delete User Profiles option on the Options menu. (Take a look at *Microsoft Windows NT 4.0 Workstation Resource Kit,* which is briefly described in the "Further Reading" section of this book.)

Backing Up and Recovering the NT 4.0 Registry

Before you modify a setting in the Registry, you should back it up, which will ensure that you can recover a clean Registry if the one you are working on is corrupted. Because Windows NT 4.0 uses a different Registry file structure than Windows 95, you can't use the Windows 95 tools to create a backup. In the following sections, we'll take a look at some tips for creating a backup of the Windows NT 4.0 Registry.

Backing Up

You have several options for backing up your Windows NT 4.0 Registry, and Windows NT 4.0 comes with a few utilities that support the backup process. The most convenient way, however, is offered by the tools shipped on the CD available with the Windows NT 4.0 Workstation Resource Kit. (See the "Further Readings" section for details.)

Using the Backup Program to Save the Hives

We know that permanent Registry information is stored in hives. Those hives are mapped into files, which are located in several folders on the hard disk, so you can create a backup of them.

The recommended way to create a backup of your NT Registry is to use the Backup program provided with Windows NT, but you've got to have a tape drive to use it. The Backup program is available after you install Windows NT. Here's what to do:

1. Click Start on the taskbar, and then select Programs, Administrative Tools (Common), and Backup.

2. Once the program has started, click Backup on the Operations menu. This opens the Backup Information dialog box.

3. Select the Backup Local Registry option. This option saves all the local hive files necessary for the Registry.

Using the Repair Disk Utility

If you don't have a tape drive available under Windows NT 4.0, you can try to save the hive files on a diskette as long as your Registry isn't too big. Windows NT 4.0 comes with a tool called Repair Disk Utility that can be used for this purpose. You start this tool by running the RDISK.EXE file, located in the Windows NT subfolder \System32.

RDISK.EXE allows you to update the repair information for Windows NT stored on your hard disk. You can also create an Emergency Repair Disk that can be used for the reconstruction of the system files if they are damaged. After starting this tool, you will see the dialog box shown in Figure C-5. Here's an overview of the dialog box options:

■ The Update Repair Info button enables you to update the repair information on the hard disk. This information is stored in the Windows NT subfolder \repair, which contains the system files in a compressed version. These system files are necessary to create an Emergency Repair Disk.

■ The Create Repair Disk button invokes a function that uses the information stored in the \repair subfolder to create an Emergency Repair Disk. The function formats a 1.44-MB floppy disk and copies the files onto the disk.

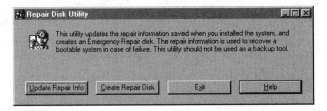

Figure C-5.
The Repair Disk Utility.

If you invoke RDISK.EXE by double-clicking the file's icon, the program will back up only the hive files for the system and software. You can force RDISK.EXE to also back up the SAM and security hives by activating the tool with the command RDISK -s. But be aware of space requirements when you use this switch: If a lot of user accounts are on the system, more space than is available on a floppy disk might be required for the SAM and security hives.

NOTE: During system installation, Setup creates a file set in the \repair subfolder. This file set contains the image of the system files after the first successful system startup. If you create an Emergency Repair Disk, you will get the post-install system configuration. To keep an up-to-date copy of your system configuration files, you should use the Update Repair Info button before you use the Create Repair Disk function.

Other Backup Methods

Depending on your system, you can use other methods to create a backup of your system files.

- If NT uses a FAT partition, you can start MS-DOS or Windows 95 on that machine and then copy the files contained in the Windows NT subfolder \System32\config to a backup medium. This enables you to use tools such as WinZip or PKZIP to squeeze the files onto a floppy disk.

- If you have already installed a second NT version, you can use the process described above to access the \System32\config folder on an NTFS partition and save the files on backup media.

- If you have access to the *Windows NT 4.0 Workstation Resource Kit* CD, you can use the program REGBACK.EXE to create a backup of the Registry files.

- You can use the Registry Editor REGEDT32.EXE to save parts of the Registry in hive files. Then you can copy these hive files onto a floppy and load them into the Registry later on with REGEDT32.EXE. This approach enables you to share parts of the Registry between two computers.

All these methods require that you keep track of your files. You should note that it is not possible to copy a hive file under Windows NT because the file is locked by the operating system.

Recovering the Registry

There are several ways to recover a corrupted Registry and restore an old version. If you have already created a backup of your Registry, you can use this backup copy to recover the Registry. In this section, we'll briefly examine some strategies for recovering the contents of the Registry.

Using the Last Version

The Registry Editors provided with Windows NT do not support an Undo function. When you delete a key, the Registry is updated and the results are stored after a few seconds in the hive files on the hard disk. You get a chance to recover a key deleted in *HKEY_LOCAL_MACHINE\SYSTEM\CurrentControlSet* if you restart your computer with Windows NT. During the system startup (in the character-based setup), the "Press Spacebar To Invoke Hardware Profile" message is displayed. If you press the spacebar immediately when this message appears, you can go back to the Last Known Good Registry configuration by pressing the L key.

Restoring the Backup Files

If your Registry is corrupted, Windows NT might not be able to start successfully. If you have the Windows NT Startup disk and the Emergency Repair Disk, you can use them to restore the system. The Emergency Repair Disk recovers the image of the Registry saved in the \repair subfolder—this is the image created during the first installation of the Registry or during the last Update Repair Info process. Once you restore the data from the Emergency Repair Disk and successfully start Windows NT, you can try to restore more of the Registry settings in several ways, which are briefly described in the following sections.

Reloading a hive file after startup   If you have a copy of a hive file (created with REGEDT32.EXE), you can reload it into the Registry after a successful Windows NT 4.0 startup. A huge problem exists with this approach, however. Windows NT requires a ReplaceKey operation for active parts of the Registry, but this operation isn't supported by the Registry Editor. For inactive parts of the Registry, you can do the following:

1. Invoke the REGEDT32.EXE program, and select the hive or key you want to update.

2. Open the Registry menu, and then click Load Hive.

3. Select the hive file in the Load Hive dialog box, and click the Open button. The Registry Editor loads the hive into the selected key.

Using a backup set   The best method of recovering your Registry is to use a backup set created with the Windows NT 4.0 Backup program. If you have a backup tape, you can use the Backup option to restore the Registry.

Starting your computer with a different operating system   If you created a backup manually by copying files, you can't copy the hive files from the backup set to the hard disk because Windows NT locks the system files currently in use. So you have to start your computer with a different operating system (such as MS-DOS) and copy the backup files to your hard disk (in the Windows NT subfolder\System32\config and in the\Profiles subfolders). Then you must restart your computer and hope that Windows NT will boot in a proper manner.

Using REGREST.EXE   If you have access to the *Windows NT 4.0 Workstation Resource Kit* CD, you can use the program REGREST.EXE to restore a backup created with the REGBACK.EXE tool, which is on this CD.

> NOTE: You can find additional information about backing up and recovering the Registry in the *Windows NT 4.0 Workstation Resource Kit*. See the "Further Readings" section for details.

Windows NT 4.0 Workstation Registry Entries

Many of the Windows 95 Registry entries examined in this book are also available in the Windows NT 4.0 Registry, but some branches in Windows NT are not available under Windows 95, and some information that both Registries share is contained in different branches. In this section, we'll take a look at the branches and entries in the Windows NT Registry.

HKEY_CLASSES_ROOT

As noted earlier in this appendix, this branch contains all data that is used for OLE and drag-and-drop operations in Windows. You can use the procedures throughout this book to identify and modify entries in this branch. This branch is mirrored in the *HKEY_LOCAL_MACHINE\SOFTWARE\Classes* key.

HKEY_USERS

This branch and the Windows 95 *HKEY_USERS* branch contain similar information. In Windows NT, this branch stores information about the user profiles for each user account. The *.DEFAULT* key contains the profile used by Windows NT if no user is logged on to the system. Every other key directly under *HKEY_USERS* contains the data for a particular user. As in Windows 95, the information about the current user is copied into the *HKEY_CURRENT_USER* branch.

HKEY_CURRENT_USER

When a user logs on to the system, Windows NT copies the user profile into this key from *HKEY_USERS. HKEY_CURRENT_USER* contains several subkeys, described in the following sections. The profiles of these Windows NT 4.0 subkeys are similar to their Windows 95 counterparts, so you can find additional information about them in the preceding chapters of this book.

\AppEvents

This subkey contains paths to sound files that are loaded for particular system events (for example, when an error message occurs). The structure of this key is similar to the same key in Windows 95.

\Console

Available only in Windows NT, this subkey defines the options and the window size for the console. (The console is the DOS window interface that is used for character mode applications.) The value names used in this key are self-explanatory. You can change the settings of this key using the property sheet for the console. This property sheet can be invoked in two ways: in the console window (select Programs from the Start menu, then Command Prompt) by right-clicking the title bar and selecting Properties from the context menu, or by opening the Control Panel and double-clicking the Console icon.

\Control Panel

Data that can be altered in the Control Panel window (such as screen settings) is contained in this subkey. (Most of its entries are similar to those in *\Control Panel* under Windows 95, so take a look at the previous chapters in this book to find out more about them.) In this subkey, you will also find the settings for the screen savers installed under Windows NT. Screen saver options are set on the Display Properties property sheet (which is on the Screen Saver property page).

\Environment

In this subkey are the names of Environment variables (like *TEMP*). To set Environment variables or change their values, open the Environment property page through the System Properties property sheet. (You can access this property sheet by opening the Control Panel window and double-clicking the System icon.)

\Keyboard Layout

This subkey contains information about the language used for the keyboard layout. You can change keyboard layout settings on the Input Locale property page, which is available from the Keyboard Properties property sheet. (Access this by opening the Control Panel and double-clicking the Keyboard icon.) The options in the Switch Locales group set the *Hotkey* value in the *Toggle* subkey to *1*, *2*, or *3*. These values correspond to the three option boxes. (The value *3*, for example, stands for the None option.)

\Printers

Information about the installed printer drivers for the current user is stored in this subkey. You can change the settings of a printer by using the property sheet of the printer driver. (Open the Printers folder in the Control Panel, right-click the desired printer, and select Properties from the context menu.)

\Network

This subkey is no longer supported in Windows NT 4.0. (Windows 95 and previous NT versions use this key to store persistent network connections.) In Windows NT 4.0, the information about persistent network connections has moved to the following branch of *HKEY_CURRENT_USER*:

> *\Software\Microsoft\Windows NT\CurrentVersion\Network\Persistent*

\Software

This subkey describes the properties of user-installed software. This subkey refers to the *HKEY_LOCAL_MACHINE* branch, in which applications store their settings. If both *HKEY_CURRENT_USER\Software* and *HKEY_LOCAL_MACHINE\SOFTWARE* contain similar data for a particular subkey, the entry in *HKEY_CURRENT_USER* takes precedence over the *HKEY_LOCAL_MACHINE* value. This allows you to override some machine-specific settings with user-specific settings.

\UNICODE Program Groups

This subkey isn't used in Windows NT 4.0 because the Windows NT shell no longer uses GRP files.

\Windows 3.1 Migration Status

This subkey exists only if Windows NT 4.0 is set up as an upgrade to Windows 3.1. These entries contain information about whether INI and GRP files are converted successfully.

HKEY_LOCAL_MACHINE

This branch defines all specific information for the local machine, such as drivers, installed hardware, port mappings, software configuration, and so on. This information is valid for all users logged on to the system. *HKEY_LOCAL_ MACHINE* is divided into several subkeys containing the following data.

\HARDWARE

This key contains the settings for the hardware used by the current computer. Figure C-6 shows the structure of this key.

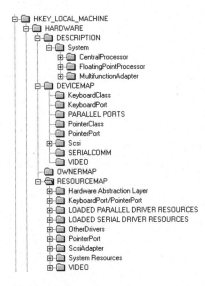

Figure C-6.
Contents of the \HARDWARE *key.*

The following sections describe the subkeys contained in *HKEY_LOCAL_ MACHINE\HARDWARE.*

\DESCRIPTION   This subkey contains information about the hardware. All entries are built from the firmware information contained in the computer. This information is detected by the NTDETECT.COM program and the NT Executive during each system startup. The *\System* subkey contains information about numeric processors and multifunction adapters (for serial and parallel ports and for disk controllers).

\DEVICEMAP   This subkey contains a subkey for each device that stores values specifying where in the Registry device-specific information is located.

\OWNERMAP   This subkey appears only on machines having a PCI bus. It contains data to associate a PCI driver with PCI devices installed on the bus.

\RESOURCEMAP   This subkey maps the device drivers to resources that the drivers use. This data is stored in raw binary format and describes IO addresses, DMA channels, Interrupts, and so on. The contents of this branch are built during each system startup, so it wouldn't make sense to write data into the keys contained here.

\SAM

This branch belongs to the Security Account Manager and contains information about user accounts. It cannot be directly accessed or changed. This key is mapped to the *HKEY_LOCAL_MACHINE\SECURITY\SAM* key.

\SECURITY

This branch contains security information and belongs to the Security Account Manager. The keys in this branch cannot be accessed through the Registry Editor.

\SOFTWARE

All information about the software installed on the machine is stored in this branch, which is shown in Figure C-7.

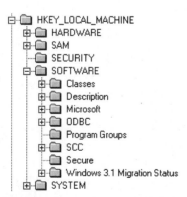

Figure C-7.
Contents of the \SOFTWARE *branch.*

The following sections describe the subkeys in the *\SOFTWARE* branch.

\Classes   This subkey contains the registered filename extensions and the Class ID subkeys for Component Object Model objects (CLSID codes). All entries contained in this subkey are mapped into the *HKEY_CLASSES_ROOT* branch of the Registry. You can find further information about the entries in this branch in Chapter 3.

\Description   This subkey stores the names and versions of software installed on the local computer. The entries in this subkey must be stored as ...*\Company\ Product\Version*. After Windows NT is installed, the *\Description* subkey contains only one entry, *\Microsoft\Rpc*, which defines data for Remote Procedure calls.

\Microsoft   Configuration settings for Microsoft programs installed on the local machine are contained in this subkey. The *\Microsoft\Windows\CurrentVersion* subkey contains information used by the Windows NT 4.0 shell. The entries in the *\Microsoft\Windows\CurrentVersion* subkey are similar to the subkeys of the same name in Windows 95. The subkey *\Microsoft\Windows NT\ CurrentVersion* contains information about services built into Windows NT.

\ODBC   Settings for any ODBC drivers installed on the local machine are contained in this subkey.

\Program Groups   In previous versions of Windows NT, this subkey stored program group information. In Windows NT 4.0, the Start menu Programs folder structure stores program group information. The *\Program Groups* subkey now contains only the *ConvertedToLinks* value. A value of *1* in this entry indicates a successful conversion of old program group files (GRPs) to the new folder structure.

\Secure   Applications can store information in this subkey. Subkeys of *\Secure* can be modified only by a system administrator. This subkey is empty after the Windows NT setup.

\Windows 3.1 Migration Status   Information about the migration status of INI and GRP files is stored in this subkey. It contains valid data only if Windows NT is installed over Windows 3.1.

\SYSTEM

This branch contains all system-specific data, which is needed during startup and which might not be configured by detection software. This branch is mapped into the *SYSTEM* hive. Figure C-8 on the following page shows the structure of *\HKEY_LOCAL_MACHINE\SYSTEM*.

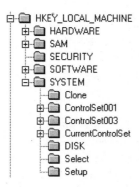

Figure C-8.
Contents of the \SYSTEM *key.*

The following sections describe the contents of \SYSTEM.

\Clone   This subkey is not accessible in the Registry Editor. It contains the last control set used for the system startup.

Control sets   Data necessary during the system startup is grouped in control sets. Multiple control sets are stored in the \SYSTEM key (usually two with the numbers 001 and 003). The *Windows NT 4.0 Workstation Resource Kit* contains further information about typical values found in this subkey. Each of these control sets has a number and contains four subkeys, described in the following sections.

- \Control. This subkey always contains configuration information (computer name, file system, and so on).

- \Enum. Hardware configuration information (data for devices and drivers loaded in Windows NT) is stored here.

- \Hardware Profiles. This subkey contains configuration data needed for drivers and devices that are used in hardware profiles. If the configuration for a specified hardware profile differs from the standard configuration, that information is stored in this subkey.

- \Services. This subkey contains subkeys for driver, file system, service program, and virtual hardware used by Windows NT. The data in these subkeys is used to load the corresponding services.

\DISK   This subkey contains entry information with a binary data stream value that defines information about the disk. *\DISK* will be available only after you have run Disk Administrator at least once. (Run Disk Administrator from the Start menu by selecting Programs, then Administrative Tools, and then Disk Administrator.)

\Select   This subkey stores information about the status of the Registry. If the system starts, the control set stored in the *\Clone* subkey is used. Following is a description of values stored in the *\Select* subkey.

- *LastKnownGood* contains the number of the control set that is known as good for a system startup.

- *Default* defines the control set that is used for a default system startup.

- *Current* is the name of the control set used during startup. The user can change this value by selecting a control set at system startup. (Press the spacebar in the character-based startup process when the message "Press spacebar..." becomes visible.)

- *Failed* is a flag indicating that a system startup has failed.

\Setup   This subkey is left over from the Windows NT system setup program.

HKEY_CURRENT_CONFIG

Added to provide compatibility between Windows 95 and Windows NT, this branch is new in Windows NT 4.0 and contains the current hardware configuration for computers with varying hardware profiles (docking stations). Although application programs can run under both operating systems, the hardware data in Windows NT and Windows 95 is stored differently. So these application programs cannot alter the Registry. Instead, the programs use the Config Manager API to access information in the *HKEY_CURRENT_CONFIG* key. The entries in this key are stored separately from the entries in this branch:

   HKEY_LOCAL_MACHINE\SYSTEM\ControlSetxxx\Hardware Profiles.

If the user selects a hardware profile during system startup, this profile is set in the *HKEY_CURRENT_CONFIG* key.

Further Reading

Here are a few books that might be helpful to programmers and advanced users who want to look in depth at topics related to the Registry. This bibliography isn't complete, of course, but the books I mention here are the standard references that all Windows 95 programmers should know about. Not included in this list are several other important titles I've mentioned in the book, such as the Win32 SDK. This SDK and other helpful information are available on the CD-ROMs shipped with the Microsoft Developer Network (MSDN) available from Microsoft.

Microsoft Windows 95 Resource Kit   By Microsoft Corporation

Microsoft Press. 1-55615-678-2. This is the definitive reference for all advanced Windows 95 users who want details about many Windows topics. Unfortunately, this book contains only a short description of the Registry keys, but the sections about the Registry Editor, the System Policy Editor, and the INF file format will be rather helpful.

Inside OLE, Second Edition   By Kraig Brockschmidt

Microsoft Press. 1-55615-843-2. This is the reference for programmers who want to understand the concepts of OLE (now often referred to as ActiveX) technology. This book also explains how to obtain the CLSID codes for OLE components.

Programming Windows 95   By Charles Petzold

Microsoft Press. 1-55615-676-6. Petzold wrote the definitive guide for Windows programmers. Of particular interest is Chapter 20, *"What's This Thing called OLE?,"* written by Paul Yao, which examines OLE components. (These details are also reflected in the *HKEY_CLASSES_ ROOT\Interface* branch of the Registry.)

Programming the Windows 95 User Interface   By Nancy Winnick Cluts

Microsoft Press. 1-55615-884-X. This book provides a valuable overview of the Windows 95 user interface architecture. For programmers, it describes the new features of the Windows 95 shell. Sections show how to implement and register Quick Viewers, drag-and-drop handlers, context menu handlers, copy handlers, and property sheet handlers.

Programmer's Guide to Microsoft Windows 95   By Microsoft Corporation

Microsoft Press. 1-55615-834-3. This book is a must if you intend to develop Windows 95 applications because it discusses the key technologies used in Windows 95 from a programmer's perspective. Here you'll find further information about the topics I briefly discussed in Chapter 7. This book is also valid for advanced Windows 95 users because it discusses many aspects of Windows in a general way (such as how to register certain Windows 95 components).

Microsoft Windows NT 4.0 Workstation Resource Kit   By Microsoft Corporation

Microsoft Press. 1-57231-343-9. You really should read this book. The Windows NT 4.0 Registry differs from the Windows 95 Registry, and we only briefly examine these differences in this book. The *Resource Kit* contains at least four chapters about NT 4.0 Registry issues, and the companion CD contains the tools for backing up and restoring the NT 4.0 Registry.

INDEX

SPECIAL CHARACTERS

A

About the Author

Günter Born holds an engineering degree in physics and has studied information science and electrotechnics. He began working as a software developer and project engineer in the German spacecraft and chemical industries in 1979, managing software development groups and consulting on several international projects with Japan, Thailand, and Europe. Currently he works as an independent writer and translator.

Born started his work with computers as a student, when one of his professors encouraged him to work through a series of equations for mechanical systems. Too poor to buy a pocket calculator and too lazy to do the calculations by hand, Born turned to an IBM 370 computer, which had to be fed with punched cards. An incorrect FORTRAN statement resulted in a long listing and wasted time, but after the program was finally running, the computer saved Born a lot of time and provided a lot of free paper, which he used for classroom notes.

His publishing career started with some mistakes. In 1987 he failed to publish an article he wrote about an 8085/Z80 Disassembler implemented in BASIC—nobody wanted to read about Basic. So he decided to learn Pascal. He borrowed an old IBM PC/XT with a Borland Pascal compiler, spent a weekend porting his disassembler to Pascal, exchanged the Basic listings with Pascal source code, and succeeded at last, publishing his article in a computer magazine. Born wrote his first book to get the money for a PC. (The royalties, as it turned out, funded only the PC.)

Since then, Born has published many articles and over 50 books and CD-ROMs about computers, ranging from computer books for children to books about application software for end users to high-end programming titles. He wrote two highly successful books about Microsoft Windows 95, and he is the author of the *The File Formats Handbook,* a standard in the programmer community and available in English, German, and Russian. Born is also the author, translator, and technical editor of several books published by Microsoft Press Germany.

The manuscript for this book was prepared and submitted to Microsoft Press in electronic form. Text files were prepared using Microsoft Word 7.0 for Windows. Pages were composed by Microsoft Press using Adobe PageMaker 6.0 for Windows, with text in New Baskerville and display type in Helvetica bold. Composed pages were delivered to the printer as electronic prepress files.

Cover Graphic Designer
Greg Erickson

Cover Illustrator
Glenn Mitsui

Interior Graphic Designer
Kim Eggleston

Interior Graphic Artist
Travis Beaven

Compositors
E. Candace Gearhart
Abby Hall

Principal Proofreader/Copy Editor
Richard Carey

Indexer
Patti Schiendelman